# THE
# SECOND

*One Person, No Vote: How Voter Suppression
Is Destroying Our Democracy*

*White Rage: The Unspoken Truth of Our Racial Divide*

*Bourgeois Radicals: The NAACP and the Struggle for
Colonial Liberation, 1941–1960*

*Eyes off the Prize: The United Nations and the African American
Struggle for Human Rights, 1944–1955*

# THE

# SECOND

---

## RACE AND GUNS IN
## A FATALLY
## UNEQUAL AMERICA

# CAROL ANDERSON

BLOOMSBURY PUBLISHING

NEW YORK · LONDON · OXFORD · NEW DELHI · SYDNEY

BLOOMSBURY PUBLISHING
Bloomsbury Publishing Inc.
1385 Broadway, New York, NY 10018, USA

BLOOMSBURY, BLOOMSBURY PUBLISHING, and the Diana logo
are trademarks of Bloomsbury Publishing Plc

First published in the United States 2021

Bloomsbury Publishing Plc does not have any control over, or responsibility for,
any third-party websites referred to or in this book. All internet addresses given
in this book were correct at the time of going to press. The author and publisher
regret any inconvenience caused if addresses have changed or sites have ceased
to exist, but can accept no responsibility for any such changes.

ISBN: HB: 978-1-63557-425-8; eBook: 978-1-63557-426-5

LIBRARY OF CONGRESS CATALOGING-IN-PUBLICATION DATA IS AVAILABLE

2 4 6 8 10 9 7 5 3 1

Typeset by Westchester Publishing Services
Printed and bound in the U.S.A. by Berryville Graphics Inc., Berryville, Virginia

To find out more about our authors and books visit www.bloomsbury.com
and sign up for our newsletters.

Bloomsbury books may be purchased for business or promotional use.
For information on bulk purchases please contact Macmillan Corporate and
Premium Sales Department at specialmarkets@macmillan.com.

*For*
*Aunt Lennie, Uncle Sam, and Aunt Barbara*
*My Soul Looks Back and Wonders . . .*

# CONTENTS

# "Why Did You Shoot Him, Sir?"

It was like a snuff film that July 6, 2016, livestream. Philando Castile sat in his car, buckled in, bleeding, dying. "Why did you shoot him, sir?" asked his fiancée, Diamond Reynolds, pain piercing her every word.[1]

Castile, who had been pulled over in a suburb of St. Paul, Minnesota, because "his wide-set nose" supposedly resembled that of a robbery suspect, had been reaching for his ID but, in order to avoid any surprises, let the police officer know that he had a gun with him: a legally permitted, right-to-carry-concealed gun.[2]

That was all the cop needed to know: Officer Jeronimo Yanez began shooting.[3]

Castile's death came just one day after Alton Sterling's down in Louisiana. He, too, was carrying a gun, which was not unusual in this right-to-carry state. Granted, Sterling had a felony conviction, so owning a firearm was for him illegal, but he had been robbed before and wanted protection. On July 5, 2016, the Baton Rouge police received a 911 call that there was a man with a weapon threatening customers at a local convenience store. As officers rolled onto the scene, they saw

Sterling sitting there, selling CDs and DVDs, just as the store owner allowed him to do and, indeed, welcomed. The threatening man was not Sterling. In fact, there *was* no threatening man. It had been a prank call. But that didn't matter. Within a few moments, police had thrown the Black man down, pinned him to the asphalt, and then started yelling that Sterling had a gun. He did. It was in his pocket, where he could hardly reach it, what with the officers squatting on both his legs and one arm. Nevertheless, the police began firing round after round into his prone body. Point-blank. Blood poured out of his chest. But not for long. Alton Sterling was dead.[4]

The back-to-back deaths of these two Black men police had shot for carrying guns should have jolted into action the Second Amendment's staunchest advocate, the National Rifle Association (NRA). In 1995, for example, the organization's denunciations flew fast and furious when it contended that law enforcement not only overreacted but went out of its way to kill gun owners. Angered by the deaths at the Branch Davidian compound in Waco, Texas, and the siege and firefight at Ruby Ridge, Idaho, both of which were sparked by federal agents serving warrants for weapons violations, Wayne LaPierre, the NRA's executive vice president, angrily wrote: "If you have a badge, you have the government's go-ahead to harass, intimidate, even murder law-abiding citizens."[5] He further denounced cops as "jack-booted government thugs [who have] more power to take away our constitutional rights, break in our doors, seize our guns, destroy our property, and even injure or kill us."[6]

Nearly two decades later that sentiment had not changed. This was evident when Nevada rancher Cliven Bundy, who had refused to pay over one million dollars in fees for grazing his cattle on public land, summoned his gun-toting, self-styled militiamen to do battle with federal authorities to prevent the seizure of his herd for restitution.

Richard Mack, a former recipient of the NRA's Law Enforcement Officer of the Year award, asserted, "If [federal agents are] going to start killing people, I'm sorry, but to show the world how ruthless these people are," women and children needed to be placed on the front lines as human shields. Mack didn't flinch as he insisted, "women needed to be the first ones shot . . . I would have put my own wife or daughters there [on the front lines], and I would have been screaming bloody murder to watch them die."[7] Larry Pratt, a speaker at the NRA's 2014 national convention, commenting on the fact that Bundy "backed them [the Bureau of Land Management agents] down with automatic rifles and other deadly weaponry," proudly called that armed confrontation "a proper, legitimate, lawful response to illegitimate, unlawful exercise of government power, particularly on the federal level."[8]

Yet how quickly the NRA's swagger disappeared when government agents gunned down Philando Castile and Alton Sterling for merely carrying guns. Sterling's death didn't even merit acknowledgment. As for Castile, the NRA broke its silence only after inordinate pressure from African American members led the gun manufacturers' lobby to issue a tepid statement that the Second Amendment was applicable "regardless of race, religion, or sexual orientation." When pressed further by many of its members to stand up for Castile, the often-fierce organization demurred, saying it was "important for the NRA not to comment while the investigation is ongoing."[9]

This situational silence did not go unnoticed. The NRA had not only loudly defended the rights of those in the Branch Davidian cult and at Ruby Ridge, men who had actually shot and killed members of law enforcement, but the organization had also doubled down on calling for *more* guns in the face of mass shootings in a public school in Newtown, Connecticut, and a movie theater in Aurora, Colorado.[10] Yet here the guardian of the Second Amendment was now deliberately ignoring the inconvenient fact that Black men had been killed for merely possessing a firearm. "Where's the NRA?" asked journalist Hanna Kozlowska. Didn't Alton Sterling and Philando Castile have Second Amendment rights, too?[11] David A. Graham, in *The Atlantic*, coolly observed that the "two shootings give a strong sense that the Second Amendment does not apply to black Americans the same way it does to white Americans."[12] *Washington Post* columnist Eugene Robinson wrote that he saw that old Jim Crow "whites only" sign plastered above the Second Amendment.[13] The message was loud and clear: Even for the NRA, Black people did not have Second Amendment rights.[14]

A BROKEN, TREACHEROUS rights landscape, of course, has always been the reality for African Americans. We know that the Fifteenth Amendment (the right to vote) was undercut by poll taxes, literacy tests, violence, and understanding clauses for nearly one hundred years and unfortunately, since 2013, has come under assault again.[15] Similarly, the amendments covering the criminal justice system—the Fourth, Fifth, Sixth, and Eighth—have offered little to no protection for African Americans because of numerous Supreme Court decisions that have embedded racism and racial profiling into policing, trial procedures, and sentencing.[16] But the Second Amendment's charge for a "well regulated Militia" and "the right of the people to keep and bear Arms" offers a particularly maddening set of double standards where race is concerned.[17] And that is what I explore in *The Second*. While numerous books have examined the impact on Blacks of a racially compromised Bill of Rights, there is almost an eerie silence on this particular amendment, which its advocates call central to citizenship.[18]

That silence is not accidental. The eighteenth-century origins of the "right to bear arms" explicitly excluded Black people.[19] South Carolina encoded into law that the enslaved could not "carry or make use of firearms or any offensive weapons whatsoever" unless "in the presence of some white person." Moreover, the state's various militias had the "power to search and examine all negro-houses for offensive weapons and ammunition." In Delaware, there could be no valid earthly reason that any "bought Servant, or Negro, or Mulatto slave . . . be allowed to bear Arms." Georgia was even more direct. Not only were Blacks forbidden from owning or carrying firearms, but white men were required to own "a good gun or pistol" to give them the means to "search and examine all negro houses for offensive weapons and ammunition." The distinction was clear: "Citizen(s) had the right to keep arms; the slave did not."[20]

Even the "well-regulated militia" interpretation of the Second Amendment ran aground on the shoals of Blackness. The militia had been active in the War of Independence, and while states wanted to keep those forces intact afterward to fend off a tyrannical president or foreign aggressor (there was no real standing army until 1947), they had actually proved to be too unreliable and ill-equipped for those roles. They were adept, however, in buttressing slave patrols to hunt down, capture, and return back to their owners Blacks who had fled bondage. More important, state militias quashed slave rebellions.[21]

Thus, the role of the militia and who controlled it—either the federal government or the slaveholding states—became a sticking point in ratification of the U.S. Constitution. James Madison, architect of the Constitution and the Bill of Rights, understood what was at stake. Just as the continuation of the Atlantic slave trade for an additional twenty years, the three-fifths clause, and the fugitive slave clause were embedded in the Constitution to purchase the South's participation in the United States of America, the Second Amendment was also a bribe.

Regardless of which legal interpretation of the Second Amendment is deployed—be it an individual's right to bear arms, the right to a well-regulated militia, or even the attendant right to self-defense—each has been used *against* African Americans.[22] The Second was designed and implemented to abrogate and deny the rights of Black people.

This has revealed a paradox. Whereas the judicial and the legislative weakening of the Bill of Rights has been instrumental in allowing the death penalty, voter suppression, and racial profiling to undermine African Americans' citizenship rights, the Second Amendment, despite numerous massacres and thousands of gun deaths, has become only more constitutionally and legally entrenched—for everyone, that is, except African Americans.[23] Let me explain.

The U.S. Supreme Court has refused to acknowledge the full extent of rampant and demonstrated racial bias in the use of the death penalty, which has made this ultimate sentence inherently "cruel and unusual" and, thus, in violation of the Eighth Amendment.[24] Instead, the court, after issuing a brief moratorium, has allowed states to continue putting the convicted, who are disproportionately Black, to death so long as the method is not as barbaric as, say, electric chairs that spark and set an inmate on fire.[25] Yet as myopic and convoluted as the rulings have been, there is a clear human rights pathway on this: The court simply has to acknowledge how profoundly embedded racism is in the criminal justice system—from racial profiling to police stops, to access to competent counsel, to jury selection, to the impact of the victim's race on the trial, to sentencing—and declare the death penalty unconstitutional. Similarly, clear-cut rulings that uphold the Voting Rights Act's pre-clearance standards would eliminate the pernicious effects of twenty-first-century gerrymandering, voter ID requirements, purged rolls, etc., on the Fifteenth Amendment's right to vote.

The Second Amendment, on the other hand, is fundamentally different. It was designed and has consistently been constructed to keep African Americans powerless and vulnerable. Regardless of the court's stance, there is no clear pathway to human rights where the Second Amendment is concerned. A series of legal decisions best illustrate this point. In *Lewis v. United States* (1980), citing the need for public safety, felons were stripped of the right to bear arms. This ruling, of course, fell disproportionately on African Americans, because an unequal justice system had unnaturally created mass incarceration and imprisoned the Black community.[26] Meanwhile, African Americans in Chicago and Washington, D.C., had faced staggering gun violence and record homicides, and responded with statutes to reduce the number of firearms in their cities. But they soon ran headlong into NRA-backed Supreme Court decisions that interpreted gun control as violating the individual's right to bear arms.[27] Guns would once again legally flood those cities.[28] Similarly, state laws that banned firearms in public housing in order to provide for the security of the residents have also been overturned.[29] Each of these—restricting felons from possessing guns, while also allowing a greater flow in urban areas for "protection" against crime, and forbidding firearms in public housing—had at its center the argument of "safety" and "security." But they had something else in common, too: African Americans were always the ones who posed the threat and always the ones who bore the brunt of the decision.

Similarly, the Second Amendment, which scholars herald as bedrock for the right to self-defense, has been quicksand for African Americans.[30] Since at least 1680, Black people have not had the right to self-defense, especially when it comes to protecting themselves from white violence.[31] Over the course of more than three hundred years, that hard reality remains as the "stand your ground" laws, first enacted in 2005, make clear. As the U.S. Commission on Civil Rights reported in its study of the racial implications of the law, the criminal justice system is "ten times more likely" to rule a homicide justifiable "if the shooter is white and the victim black" than if an African American kills someone white and claims self-defense.[32] In fact, the report notes, stand-your-ground laws actually worsen and increase the racial disparity outcomes of self-defense claims.[33] When the NRA provided the template of this law for Florida's legislators, it "wanted the legal equivalent of carte blanche for the exerciser of a Stand Your Ground right."[34] The NRA got it.

To be clear, this is not a pro-gun or anti-gun book. Guns are not the key variable here. It's Black people. Their legal status—enslaved, free Black, denizen, Jim Crowed citizen, or citizen of "post-racial America"—did not change the way the Second Amendment worked against their rights. From colonial times through the twenty-first century, regardless of the laws, regardless of the court decisions, regardless of the changing political environment, the Second has consistently meant this: The second a Black person exercises that right, the second they pick up a gun to protect themselves (or not), their life—as surely as Philando Castile's, as surely as Alton Sterling's, as surely as twelve-year-old Tamir Rice's—could be snatched away in that same fatal second.

Once all the distracting arguments about individual versus collective gun rights are stripped away, it becomes clear that this debate is quite simply dwarfed by a much broader national discussion about rights and equality. The NRA's insistence on framing the "Second Amendment: A Citizen's Right" has dominated the argument, with the only question being a citizen's right to do what?[35] But that is not the question. The Second Amendment is so inherently, structurally flawed, so based on Black exclusion and debasement, that, unlike the other amendments, it can never be a pathway to civil and human rights for 47.5 million African Americans. That's the painful answer to Diamond Reynolds's question.

*One*

# "Sheep Will Never Make a Revolution"

In 1776, in an act of incredible bravado, the rebels penned and signed the Declaration of Independence; they refused to be a mere collection of colonies subservient to the most powerful nation on earth, Britain. But after all the bold pronouncements and flowery language, hard, cold reality began setting in. How were they going to finance, much less fight, a full-scale war against a foe that "was superior . . . in manpower, in naval and army technology, and as some have argued, in seasoned military leaders?"[1]

This was not a rhetorical question. The shot heard round the world at Lexington, the bloody guerrilla warfare at Concord, and the outright battle at Bunker Hill made it clear that the American rebels were going to require more men, more arms, and definitely more money if they were going to stand a ghost of a chance.[2] The rebellious patriots were even rumbling about the need to build a fleet strong enough to take on the vaunted and feared Royal Navy.[3] None of this was going to be cheap. Representatives from Pennsylvania and others from the North acknowledged this bracing truth and, therefore, suggested a wartime taxation plan based on the head count of the 2.5 million people who lived in the thirteen colonies. That kind of financing, they argued, could provide enough revenue to equip their military and defeat King George III's forces.

There was a major problem with that formulation, however. The South, which was more dependent economically, politically, and culturally on human bondage than the Northern colonies were, balked.[4] South Carolina, where more than half the population was Black, insisted that the rationale behind a head count was faulty.[5] Namely, how were slaves going to be counted when they were not people? Thomas Lynch of South Carolina explained it in terms he hoped even someone from Massachusetts or Pennsylvania could understand: Sheep in the North weren't taxed: why should the South's property be?

Benjamin Franklin, the grand old man among the patriots, sat there in the Second Continental Congress listening and then "pungently replied that there was 'some difference between' slaves and sheep as 'sheep will never make a revolution.'"[6] Stung by Franklin's all-too-accurate insight, South Carolina's delegates countered with "the ultimate threat. If the northern states insisted on this point, 'there is an End of the Confederation.'" Pennsylvania and its compatriots could fight this war against the British alone. Without the South.[7]

REGARDLESS OF THE South's outrage, Franklin had zeroed in on the core of the matter. Despite all the fulminations and mental gymnastics about "property," the enslaved, as everyone knew, were human beings who resented mightily their bondage.[8] In fact, they had already demonstrated that, at every opportunity, they would do whatever it would take to be free.[9] If that meant running away, they would do it.[10]

If that meant pounding on the court system or the religious establishment by "petitioning for their liberty . . . or suggesting that slavery was an abomination before God," they did it.[11] If that meant launching a revolt, an insurrection, an uprising, then so be it.[12] Thus, despite all the self-congratulatory kudos for "civilizing" Africans and trying to anesthetize whites with the myth of Black docility and complacency, Southern plantation owners actually understood not only that slavery "bred insurrection" but that those revolts "threatened the entire social structure of white Southern communities."[13]

The planters responded to this challenge by adopting a three-part strategy to break the will, or at least the ability to fight, of a people who had been snatched from their homeland and brutalized and who were overwhelmingly "hostile to those who controlled their labor."[14] In a series of moves that would scar the United States well into the twenty-first century, colonial Virginia deployed this triad of brutal control. It denied the enslaved the right to bear arms; ignored the right to self-defense for Black people; and put in place a "large-scale military machinery," the militia, "to crack down [on] any conspiracies or uprisings."[15]

As early as 1639, Virginia prohibited Africans from carrying guns because "what white Southerners feared the most . . . [was] an armed black man unafraid to retaliate against both the system of slavery and those who fought to defend it."[16] Nevertheless, insurrectionist scares rocked the colony in 1687, 1709, 1710, 1722, 1723, and 1730.[17] In 1680, as racialized chattel slavery congealed, the legislature crafted a law denying the enslaved *and* free Blacks the right to self-defense if attacked by their "'master' and/or Whites."[18] Next, in 1723, the colony's statute explicitly stated that "no negro, mulatto, or indian [*sic*] whatsoever" should have a gun "under penalty of a whipping not to exceed twenty-nine lashes."[19] One key point of the laws, the "Virginia governor explained to royal officials," was to "impose a 'perpetual Brand' on blacks as different and inferior to whites."[20] The colony also passed a series of laws to beef up the readiness and firepower of the militia because, as one Southerner explained, "it was necessary that a militia should be kept constantly on foot to keep them [the enslaved] in awe."[21]

IN COLONIAL SOUTH Carolina, rice production was a special type of breeding ground for uprisings because it required an inordinate amount of Black labor, Black expertise, and the attendant Black subjugation to bend this workforce into submission and yield a handsome profit.[22] Plantation owners were thus notorious for "barbarities such as scalding, burning, castrating, and extracting the tongues or eyes of slaves."[23] That combination of the insatiable desire for enormous profits coupled with the sadistic brutalization of bonded African labor created an overwhelming fear among whites of the enslaved's capacity and desire for retribution. And they needed to be fearful. The vast majority in South Carolina were "Angolan" Africans or from Kongo. As one of the slave merchants explained, those Africans were "the meanest of all."[24]

That recognition and the resulting fear, however, did not stop the mass importation of kidnapped Africans, who by 1710 already outnumbered whites in South Carolina. Instead, the response was to double down on the brutality and other measures necessary to ensure control of what would eventually be 57.5 percent of the total population.[25] From 1671 to the early 1700s, the colony worked mightily to build, adjust, and then overhaul its slave-patrol guidelines until it had "effectively turned its white population into a community police force."[26] The deputizing of all white males and the attendant increased slave patrols were supposed "to promote white community safety."[27]

It was an illusion. Despite all the precautions, in 1720 a near revolt shook South Carolina. As one Carolinian noted, "The negroes [had] . . . a very wicked and barbarous plott" in which they planned to rise up and "destroy all the white people in the country and then to take the town in full body."[28] As could be expected, the punishments were swift and brutal. Some of the would-be insurrectionists were "burnt some hang'd and some banish'd."[29]

The colony then reorganized its militia, banning even the trusted slaves who were supposed to help fend off the threat to white Carolinians by incursions from the Spanish in Florida as well as the "Creek" and other indigenous people.[30] Although this step seemed drastic, the planters believed it was necessary. Whether they trusted them or not, the plantation owners voiced concerns that if they didn't use "great caution . . . our slaves when armed might become our masters."[31] South Carolina then formally merged the separate slave patrol with the militia to strengthen the colony's internal and external defenses.[32] Reorganized and motivated, the militia "searched slave quarters . . . looking for weapons of revolt—guns, scythes, knives, but also writing paper, books and other indications of education."[33]

But peace did not come in the wake of retaliatory violence or enhanced policing. The next year, 1721, a report from South Carolina eddied across the ocean to the king of England that "black slaves . . . were very near succeeding in a revolution, which would probably have been attended by the utter extirpation of all your Majesty's subject in this province." As the fear and pressure mounted, the colony responded with the Negro Act of 1722, which spelled out how Blacks would be punished if they had any "arms, powder, bullets, or offensive weapons in order to carry on such mutiny or insurrection."[34]

That didn't work either. By 1730, there was a report of yet another attempted revolt: "The Negroes . . . conspired to Rise and destroy us" came the plaintive wail. The enslaved planned to "rush into the heart of the city, take possession of all the arms and ammunition they could find, and murder all the white men." Then, the report continued, they were going to head straight for the plantations to wipe out the slave owners. If the plot had not been uncovered—the relief apparent in every syllable—"we had been all in blood." The reaction to the planned uprising was, of course, full of the sadism that defined slavery—some of the enslaved were tortured to extract confessions and identify the possible ringleaders, who were then subsequently "tortured to death, while many others were subjected to severe bodily punishment."[35] In a brutal version of wash-rinse-repeat, the "cycle went: deadly fear, black death, and appeals for more funds toward slave control."[36] But the enslaved were unbowed. In fact, as historian Walter Rucker noted, there were no "fewer than six revolts or conspiracies" between 1736 and 1740.[37]

The most jarring was in 1739. Twenty enslaved men, as part of a labor gang, were building roads near the Stono River. Out there day after day, they surveyed the terrain, the people, the routines, the cache where weapons were stored, and the depth of the personnel on the various shifts. After a while, led by a man named Jemmy, they had gathered all the intel they needed.[38]

Under the cover of the Sabbath, on Sunday, September 9, they struck. They stormed the storehouse where the weapons were sold, then overpowered and decapitated the two clerks.[39] Seizing the now unguarded firearms, drums blazing and banners flying, they called for others to join them in this battle for freedom and, with a force of ninety, carved a path of death and destruction through the colony en route, it appears, to Florida, where "runaways had long become free as part of an official Spanish policy."[40]

As could be expected, South Carolina's militia went after them in hot pursuit.[41] The mission was clear: Under no circumstances could the

Stono rebels reach Spanish Florida. A series of pitched battles over the span of a week, followed by a yearlong mopping-up operation, eventually overwhelmed the rebellious fugitives. But the Stono Rebellion, "the bloodiest example of slave resistance in colonial North America," was the planters' worst nightmare. Blacks, in a quest to break free, were willing and able to kill whites without remorse, without fear. More than sixty dead bodies proved that.[42] The planters were, as a consequence, determined to make as grisly an example of the vanquished as possible. The enslaved "were tortured, shot, hanged, and gibbeted alive." Then another fifty slaves "were taken by their Planters who Cutt off their heads and set them up at every Mile Post they came to."[43]

Although the rebellion was quashed, the realization that the enslaved would not just theoretically but actually rise up showed how precariously perched the entire institution of slavery really was.[44] Already shaken to the core by Stono, whites were on high alert. They needed to be. Two captains complained that yet another slave conspiracy— uncovered after Stono—had them on round-the-clock guard duty. "We shall Live very Uneasie with our Negroes while the Spaniards continue to keep possession of St. Augustine," they bemoaned. Again, the consequences for plotting to seize their freedom were brutal. Five of the insurgents were hanged, "twenty-one had their ears cropped, thirty-one were branded, and forty-six were whipped."[45] The blood had barely dried from all the flayed flesh, lynching, and maiming before there was another "full-scale slave conspiracy . . . in Charles Town itself."[46]

South Carolina's response was twofold and brutal. First, in 1740, the legislature "issued monetary rewards for the scalp of any slave found . . . attempting to escape to St. Augustine."[47] Second, lawmakers quickly moved to codify, as never before, exactly what the enslaved were, what they could not do, and, equally important, what could be done to them.

The Negro Act of 1740 had as its foundational principles that Negroes were "absolute slaves" including those not even born yet. They were "property." They were instinctually criminal. And therefore they must be "kept in due subjection and obedience." With that as the underlying premise, the statute, which became the model for slave codes throughout North America, required heavy-handed white control that curtailed the enslaved's movements, literacy, right to self-defense, and access to firearms. Any actual variance from these strictures, such as hitting or killing someone white or carrying a gun, could happen only with the explicit consent of and benefit to a white person. If the enslaved stepped outside those parameters, severe punishment, including death, awaited them.[48]

Meanwhile, whites, particularly on plantations, were stacking up the arms. Scholars who pored over the probate records revealed that "50% of all wealthholders in the Thirteen Colonies in 1774 owned guns." That percentage soared to 69 percent when isolated to the South. North Carolina (77 percent), South Carolina (70 percent), Virginia (68 percent), and Maryland (62 percent) were all well above the average for the thirteen colonies. Indeed, 81 percent of slave-owning estates had firearms, and plantations with the largest number of enslaved people were 4.3 times more likely to have guns than those with few or no slaves.[49]

The fear of the enslaved's retribution and the determination to keep them, and the relatively small number of free Blacks, under control were not just Southern phenomena, though. Slavery and its tentacles were nationwide both in terms of human bondage and economic benefits. In the early eighteenth century, "approximately half the tonnage of New England shipping had been in transporting slaves."[50] In New York, 14 percent of the population was enslaved; in New Jersey and Rhode Island, 8 percent.[51] This had influenced the shape of the northern colonies' laws as much as it had those in the South. As early as 1680, Massachusetts banned "Negroes and slaves" from the militia because the colony feared what would happen if they were armed.[52] New York did the same after a slave insurrection scare in 1741.[53] Even the supposedly anti-slavery Quakers, who dominated colonial Pennsylvania, passed a statute saying, "If any negro shall presume to carry any guns, . . . pistols, . . . or other arms or weapons whatsoever, without his master's special license . . . he shall be whipped with twenty-one lashes on his bare back."[54] All thirteen colonies, in fact, had some arms-control law forbidding the possession of guns by "suspect groups— Indians, slaves, . . . and sometimes, free Blacks."[55]

THESE WERE THE conditions of racial subjugation and suspicion as the War for American Independence began. Historian James T. Kloppenberg noted that "racism [was] shared by many white champions of democracy" and that rampant anti-Blackness underlying those laws of disarmament would affect the colonies' ability to wage war effectively.[56] The patriots had mounted a dual fighting force consisting of the local militias and the Continental army, led by George Washington, to take on the British. As the Americans recruited volunteers for this monumental task, the sign on the door by November 1775 read "whites only" even though Blacks, including Crispus Attucks, who was the first patriot to die in this war, had taken "part in the hostilities in and around Boston even before the creation of the Continental Army."[57]

In 1775, North Carolina issued a decree to "search for and seize 'all kinds of arms whatsoever' which Negroes might possess." And added that those who regularly searched Negro quarters for "guns and other weapons would receive a tax cut and be exempt from road work, militia duty, and jury service."[58] Delaware, New Hampshire, Massachusetts, and New York banned Blacks from military service. As did New Jersey, which required "all Negroes with guns or other weapons . . . to turn them in 'until the present troubles are settled.'"[59]

One of the major problems with this strategy, however, was that the longer the war dragged on, the more difficult it became to find enough white men willing to become soldiers.[60] By 1777, Congress hoped to have "roughly 75,000 men, but the Continental army peaked that year in October with 39,443 men, almost 20 percent beneath its pinnacle in 1776."[61] It soon became clear that the shortfall was not an aberration. The militias could not fill that void. The American rebels were confronted with both chronic manpower shortages and the reality that the state militias were completely unreliable and would sometimes simply run away rather than fight.[62] This was compounded by the November 7, 1775, proclamation by Virginia's royal governor, the Earl of Dunmore, that the British would emancipate every male slave of a rebel "who could and would bear arms for King George III." Benjamin Franklin, in fact, worried that the royal governors of North Carolina and Virginia, with all their promises of emancipation, were "exciting an insurrection among the Blacks." North Carolina's William Hooper, a delegate to the Continental Congress, echoed that concern as he complained that Dunmore's proclamation meant that "our negroes are to be armed against us."[63]

Combined, the stark realities of not having enough white troops, unreliable state militias, and armed slaves emboldened by the promise of freedom compelled Congress to strongly reconsider the "whites only" criteria for the Continental army.[64] Nonetheless, the colonies' new recruitment policy slammed into the palpable angst, voiced by George Washington himself, that if the enslaved or free Blacks were armed, it would only "further irritate those remaining in servitude."[65]

But time had run out to deliberate any further. With the British closing in and a Continental army stretched to its very limits, it was do or die. At that moment, most white Americans made the decision to live. They needed Black men to take up arms against the British if the United States was ever going to become more than a failed revolt against the king. In 1777, Connecticut "allowed masters to free their slaves to permit their enlistment in the Continental Army." Massachusetts made free Blacks *and* the enslaved eligible for military service. Rhode Island "began offering outright freedom as a reward for service to enslaved African Americans who would enlist." Even Virginia, the colony with the largest number of slaves, opened up its recruitment criteria to allow free Blacks to serve in the Continental army. This, however, only spurred enslaved Black men to claim that they were not bonded and then enlist.[66] Opening up access to military service to Blacks had the desired effect. There were now "negroes in abundance" serving in the Continental army, and by 1778 it had "become a racially integrated force."[67] Still there were limits, and South Carolina expressed that boundary in the most emphatic, unequivocal way.

AFTER OCCUPYING NEW York and trampling over New Jersey, only to eventually face a stiffened Continental army, the British decided to take the war to "the soft underbelly of the rebellion," the South.[68] It seemed an easy call. Savannah and Charleston were just sitting there ripe for invasion and occupation; they simply weren't ready. While the states in the North and upper South had relented and begun to recruit Black soldiers, South Carolina had refused. But now, in the British crosshairs, there weren't enough available white men to staff both the militia—which, as the "threat of slave rebellion hung heavily" in the air, had been "beefed up to enforce the plantation system"—and the Continental army.[69] Colonel John Laurens, an aide-de-camp to George Washington and the son of prominent South Carolinian Henry Laurens, had a bold plan to solve this problem. He wanted to put weapons in the hands of the enslaved. The question, however, was whether South Carolina, facing an impending force of more than eight thousand British and Hessian soldiers, would be committed and dedicated enough to the very idea of a United States to go for it.[70]

To add additional weight to this decision, on December 29, 1778, the British, guided by an enslaved African, maneuvered easily around the American forces in Georgia led by Major General Robert Howe. The Redcoats "went ashore at daybreak and with minimal casualties by sundown were masters of Savannah." Howe was utterly confused and had no idea "what had happened." Despite his befuddlement, what was clear to everyone else was that with Savannah captured and occupied, the British were ready to turn their sights fully on Charleston.[71]

South Carolina's legislative assembly knew what it had to do as it considered Laurens's proposal. It could either swallow its "alarm" and "horror" over arming the enslaved to drive the British back into the sea, or it could refuse and risk the national independence that so many had already died for. The choice was actually quite simple. The United States could be sacrificed. The majority, in fact, questioned whether "this union was worth fighting for at all." They were appalled and "disgusted" that Congress would even recommend something so abhorrent as arming the enslaved. "Not even imminent occupation could induce them to contemplate black enlistment." Instead of staying in the fight and using every weapon and resource that the colony could muster, they recommended that South Carolina surrender to the British, declare its neutrality in this war, and take its chances with the king.[72]

In South Carolina's estimation, armed Blacks were infinitely more dangerous and frightening than the might of the British military and the wrath of a king dealing with American traitors. By November 1779, "South Carolina had only 750 men fit for active duty."[73] Still, the legislature refused to budge. The Continental army's Major General Nathanael Greene, a Quaker from Rhode Island, who was sent south to defeat the British, was flummoxed.[74] South Carolina's obstinacy was infuriating. "There were not enough whites in the state," he explained to the governor, "to raise a force in any other way than by slave enlistment, especially since 'the natural strength of this country in point of numbers appears to consist much more in the blacks than in the whites.'"[75] And still, South Carolina refused. Greene complained to George Washington that "the rejection of the proposal" could be summed up in a few words: the "dread of armed blacks."[76]

While the wealthy rice plantation owners who dominated South Carolina's government refused all entreaties and pleas from Congress to fully join in this fight for the United States, the patriotic press, needing to still hold the northern and southern colonies together in this war, laid the blame for the debacle in Charleston and Savannah at the feet of the enslaved.[77] The overriding story was that, in America's darkest hour, it was actually Blacks who abandoned the fledgling United States. What was so unforgivable was the "largest unknown slave rebellion in American history," as seventy thousand to one hundred thousand fled from the plantations and flocked to the protection and the promised freedom of the king's forces.[78]

Blacks were already suspect because of years of repeated insurrections; this rush to British emancipation made betrayal the easy fallback national narrative. "The Negroes will always in time of war, prove injurious to the country wherein they live," wrote one pamphleteer.

"The Country or State which possesses a considerable number of slaves, is incapable of defending itself against invasions from abroad."[79]

That tale of Blacks fighting for a tyrannical king, against freedom-loving Americans, "engulf[ed] nearly all counterexamples of blacks . . . aiding the cause."[80] Nothing that Blacks—free and enslaved—did could overcome the ethos of Black betrayal and treachery. Even the sizable numbers who enlisted in the Continental army, whose terms of service were significantly longer than whites and whose rates of going AWOL were substantially lower, weren't enough.[81] In this national zeitgeist, Blacks were beyond simply un-American; they were "worse: an enemy within."[82]

As the war ended, it was in this mythologized landscape that only whites fought for liberty. It was only whites who stood toe-to-toe with the tyranny of monarchy. It was only whites who defeated the British, and therefore, it was whites who were now ready to build a nation committed to "deriving their just powers from the consent of the governed."[83]

The first iteration of this new government, the Articles of Confederation, drafted in 1777 but not ratified until 1781, however, proved so unworkable that within a few years, the nation was on the verge of collapse.[84] The configuration of a very weak central government meant that an unwieldy amalgamation of states was printing their own currencies, making their own foreign policy, and setting up tariff barriers among themselves. They couldn't agree on a taxation plan, couldn't pay off the debts from the war, and couldn't make the British live up to the Treaty of Paris (1783) and compensate slaveholders for those who fled bondage.[85]

James Madison, a Virginian, slaveholder, congressman, and confidante of both George Washington and Thomas Jefferson, surveyed the scene. It was dismal. America was in "disarray." The situation was so bad that a revolt in Massachusetts of poor farmers led by Daniel Shays, who resented a taxation plan that had led to staggering debts and fore-closures, had "gravely shaken" the confidence that the Confederation could survive. Shays's Rebellion had seized courthouses and threatened the state's arsenal in Springfield. The state militia couldn't stop the uprising; in fact, some members actually joined the rebellion. Desperate, Congress tried to raise a military force but "the thirteen states refused to pay for federal troops." Wealthy Bostonians then had to raise the money to "underwrite a state force of 4,000," which eventually routed Shays's rebels. But the damage was done.[86]

America was in trouble.[87] The threat of an agrarian coup that had "shut down courts and threatened a full-scale civil war in the Bay State," the "hopeless weakness of the country's military power," the financial chaos, and, for Georgia, the inability to recapture fugitive slaves who ran to "the insidious protection afforded by the Spaniards" compelled all the states to find some way to salvage what had been won in the war and was now clearly slipping away in the peace.[88] In Philadelphia in 1787, Madison led the charge to scrap the Articles of Confederation and draft a new Constitution. He was determined to make the national government strong and embody the ethos that led to the War of Independence against Britain.

But those intentions of creating a strong, viable republic committed to its lofty ideas crashed headlong into the unspoken reality of America: "Slavery was the largely unmentioned monster in the basement of the new nation."[89] It was so fearsome that its name, like a dreaded demon, was never to be mentioned in the Constitution lest it erupt out from its darkened and dank lair and tear the fragile nation apart. There was something else besides fear, though, that required slavery to remain like a terrifying wraith haunting the nation's founding document: guilt.

John Dickinson, a delegate from Pennsylvania who drafted the original Articles of Confederation, noted that the very omission of "'the WORD' slavery . . . [from the Constitution was to] conceal a principle of which we are ashamed."[90]

Nevertheless, while unspoken, slavery's ominous, conscience-haunting paradoxical presence was everywhere.[91] Twenty-five of the fifty-five delegates to the Constitutional Convention owned slaves, including George Washington, who brought three of his enslaved people with him to Philadelphia.[92] Conversely, between 1777 and 1784, Massachusetts, Rhode Island, New Hampshire, Connecticut, Pennsylvania, and the state-to-be Vermont had all put sunset clauses on slavery "within their borders."[93] In fact, Massachusetts had eliminated slavery altogether by the time of the Constitutional Convention.

And while some of the prominent Virginians who owned slaves, such as George Mason, Thomas Jefferson (who was not in Philadelphia), and James Madison, were squeamish about slavery, South Carolina's delegates had no such qualms. There was no Banquo's ghost hovering over the Palmetto State to stir the conscience or wrack slave owners with guilt. Instead, their appetite for more enslaved labor was "voracious" as they sought to "replace the many thousands who had emancipated themselves during the war." Indeed, because of the ongoing importation of Africans, the number of those in human bondage had reached nearly seven hundred thousand, with half a million "centered in Maryland, Virginia, and the Carolinas."[94] One of South Carolina's first governors, Rawlins Lowndes, was unequivocal: "Without Negroes, this state would degenerate into one of the most contemptible in the union . . . Negroes were our wealth," he said, "our only natural resource."[95] Charles Pinckney, a powerhouse in South Carolina and a delegate to the Constitutional Convention, also argued without any equivocation or hesitation that slavery was "justified."[96]

This juxtaposition laid bare the dilemma. There were two divergent goals for the Constitutional Convention. The Deep South was intent on strengthening the slaveholders' power and the institution of slavery. That is why they were there. Meanwhile, the other delegates were determined to create a viable nation. The asymmetry in aims allowed the dream of the United States of America to be held hostage to the tyranny of slave owners. If South Carolina and Georgia, in particular, did not get nationwide protection for slavery, did not get to have inordinate power in the halls of government, and did not get to enrich their wealth on the backs of the Atlantic slave trade, they "threatened to bolt."[97] Repeatedly, during the deliberations they made clear that human bondage was their price for signing onto the Constitution.[98] If Americans wanted a United States, it was going to cost Black people dearly.

John Rutledge of South Carolina, for example, issued an extortionist warning about any attempt to curtail the Atlantic slave trade, which Gouverneur Morris of New York had blasted as "cruel" and "in defiance of the most sacred laws of humanity." Rutledge countered, "If the Convention thinks that North Carolina, South Carolina, and Georgia will ever agree to the plan [for a Constitution] unless their right to import slaves [from Africa] be untouched, the expectation is in vain."[99] Madison understood the implication. He, in fact, conceded that if the Atlantic slave trade had been immediately banned, "the southern states would not have entered into the union of America."[100] And, he continued, as "great as the evil is" of the Atlantic slave trade, "the dismemberment of the Union would be worse."[101]

Similarly, when it came to the method for allocating congressional representatives based on a state's population, the South, which had previously argued that the enslaved were nothing but untaxable property, now did a complete about-face. Charles Pinckney "saw no reason why black slaves ought not 'to stand on an equality with whites'" when counting the number of inhabitants. Elbridge Gerry of Massachusetts was exasperated with this sudden shifting ground. Just a few years earlier, they were property. Even in the current discussions at the Constitutional Convention, they were property. And now, full equality with whites?! "Are they [slaves] men?" If so, he said, "then make them citizens and let them vote. Are they property? Why then is no other property included? The houses in this city [Philadelphia] are worth more than all the wretched slaves which cover the rice swamps of South Carolina." William Paterson of New Jersey then questioned aloud whether South Carolina and Georgia counted the enslaved when determining representation in the state legislature. He already knew the answer: "If Negroes are not represented in the states to which they belong, why should they be represented in the general government?" Of course there was no logical answer. But there was the ever-present Southern Damocles's sword hanging over the Constitutional Convention threatening to destroy the United States if the plantation-based regimes didn't get their way. North Carolina's William R. Davie issued the warning: "It was high time now to speak out," he declared. If the enslaved would not be counted "at least as three-fifths," which was a "compromise" Madison had proposed during the heated debates earlier in the Continental Congress, then, Davie scowled, "the business was at an end." The South had no problem in walking away from the Constitutional Convention and the United States of America. Northern delegates then scrambled to find some "cosmetic" language to twist the clause "in such a way that it did not appear that slaves were being directly counted simply to determine representation." Article 1, Section 2, Clause 3, therefore, read: "Representatives and direct Taxes shall be apportioned among the several States which may be included within this Union, according to their respective Numbers, which shall be determined by adding to the whole Number of free Persons, including those bound to Service for a Term of Years, and excluding Indians not taxed, three fifths of all other Persons." That piece of immoral legerdemain sailed through and by 1820 had "translat[ed] into 18 additional congressional representatives" for the South. Rufus King, a delegate from Massachusetts, while labeling the three-fifths clause "one of the Constitution's 'greatest blemishes,'" also admitted that that horrific concession to the slaveholders "was a necessary sacrifice to the establishment of the Constitution."[102]

And that was the deal. Human sacrifice. African-descended people would be offered up on the altar of slavery and anti-Blackness to appease the Southern gods. By the time the convention discussed the fugitive slave clause and the responsibility of the national government to suppress slave insurrections, euphemistically termed "domestic violence," there wasn't much Northern fight left. The language on the militia was "all-embracing . . . empowering the national legislature to 'call forth the aid of the militia' not only to 'repel invasions' but also 'to execute the laws of the Union' and to 'suppress insurrections.'"[103] There was some grumbling from a Northern delegate about "Philadelphia militiamen . . . being forced to bear arms against slave rebels in Georgia," but both the militia and fugitive slave clause easily sailed through to be included in the Constitution.[104] Madison explained that the militia clause in the Constitution "gave the states a 'supplementary security' by allowing Congress to enlist the help of other states in suppressing insurrections (including slave uprisings) or resisting invasions."[105]

Charles Pinckney's cousin, Charles Cotesworth Pinckney, who was also a delegate in Philadelphia, came back to South Carolina proud of what the Southerners had accomplished. He informed his fellow lawmakers about the fugitive slave clause. "We have obtained a right to recover our slaves in whatever part of America they may take refuge, which is a right we had not before." There was also a sense of pride that the Constitution would now force the federal government to assist in suppressing slave insurrections if the local militia couldn't contain the uprising. And, of course, the U.S. Constitution also permitted the Atlantic slave trade to continue for at least twenty more years. Charles Cotesworth Pinckney boasted, "We have made the best terms for the security of this species of property it was in our power to make."[106]

But the South wasn't done. Patrick Henry, Revolutionary War hero and Madison's Virginia nemesis, still was not pleased. Henry worried that the central government had far too much power, and he and the other anti-Federalists launched a campaign to scuttle ratification of the Constitution. In Richmond, where Virginia's legislators had gathered to discuss and vote on ratification, he went for the jugular. Henry argued that the draft gave the federal government the power to end slavery. "They'll take your niggers from you," he warned the Virginia legislature.[107]

Then Henry and George Mason "focused with vehemence" on a scenario laying out how that could happen—the militia. While South Carolina reveled in the benefits of the federal government's having the capacity to intervene by amassing the manpower to quell even the most violent slave uprising, Henry and Mason saw it very differently. George Mason, who owned hundreds of slaves, laid out a scenario in which the U.S. Congress could call on the state's militia during wartime, leaving "Virginians defenseless." It was the militia, he reminded his colleagues, that kept the state safe from the enslaved during the Revolutionary War. One Federalist retorted that it was absurd to think Virginia would be left without protection. If anything, given the repeated slave uprisings, it was "the Southern states . . . who were in fact most likely to need help from elsewhere."[108]

Patrick Henry, sensing that Mason's arguments weren't quite landing, then jumped back into the debate and spelled out another nightmare scenario. "Slavery is detested" in the North, he fulminated.[109] The question hanging in the air, as historian David Waldstreicher noted, was: "What would keep a Congress dominated by Northerners from refusing to defend the state from a slave rebellion?" The very thought of it, Henry shivered, "scared him." But there was more. Never forget, he goaded his fellow Virginians, that "the Continental Congress had asked for southern slaves to be armed."[110] Now, he continued, those Northern states, especially the ones that have already put emancipation clauses in their laws, would not hesitate to have Congress order that "every black man must fight . . . that every black man who would go into the army should be free." As he stared directly at Madison, Henry dared the Constitution's author to deny it. "The majority of Congress is to the north," Henry pressed on, "and the slaves are to the south." That very configuration spelled trouble. Unable to trust the North, he explained, "I see a great deal of property of Virginia in jeopardy." In order to protect what was rightfully ours, he insisted, "We ought to possess them in the manner we inherited them from our ancestors." Blacks' freedom, even through some type of military service, was simply "incompatible with the felicity of our country."[111]

The tendentious harangues, while not sabotaging the Constitution, had made an important dent. George Mason managed to wring a major concession out of Madison in order to get ratification through the Virginia legislature—a promise to include a Bill of Rights.[112] It was an omission that hadn't even occurred to James Madison, who was "dogmatically attached to the Constitution in every clause, syllable and letter." He had initially dismissed a Bill of Rights as a "mere parchment barrier," but its omission was a "significant political error" because seven state constitutions had some vague statement about the basic freedoms upon which the federal government could not encroach. Madison soon came to realize that his tunnel vision could prove to be a "costly political mistake." The Southern states had already voiced fears about "federal control of the militia" and "whether the federal government would attempt to destroy the slave system." It soon dawned on him that if he stood any chance of getting enough states to ratify the Constitution—North Carolina had already rejected it, Vermont and Rhode Island didn't even call it up for a vote, and six states "had proposed over 100 distinct changes"—the very first meeting of Congress had to deliver a Bill of Rights.[113]

MADISON, ONCE AGAIN, took charge. He "overawed the House of Representatives with his unrivaled command of legislative machinery and by his powers of persuasive argument."[114] He "single-handedly" drafted the initial seventeen amendments, maneuvered them through the U.S. House of Representatives, then massaged the negotiations in the Senate to reduce the number of enumerated rights down to twelve. Yet, while there was definitely inordinate skill at work, Congressman Theodore Sedgwick of Massachusetts thought there was something else, too. Fear. Madison was so "obsessive," Sedgwick noted, that he acted as if he was "constantly haunted by the ghost of Patrick Henry." Senator Robert Morris of Pennsylvania was also convinced that whatever happened in Virginia had Madison "so cursedly frightened . . . that he dreamed of amendments ever since."[115]

What Madison actually feared was that the anti-Federalists, like Patrick Henry's cronies in Congress, would add the kind of amendments that would undermine a strong central government and send the United States hurtling back to the unworkable conditions of the Articles of Confederation.[116] He wanted amendments that would leave the "structure and stamina of the Govt. as little touched as possible."[117] What those amendments look like reveal much about the man as well as the political forces shaping the Bill of Rights.

Madison conveyed that he believed the "great rights" were "trial by jury, freedom of the press, and 'liberty of conscience.'"[118] On the other hand, the right to bear arms and a well-regulated militia, in both his discussion in the House of Representatives and with Thomas Jefferson, did not make his list. In fact, he wasn't alone. That right was nowhere to be found in more than "two thirds of the state constitutions." And when it was there, Massachusetts and North Carolina had limited it to defend the state, while Pennsylvania and Vermont defined it as the right for self-defense and for the state. That's it.[119] But nonetheless, it was going to rear its head because if there was going to be a Constitution and a United States of America, the Federalists had to respond to Mason's, Henry's, and other Southerners' assertions "that the federal government would, in one way or another, render the militia impotent as a slave control device."[120] Representative Lambert Cadwalader of New Jersey, therefore, hoped that Madison's amendments would "calm the turbulence of the opposition in Virginia and some of the other states and certainly bring North Carolina into the Union."[121]

THE SECOND AMENDMENT was, thus, not some hallowed ground but rather a bribe, paid again with Black bodies. It was the result of Madison's determination to salve Patrick Henry's obsession about Virginia's vulnerability to slave revolts, seduce enough anti-Federalists to get the Constitution ratified, and stifle the demonstrated willingness of the South to scuttle the United States if slavery were not protected.

The question of the role of the militia was key to all of this. While Article 2, Section 8, Clauses 15 and 16 of the Constitution delineated the role of Congress in calling out the militia for a variety of tasks—executing the laws of the nation, repelling a foreign invasion, and quelling domestic insurrections, it was the latter that was crucial for the Second. As defenders of America's laws, the militia had a tenuous and shaky role. In Massachusetts, recall that during Shays's Rebellion, many members of the militia actually joined with the rebels to disrupt, defy, and overturn the law while others dug in and refused to engage in battle. Congress couldn't get any of the states to pay for amassing a force large enough to take on Shays's troops. It required a squadron of mercenaries, paid by Boston's elite, to stop the uprising. In short, Shays's Rebellion hovered like a dark cloud over the proceedings, and there weren't a lot of expectations about the militia's ability to uphold the law.

Meanwhile, what the anti-Federalists, in particular, were afraid of was a standing army controlled by the U.S. government. And the militia, ostensibly, was to counter the threat of a professional military ready to pounce and destroy liberty.[122] The ghost of the British Redcoats was the source of that traumatic memory, and its effects are apparent in what would become the Third Amendment, banning the quartering of troops in private homes. The colonists resented mightily the king's soldiers sleeping in their homes, eating their food, and worse. Much worse. Moreover, the war had also led to the Continental army taking over colonists' homes to house the troops. In this new nation, regardless of whose army, the vow was "never again."[123] The memory was so intense that, years later, George Washington's 1796 Farewell Address warned against "overgrown military establishments," and it wasn't until 1947 that the United States created a Department of Defense to indicate the permanence of U.S. military forces—the dreaded standing army.[124]

As for repelling a foreign invasion, that idea had already been disproved. George Washington knew all too well how ill-equipped the citizen/farmer/saloon keep/blacksmith militiaman was to confront a professional army.[125] There were far too many times during the War of Independence when the militia would not show up, would run away, or would decide to just go home in the middle of a battle. At Bunker Hill, for example, although the militia initially pounded the British and inflicted a 90 percent casualty rate, it was the *Americans* who had to retreat because "a steady trickle of desertions had drained [the defenders] like a leaky pipe" and "fresh militia troops nearby refused to come forward."[126] The discipline, the reliability, and the training were simply not there. Even the Southern militias, when up against a professional army, were wholly inadequate. "Virginia's militia . . . had disgraced itself by bolting before firing a single shot in the critical battle of Camden, South Carolina." It was obvious, whether North or South, that no militia was going to stop a foreign invasion. The war proved that beyond a reasonable doubt.[127]

What the militia could do rather well, however, as George Mason noted, was keep slave owners safe. It was the militia that was instrumental in shutting down the massive Stono Rebellion. Indeed, that Sunday in 1739, all the white men, as the law required, had gone to church with their guns, and when the alarm rang, they were prepared to hunt down those who dared seek freedom in Spanish Florida.[128] As historian Sally Hadden noted, slave "patrols alone were thought to be an inadequate response to a large-scale insurrection. Typically, if the rebellion was (or was believed to be) a large one, senior militia officers would be alerted and whole militia units could be called up for service . . . and eventually the patrols could be subsumed within larger militia units."[129]

The Southern militias not only quelled rebellions; they were also there to prevent another Stono. They oversaw the slave patrols and regularly searched the homes of the enslaved for weapons.[130] Georgia even upped the ante with a "standing warrant to search any black's house," enslaved *or* free, for "offensive weapons and ammunition."[131] In short, James Madison, the Virginian, knew "that the militia's prime function in his state, and throughout the South, was slave control."[132]

ALTHOUGH THERE ARE very few records concerning the actual drafting and debate of the Second Amendment, Madison's first completed attempt reflected his concerns for "liberty of conscience" and perhaps the unease voiced during the Constitutional Convention about forcing Quakers to take up arms to put down a slave rebellion in Georgia.[133] He wrote:

> The right of the people to keep and bear arms shall not be infringed; a well armed and well regulated militia being the best security of a free country; but no person religiously scrupulous of bearing arms shall be compelled to render military service in person.[134]

That amendment, of course, was just one of seventeen. Even though Madison had whittled the hundreds of proposed amendments pouring in from the states down to that number, for many of the Federalists, that was seventeen too many. It was a hot and humid late July through early August in 1789, tempers and patience were frayed. Their attention was, therefore, on getting this newfangled government up and running, and the amendments seemed like a distraction. Their discussion about the enumerated rights was, as a consequence, "remarkably short, snappish, and driven by the politics of the moment rather than by appeals to lofty ideals." The Federalists and anti-Federalists were at diametrically opposed ends of the spectrum on the amendments. The former arguing that they were unnecessary, and the latter demanding that they go further because the federal government's power had yet to be curtailed.[135]

Before the polarizing differences between the two could destroy even the faintest possibility of ratification, Madison tried to rush through a floor vote on his raft of amendments, but the wily legislator hit a major stumbling block. Massachusetts's Elbridge Gerry decried the vague language about the militia, insisted on the need to be more explicit about the fact that the point of citizen soldiers was to prevent the rise of a standing army, and railed against the devilment that could arise if the federal government declared everyone a "conscientious objector" and thereby rendered state militias weaponless and impotent. He was soon joined by a chorus of twelve other congressmen.[136]

This mini revolt was stretching Madison to the outer limits of his skill set. He was exhausted. The House of Representatives simply did not grasp what he had come to understand so clearly after emerging from his battles with Patrick Henry and George Mason. The raucous debates in Virginia portended a future, if he didn't prevail now, with a weak central government and all the dystopian ills of the unworkable Articles of Confederation. And he knew that *weak* was exactly what the anti-Federalists wanted. Patrick Henry made it so clear that a strong central government, dominated by Northerners, posed an existential threat to the institution of slavery. During those debates in Virginia, Madison had tried "to cite the fugitive slave clause and slave trade agreement as proof that slavery was safe under the Constitution." Other Federalists brought up the three-fifths clause. Henry contemptuously dismissed all of them. They weren't enough. He flat out "opposed the creation of a national Congress that could legislate at all about how life was lived in Virginia." Slavery required states' rights. Strong, impenetrable states' rights. In fact, despite Georgia ratifying the Constitution, "threats to slavery worried ratification conventions in the South."[137] Madison, therefore, had to find a way to keep the central government strong yet still provide the pro-slavery safeguards to mollify the powerful plantation owners that dominated the state legislatures. One amendment in particular, it seemed, would do that. This enumerated right not only elevated militias, whose primary and most important function was controlling the Black population, but ensured that the federal government's constitutional role would not interfere in the states' ability to use those forces when necessary.[138]

But instead of getting the Bill of Rights up on the floor for a vote, the House pushed the discussion into an ad hoc committee led by Federalist John Vining of Delaware. There, Roger Sherman from Connecticut, who was described by John Adams as an "Angell" and by others as someone "as cunning as the devil," thought all the amendments were superfluous and wholly unworthy of the Constitution. To Madison's chagrin, Sherman had the clout and the legislative heft to drive that viewpoint home and turn the Vining Committee into an amendment graveyard. Madison had to act quickly. He called on the one person who had the power and respect to convince Sherman to back down. George Washington. Within days, Sherman received a letter from the president: "I see nothing exceptionable in the proposed amendments," Washington wrote. "Some of them, in my opinion, . . . are necessary to quiet the fears of some respectable characters and well meaning Men."[139]

After that, Sherman's objections melted away, and Vining's committee reported out a revised draft, reducing the number of amendments, reshuffling them, and altering the wording in Madison's militia amendment to remove the conscientious objector clause and "to make clear that the amendment applied specifically to an organized, officially sanctioned body," instead of something akin to Shays's "mob."[140] The revisions then went to the Senate for further edits—eliminating language that a militia was composed of "the body of the people," making clear that it was "limited to men sanctioned by the state"—and after a bit of back-and-forth with the House, the draft was legislatively polished, though grammatically clunky, and would emerge from committee as the Second Amendment.[141]

> A well regulated Militia, being necessary to the security of a free State, the right of the people to keep and bear Arms, shall not be infringed.

The full Bill of Rights, with its ten amendments, was now ready for state ratification. As legal scholar Michael Waldman noted, however, the "other amendments pointed forward; the Second Amendment, backward."[142] In a landmark document whose preamble begins, "We the People of the United States, in Order to form a more perfect Union, establish Justice, insure domestic Tranquility, provide for the common defense, promote the general Welfare, and secure the Blessings of Liberty," the Second Amendment continued to buttress slavery. The language is "what Patrick Henry claimed to want during the ratification debate in Richmond": a bribe to the South using the control of Black people as the payoff. And Madison delivered.[143] Through awkward wording and punctuation about the right to bear arms *and* the well-regulated militia, he provided "another constitutional provision prohibiting Congress from emasculating the South's primary instrument of slave control."[144]

On September 25, 1789, Congress sent the amendments to the states. In less than two years, three-fourths of them had ratified the Bill of

Rights, and the Second Amendment came into being on December 15, 1791, steeped in anti-Blackness, swaddled in the desire to keep African-descended people rightless and powerless, and as yet another bone tossed to keep the South mollified and willing to stay aligned with the grand experiment of the United States of America.[145]

*Two*

# Keeping a Ferocious Monster in Chains

The determination to keep Black people subjugated by law and excluded from the array of rights that defined the revolutionary era "poisoned the entire society."[1] Legislatures passed a series of statutes that "cracked down on free people of color with unprecedented ferocity."[2] Similarly, the "regulation of slavery . . . never ceased adapting, reacting, evolving, and expanding" to try to stage-manage the impossibility of easily holding millions of people in bondage.[3] The governor of the Mississippi territory fearfully imagined the powder keg that was bound to explode in America's slaveholding democracy: "That we deprive them of the sacred Boon of Liberty is a Crime they can never forgive."[4]

The fear of retribution for slavery and the flat-out denial of citizenship only strengthened the anti-Blackness of the Second Amendment and shaped whether Blacks, even free Blacks, had the right to bear arms, the right to a well-regulated militia, or even the basic right to self-defense.[5]

\* \* \*

CONGRESS, THUS, FOLLOWED up its work on the Bill of Rights with a heated debate about the ongoing existence of slavery and by passing two new, important laws. First, there was a petition crafted by Pennsylvania Quakers, signed by the revered but dying Benjamin Franklin, and introduced by the Speaker of the House "calling for a national commitment" to end slavery. It landed like a stick of dynamite among the solons. Some legislators tried to just snuff out the flame, hoping that no one would see the "explosive" issue of slavery smoldering in a House of Representatives built on the three-fifths clause. Others scrambled to throw the dynamite out the window before it destroyed what Madison had so deftly welded together. The congressmen from Georgia and South Carolina, however, were not going to ignore the attempt to blow up the House of Slavery. This was "racial treason" and they went right after the bomb-throwers. James Jackson of Georgia and William Loughton Smith of South Carolina launched into a four-hour filibuster, before the term was even used, to "harangue," threaten, and berate the other congressional representatives about "these cursed negro petitions." Jackson's ire was particularly focused on the Quakers who threw that antislavery bomb into the House of Representatives, and he swore that anyone who tried to emancipate the South's slaves would soon find themselves "in danger." Mortal danger.[6]

Madison, seeing the nation he had patiently helped build teetering once again on the brink of collapse because of slavery, intervened. After he read the committee's report for the Franklin-backed petition, he knew trouble was inevitable. The committee recommended that Congress place an exorbitant tax on the importation of slaves so that it would be too expensive to engage in that nefarious business. As his biographer Joseph Ellis noted, Madison had mastered the "Virginia straddle," talking Northern but thinking Southern.[7] This time was no different. He knew "that slavery contradicted the Revolution's founding commitment to human equality, that southerners (including his own constituents) would resist yielding control over their slaves to a national government . . . , and that political combat over slavery would likely explode the two-year-old constitutional impact." Madison had to remember only the blistering constitutional ratification debates in Virginia just a few years earlier. Patrick Henry had predicted then that if Congress didn't go after slavery via the militia, it would do so by taxing the South's peculiar institution into oblivion. At the time, Madison had dismissed that idea as fantasy and thought he had allayed Henry's primary fears about the militia with the Second Amendment. But now, like a monstrous hydra, here came the other head threatening the existence of the nation he had labored so hard to create. Therefore, although he knew slavery was an abomination, Madison stripped the committee's language down and whittled it away until it was unequivocal: "Congress have no authority to interfere in the emancipation of slaves, or in the treatment of them within any of the States."[8]

WHILE ENDING SLAVERY was pushed off the legislative agenda, defining "American" was pulled onto it. The first bill, in 1790, explored who could become a U.S. citizen and, therefore, who had access to rights. The congressional debates centered on three questions: What qualities made someone worthy of U.S. citizenship? How long would he or she have to reside in the United States for the government to make that assessment? And was there some kind of stairstep semi-citizenship status whereby a person would have some (but not all) of the rights and immunities that came with being an American citizen?[9] Underlying all these questions were the foundational ones: Who was "worthy," and how was that characteristic going to be decided? Legislators asked, Was there some appropriate amount of time spent in the United States that would be a good barometer? Would an oath of allegiance be enough? How about, one asked facetiously, holding an "inquisition"?[10]

They could not agree on much except that "African Americans were not considered qualified for citizenship or for other rights."[11] Congress erected a racial threshold that would not be substantively crossed until 1952, when the legislators finally "eliminated race as a basis for naturalization."[12] Before then, however, the Naturalization Act of 1790 declared that only white immigrants who had lived in the United States for at least two years could become naturalized citizens. Equally important, their children who were under the age of twenty-one at the time of the parent's naturalization would also be U.S. citizens.[13] By designating white immigrants as the touchstone for citizenship, Congress carefully ignored that in the first national census in 1790, there was no information about ancestry, parental homeland, or national origin. In fact, there was no mechanism whatsoever to determine immigrant status. So it wasn't actually "immigrant" that became the defining characteristic for American citizenship. The only thing the nation could rely on was phenotype. White skin.[14]

As historian Martha S. Jones noted, "No single piece of congressional legislation was felt more . . . than the Naturalization Act of 1790."[15] That "whites only" barricade created a rightless, race-contingent netherworld for everyone else, including free Blacks.[16] They were to be no more than "denizens," mere "halfway members" in American society.[17] Their claim to U.S. citizenship evaporated the moment it was exposed to the air of white fear, white suspicion, white contempt, and white rage.[18] Even the freedom that some Blacks achieved by fighting in the War of Independence vanished once the crisis had passed. In 1806, the Virginia Supreme Court of Appeals ruled, "In the case of a person visibly appearing to be a negro, the presumption is that he is a slave." The burden of proof was on them to prove otherwise.[19]

And that very burden meant that there was nothing they could do, no level of patriotism, no amount of God-fearing godliness, no depth of bravery, no proof of being born in the sweet land of liberty, and no "evidence of time-in-residence . . . [that] could alter their natural-born state of unfitness."[20] Of course free Blacks chafed. This was the land, Bishop Richard Allen of the African Methodist Episcopal Church would note, that African-descended people "watered with our *tears* and *our blood* and is now our *mother country*."[21] It was, therefore, impossible to blithely accept how white immigrants gained the benefits of American citizenship, yet Blacks who had been born in the United States, fought for the United States, and had no other homeland besides the United States could not achieve anything more than the lethal limbo of being "halfway members."[22]

White skin, by law, carried the presumption of worthiness, while far too often Blacks, who had earned their freedom through manumission, military service, or buying themselves out of bondage, were defined "as a threat to the general welfare, if not an outright liability."[23] Even anti-slavery Northerners were worried that free Blacks "becoming citizens [would] be dangerous to the public." Vice President John Adams opined that "Negroes . . . turned loose upon a world" would know only how to "live by violence or theft or fraud."[24] The South was even more fearful. James Monroe, governor of Virginia, warned that free Blacks, who were nearly 10 percent of the state's Black population, were a "publick danger."[25] They purportedly sold liquor to the enslaved, received stolen goods from them, harbored fugitives, and, worse, plotted uprisings.[26]

The "publick danger" posed by free Blacks that rattled Monroe most, however, focused on something even more frightening than violence.

Hope. Uncomfortably coexisting with the elegiac "we hold these truths" was America's foundational belief that "God intended the African for the *status* of slavery."[27] That Blacks could actually be "free," therefore, sent a strong, unwanted signal to those entrapped in human bondage. George Washington was greatly concerned, as he brought his enslaved entourage to his presidential residence in Philadelphia, a city where free Blacks were nearly five times more prevalent than those "still tethered to the institution of slavery." He worried that "the idea of freedom might be too great a temptation for them to resist." His wife, Martha Washington, was even more determined to "shield . . . her slaves from the contagion of liberty."[28]

Despite the Washingtons' fears, however, the North "was no Eden." As the number of free Blacks increased, so, too, did the laws to curtail their access to rights. In most states, Blacks could not vote or testify against a white person in court or sit on a jury.[29] "Other than Maine, no state admitted to the union in the nineteenth century's antebellum period allowed blacks to vote."[30] In 1821, while eliminating the one-hundred-dollar property requirement for white men to vote, New York increased the threshold by 150 percent for Blacks.[31] In 1837 the Pennsylvania Supreme Court, based on the colony's 1701 charter, the state's 1776 and 1790 constitutions, and the U.S. Constitution, ruled that only freemen had the right to vote and, equally important, that free "blacks were not considered to be freemen." In fact, "black men held a status inferior to that of freemen" and thus could not enjoy the inalienable rights of those who were free, those who were citizens.[32]

Many of the Midwest states agreed. Illinois and Indiana forbid free Blacks from moving there. Some, like Ohio, actually required bonds up to one thousand dollars from Blacks to "guarantee good conduct." Iowa fined them two dollars a day for remaining in the state for more than three days, as if they were unwanted guests. As late as 1857 in

Oregon, a lopsided 8,640–1,041 election banned Blacks from settling in the territory, which was codified in the state's 1859 constitution and not repealed until 1926.[33]

The South was even more determined to snuff out the vaporous rights of free Blacks. In 1783, Maryland had already created a special liminal category—"free blacks denied the rights of freemen"—that had them precariously perched between the enslaved and whites. Then, within a few years after the ratification of the U.S. Constitution, Delaware, Maryland, and Kentucky stripped free Blacks of the right to vote. In Louisiana, free Blacks were banned from traveling between states.[34] In South Carolina, Black seamen were thrown in jail when their ships docked and were not released until their vessels were ready to leave the harbor.[35] Georgia would eventually pass a law that free Blacks had to actually be registered with the courts to remain in the state.[36] Virginia and Florida would craft legislation that used the criminal justice system to convict free Blacks of some trumped-up charge and then sell them into "their true condition . . . absolute slavery."[37]

Not surprisingly, given the omnipresent sense of suspicion and danger associated with Blackness, this exclusion carried through to guns. It was "illegal in most states for [free Blacks] to possess a shotgun, musket, rifle or shot unless by special permit."[38] In Virginia, a free Black man named Peter Mathews gingerly asked to be released from all the restrictions that limited his ability to conduct business, such as going to court and testifying against white debtors. His respectful requests put a target on him. A group of vigilantes broke into his home "searching for a cache of weapons." He tried to explain that an "old pistol without flint, a broken sword, and an old cutlass" were hardly the beginnings of a revolution. But Blacks with guns, outside the control and approval of whites, was a revolution that was not to be tolerated.[39]

The second major law passed by Congress, therefore, was all about getting guns and control into white men's hands. Prior to 1790, numerous states, especially in the North, allowed free Blacks to be members of their militias.[40] The Uniform Militia Act of 1792 sought to change that. This federal law required every *white*, able-bodied male between eighteen and forty-five to join his state's militia. "More significantly, it required them all to buy a gun."[41] This was an act of citizenship and an act of self-defense. Whites believed that they "lived in an enemy camp."[42] The threat was always there.

Ironically, the Age of Revolution contributed greatly to the foreboding threat of being overtaken, ruled, or killed by Black people. Enlightenment ideas about freedom, liberty, and people-powered and people-centric governments had, of course, wrested the thirteen colonies from King George III and toppled the Bourbon monarchy in France. Those ideas, however, had also sparked a revolution by hundreds of thousands of enslaved people in Saint Domingue, current-day Haiti. What happened there led many Southern whites to look upon Haiti as "a very hell of horrors," according to Frederick Douglass, who remarked that its "very name was pronounced with a shudder."[43]

The Haitian Revolution began in 1791 in a French-owned colony that not only produced the most wealth for France but also held more than half of the entire Caribbean's enslaved population.[44] Sugar and coffee were the beasts that fed that engine.[45] The work was backbreaking. The planters sybaritic and sadistic. The enslaved's life brutishly short.[46] But with the revolutionary turmoil in the French metropole, which began in 1789 and led to the guillotine execution of King Louis XVI, whites and mulattos in Haiti had squared off in a scramble for power in this all-important colony. While they pummeled each other, on August 22, 1791, "slaves in the rich northern plain had risen in concert, destroying plantations, burning cane fields, and mercilessly attacking surprised slaveholders, overseers, and their families."[47] The colonizing government "found the enemy at their gate, their houses in flame, and every public and private place filled with assassins."[48]

Almost from the very beginning, America's Founding Fathers were rattled. South Carolina governor Charles Pinckney expressed to George Washington the slaveholders' ultimate fear: "I am afraid if not checked in time it is a flame which . . . may eventually" torch "the Southern States." He shuddered as he looked at Saint Domingue and saw "the almost indiscriminate Slaughter of all the whites who had fallen into their hands—The conflagration of the largest & most valuable Sugar Estates on the Island—The general destruction of property, & a probable famine are particularly unpleasant to us who live in Countries where Slaves abound."[49] Washington was also distressed. "Lamentable!"—there was no other word for it—"to see such a spirit of revolt among the Blacks."[50] Nathaniel Cutting, who held a variety of positions in the government, walked Jefferson through the frightening carnage. "They have disarmed the whites in almost every Parish . . . They have afterwards in the most cruel manner murder'd in cool blood great numbers of those whom they had thus render'd defenceless. Their savage barbarity has spared neither age nor sex." And, he continued, "Their treatment of Matrons, Virgins and Infants, would make a Nero blush."[51]

Military power from Spain, Britain, and France descended on the island to quell the uprising and establish their own authority over this very rich colony. The enslaved, however, fought off wave after wave over the span of more than a decade and sent Europe's most powerful armies reeling. For the British, who had lost ten thousand men in less than two months, it was like "fighting to conquer a cemetery."[52] Napoleon sent "the largest expedition that had ever sailed from France, consisting of 20,000 veteran troops, under some of Bonaparte's ablest officers," including his brother-in-law Charles Victor Emmanuel Leclerc.[53] What was supposed to be a quick little victory, however, with the mighty French disarming all Black Haitians and regaining full control of the island, instead turned into "arguably the most brutal, racist war ever fought on French soil."[54] Leclerc's military strategy was barbaric and "genocidal."[55] He wrote to "Napoleon that all people of color over twelve years of age had to be killed." And he tried to accomplish that goal. "Blacks as well as mulattoes were killed at the drop of a hat—drowned, hung, shot, or devoured by bloodhounds especially imported from Cuba for this purpose."[56] Before his capture, the Haitian leader Toussaint Louverture, knowing that the only way to defeat a vastly superior army was through a scorched-earth strategy, ordered his troops:

> Don't forget that the only resources we have until the rainy season rids us of our enemies are destruction and fire. Know that the earth worked by our own sweat must not provide a single morsel of food to our enemies. Obstruct trails, throw cadavers and horses in all the springs; annihilate and burn everything, so that those that come to put us back in bondage always encounter here a portrayal of the hell they all deserve to go to.[57]

And the French entered that inferno. They took one fiery blow after the next as the Haitians waged a textbook version of guerrilla warfare. Then, just as Louverture predicted, the rainy season came, as did the mosquitoes and yellow fever.[58] Beaten. Sick. Decimated. Inconceivable surrender became Napoleon's only option as more than "80 percent of the French army sent there died on the island."[59]

THE UNTHINKABLE HAD just happened. For white slaveholders in the United States, the Haitian Revolution had set a "terrifying precedent."[60] It "rendered white supremacy vulnerable and thereby surmountable."[61] Southern slave owners knew it and trembled; it was "their darkest fears realized."[62] But it wasn't just about military prowess, however.

It showed something else that was equally frightening. Initially, the Saint Domingue plantation owners thought that the insurgents did not have "*combinaison d'idées nécessaire*" to sustain a successful revolt.[63] The ideas that drove the American and French Revolutions were supposed to be "FOR WHITES ONLY."[64] But the Haitian Revolution's leaders had welded *egalité*, *liberté*, and *fraternité* into a mighty sword for Black liberation.[65] They, in fact, exceeded the parameters of the American Revolution by making the struggle not only about civil liberties but about racial equality.[66] Historians have therefore traced the resonance of those ideas through a series of slave revolts in Louisiana in 1795 and 1811, as well as in Virginia in 1800, 1822, and 1831.[67]

Contemporaries saw it, too. Albeit with a twist. Nathaniel Cutting attributed the "Rapine, Murder and Devastation" in Saint Domingue to "certain mistaken ideas of the Rights of Man."[68] Thomas Jefferson had warily eyed the uprising since 1791 and "could . . . see himself as the target of a justifiable revolution by his own slaves."[69] He warned James Madison about Haiti: "If this combustion can be introduced among us under any veil whatever, we have to fear it."[70]

Indeed, the proximity to the United States, as a slaveholding, maritime nation with a number of key port cities, made it a vector for unbridled fear, especially as thousands of white planters fled "from

Saint-Domingue to the comforting shores of the southern United States." They brought not only "tales of black rebellion and atrocities" but their enslaved as well.[71] In Baltimore, in 1793, when fifty-three ships landed with about one thousand whites and five hundred slaves from Saint Domingue, the city council responded to the supposedly "reasonable fears" among the city's whites and granted the residents access to "public arms"—weapons—"for the use of the volunteer militia units."[72]

In Charleston, Thomas Pinckney worried that South Carolina would soon "be exposed to the same insurrections" that had engulfed Saint Domingue. In 1792, he tried to "insulate" his state "from the contagion [by] banning the importation of French slaves." He also noted that the slave revolt in Saint Domingue did "thoroughly prove the Policy of having our Militia always in a situation to act with promptness and Effect as Circumstances may require."[73]

Meanwhile, as white planter refugees and their enslaved continued to pour into Louisiana, which would soon become American territory, "growing fears of insurrection" rippled from Pointe Coupée to New Orleans.[74] In that steamy hotbed of human bondage, "the ideas of liberty, fraternity, and equality were spread to the far corners of the colony, including the slave quarters."[75]

When 137 merchant ships from Saint Domingue, protected by a "heavily armed convoy of French warships," showed up at Hampton Roads, Virginia, the panic among whites reached a fever pitch. They brought "too many negroes . . . with them," came the complaints. And now, the criticism continued, "local slaves had begun deserting plantations . . . and behaving 'in an insolent manner.'"[76] The press was sure that "the St. Domingo negroes have sown those seeds of revolt."[77] Governor James Monroe feared that Virginia's enslaved population would be "infected with the malady of insurrection" because, he surmised, the enslaved from "Santo Domingo . . . must produce an effect on all the people of color . . . especially our slaves." Monroe wasn't wrong.[78]

Freedom and independence had now become what the Founding Fathers feared—a lethal virus that could not be quarantined in a whites-only world. Jefferson despondently warned that "the revolutionary storm, now sweeping the globe, will [soon] be upon us."[79] White slave owners lived in fear that "the contagion of liberty that had been released by the American Revolution was dangerously spreading to the 'wrong' people." The enslaved.[80] And that was the critical lesson of Saint Domingue. "American blacks inspired by the Haitians were to be feared above all else."[81] Every one of them could now be infected with "ideas about emancipation and liberty; each one was, in the eyes of Americans, a potential conspirator."[82]

That fear was palpable for those who were making life-and-death decisions for the nation. Pinckney was concerned. Washington was concerned. Jefferson and James Madison were also concerned. In March 1792, while mentioning to a colleague that "the Militia bill" was headed to the Senate, Madison offered, in the very next sentence, that the news "from St. Domingo paints the distress of the Island in the most gloomy colours."[83]

The nation's legislature was doing its part to brighten the picture. First, there was the evisceration of the attempt to have Congress end slavery. Then that effort was followed with the definition of whites (and only whites) as worthy of being or becoming American citizens. The next piece of legislative business, the Militia Acts of 1792, which Congress passed under the shadow of the Haitian Revolution, further solidified the parameters of race, rights, and citizenship. This "was to be a white man's republic defended by white arms."[84]

Nothing, not even another mass revolt by white farmers angry over a tax law, could shake that foundational principle. The Whiskey Rebellion in 1794 was the culmination of a multiyear violent resistance to a tax on domestically produced distilled alcohol. In 1791, Secretary of the Treasury Alexander Hamilton proposed the tax, arguing that it would be a solid revenue generator on a luxury item and that it would encourage sobriety. Most important, it would deal with the massive government deficit, which amounted to 27 percent of the federal budget. But whiskey was no luxury item; the tax hit hardest the poor farmers in the western reaches of the United States, around Pittsburgh, and areas of Virginia and Kentucky. At that time, because Spain controlled the Mississippi River and wouldn't grant the U.S. shipping privileges, those farmers couldn't get their grain to market via the easiest and most cost-effective way. They could, however, distill it, use it in the cash-strapped barter economy that flourished in the area, and keep their financial heads above water. The whiskey tax changed all that.[85]

Virtually everything about the tax, from the way it carved out a sizable chunk of the farmers' annual income, to the complicated book-keeping required by law, to the timing of when the tax had to be paid, which was well before the farmer had any profit whatsoever from the crops, caused massive resentment at both the tax and the federal authority that required it. As the Pennsylvania farmers dug in and resisted, the federal government responded by invoking a section of the law that allowed tax collectors to seize the properties for failure to pay. The farmers retaliated with a series of attacks against federal agents, several of whom endured the torture of being tarred and feathered. Year after year of this resistance hardened the farmers until they had amassed a six-hundred-man militia that launched an assault on the sprawling compound, Bower Hill, of the chief federal excise tax collector, John Neville. "This was no rag-tag gathering to brutalize a tax collector, but a serious military encounter." U.S. soldiers had to swoop in from nearby Fort Pitt to get Neville out safely. But the farmers' militia seemed intent on destroying any vestige of American power and, unable to get to Neville, went into battle against the U.S. Army. And won. The farmers had scored a major victory, carried their own flag, and dreamed of their own new country, Westylvania, and they appeared ready for a larger war.[86]

So was Alexander Hamilton. He had been urging a military strike for years to no avail. But now with the full-blown Whiskey Rebellion, it looked as if George Washington, who had been vacillating, was finally ready. Amassing militia from Pennsylvania, New Jersey, Maryland, and Virginia, on September 9, 1794, the president led the troops into battle. Yet even before Washington's forces reached Pittsburgh, "the leaders of the insurrection were running for cover." Barely a shot was fired.[87]

While it may have ended in a whimper, it certainly didn't start out that way. This was one of the first major tests of the barely new federal government. More than six hundred insurgents had defied the law, repeatedly mutilated tax collectors, and engaged in a shooting battle against U.S. soldiers. Surely, there would be consequences. Yet, only a handful of the rebels were tried in court, even fewer were convicted, and eventually they all received presidential pardons.[88] Most important, unlike in slave insurrections, there was no clamor for state and federal laws to disarm all white men so that the community could feel "safe," although it is clear from the reports coming out of Western Pennsylvania that many felt threatened, silenced, and cowed. This legislative ennui about musket- and rifle-toting insurgents also ignored that, from Shays's Rebellion to the Whiskey Rebellion, white men were the ones who had taken up arms against the United States of America. And in a pattern that would repeat itself well into the twenty-first century, there were little to no consequences for that.

THE PLANNED SLAVE uprising in Virginia in 1800, however, would have a very different ending. It was led by Gabriel, a strong, tall, literate, enslaved blacksmith on Thomas Prosser's plantation in Henrico County, whose religion was freedom and who wanted to live in a real republic. One where those who labored were able to keep their wages. "All of them."[89] A republic where those committed to democracy could live freely. For Gabriel and the hundreds who plotted, planned, and dreamed with him, this wasn't about a Black republic. This was about a multiracial, multireligious, multiethnic republic.

Gabriel would pay for that dream with his life.

He and several hundred slaves, a handful of free Blacks, and two white conspirators from France had drank heavily from the language of revolution and freedom. The rebels' flag would read "Death or Liberty," a stinging inversion of Patrick Henry's revolutionary motto. One of the key co-conspirators, Jack Ditcher, although illiterate, was well versed in the language of freedom when he said, "We had as much right to fight for our liberty as any men."[90] Another put it even more profoundly: "I have nothing more to offer than what General Washington would have . . . had he been taken by the British and put to trial . . . I have adventured my life in endeavouring to obtain the liberty of my countrymen, and am a willing sacrifice in their cause."[91]

But it wasn't just the American Revolution that influenced Gabriel. Haiti provided its own language. Gabriel understood that "Louverture demonstrated that black liberty could be won and that black rebellion could be successful, especially if [whites] were bitterly divided."[92] And divided and bitter barely captured the toxic fissures between the Republicans and the Federalists, respectively headed by Vice President Thomas Jefferson and President John Adams. Those ruptures, especially with a presidential election looming and rumblings about a call to violence if one party's candidate or the other did not win, showed a cleavage that Gabriel was convinced he could drive a successful revolt through.[93]

The plan called for three battalions of Gabriel's carefully recruited forces to hit key targets en route to the capital of Richmond and, while there, to kidnap Governor Monroe and hold him hostage. But Gabriel admonished that this was not to be some race war. "Quakers, the Methodists, and [all] Frenchmen . . . were to be spared" because of "their being friendly to liberty." In addition, he "intended also to spare the poor white women who had no slaves."[94]

One of the major stumbling blocks Gabriel encountered in his plan was a lack of guns. His forces were armed with the swords that he and his brother had made over the past few months, but blades were no match against bullets. The solution was simple enough: Go to Virginia's armory on Capitol Square and seize what they needed. One group of insurgents would set fire to a warehouse as a diversionary tactic. Then another group would head to the square where "several thousand stands of arms were piled up in the Capitol and Penitentiary."[95] The third group would "grab the money in the treasury." Then, after taking the state's warehouse of muskets, rifles, shot, and powder, and with enough money to pay the insurgent soldiers, the war of liberation could begin in earnest.[96]

As widespread and audacious as the conspiracy was—hundreds of people spread out over two counties and three towns—the vow of secrecy, for the most part, held. A rumor did surface a few weeks before the planned uprising and had actually percolated up to Governor

Monroe, but it was so "vague and uncertain" and, frankly, "preposter-ous"—a widespread slave revolt—that he didn't believe it and "took no action."[97]

While the insurgents held fast, however, the skies did not. On August 30, the evening of the planned revolt, a storm like no other unleashed a torrent of wind and rain, swelling the waterways and muddying the roads. Travel was virtually impossible. Hundreds of insurgents who needed to be at a key bridge were instead trapped behind walls of water and rivers of impassable mud. One slave, a man named Pharaoh, sitting out there drenched and unable to get to the rendezvous point, with thunder and lightning rattling every nerve in his body, cracked under the strain. He decided that he could secure his freedom another way. A safer way. He told a white planta-tion owner about the plot, hoping that manumission would be his reward.[98]

Hearing the news, the governor was stunned and "alarmed." The insurrection was only "discovered on the day when it was to have taken effect," he told Jefferson.[99] Monroe and other city and state officials were "in a state of absolute terror."[100] He immediately called out the militia, which, "like that of all southern states . . . existed to prevent slave insur-rections." First there was the Fourth Regiment Richmond, whose mission was to hunt down Gabriel and the other insurgents. Knowing that whoever got to the stash of guns first would win, the Nineteenth Regiment rushed to stand guard over the weapons, which Monroe had ordered to be moved to the penitentiary. Meanwhile, other bands of militia from around Virginia joined in the hunt. Within two weeks there were "about five Hundred Militia" determined to track down and quash any attempt at a slave revolt.[101] Monroe explained that there had to be "a display of our force and measures of defence . . . to intimidate those people."[102]

That unnatural bustle of activity to round up the conspirators forced many Virginians to come to grips with the full extent of Gabriel's plot and number of accomplices. This wasn't about one or two unhappy slaves. This was about three towns' and two counties' worth of well-organized insurgents who, if it hadn't been for the storm, might have inflicted enormous damage.[103] Gabriel's conspiracy "shook Virginians . . . because it seemed incontestable proof that Santo Domingo had been boiling right underneath them."[104] Monroe, in fact, confided to Jefferson, "We have had much trouble with the negroes here"; Gabriel's rebellion was "unquestionably the most serious and formidable conspiracy we have ever known of the kind."[105]

While Monroe was not prepared to articulate why they had so "much trouble," others stepped into that breach and gave public voice to Jefferson's own private fears about the "combustion" of revolutionary ideas circulating among an oppressed Black population. What patriots saw as heroic in whites, such as Patrick Henry's clarion call "Give me liberty or give me death," was dangerous when espoused by Blacks. One man remarked, for example, that too "many of the slaves . . . displayed a proud 'sense of their [natural] rights, [and] a contempt of danger.'"[106] The editor of the *Virginia Gazette* wrote that it was "evident that the French principles of Liberty and Equality have been infused into the minds of the negroes, and the incautious and intemperate use of these words by some whites amongst us have inspired them with hopes of success."[107] The real problem, another man wrote in the *Virginia Gazette*, was that "liberty and equality [are] . . . dangerous and extremely wicked" when bandied about among the enslaved. Slavery and freedom were wholly incompatible, he continued, and if Virginia insisted on slavery, then "we must re-enact all those rigorous laws which experience has proved necessary to keep it within bounds. In a word, if we will keep a ferocious monster in our country, we must keep him in chains."[108]

There had to be, undoubtedly, horrific consequences for those who dreamed of a real republic. And so, week after week, a series of public hangings, many in the town square, rolled through, three, four, five men at a time, until Gabriel himself was led to the gallows to hang alone. The editor of the *Virginia Argus* hoped "that these examples may deter all future attempts of this diabolical nature."[109] Although that was clearly the intent, Monroe had grown a bit squeamish after the public hangings had reached the double digits and sought Jefferson's advice on how to proceed: "10. have been condemned & executed, and there are at least twenty perhaps 40. more to be tried, of whose guilt no doubt is entertained." But, he continued, when is enough enough?[110]

Even with twenty-seven men hanged, others permanently ejected from Virginia, and some sold to slavers deep into the pure brutality of South Carolina and Georgia, though, there still was not peace. The "nation, from Massachusetts to Mississippi, was terror-stricken."[111] Gabriel's revolt compelled Virginia and other states to pass a series of laws to shore up the defenses against slave insurrections and further curtail the already limited freedom of free Blacks.

Virginia instituted "a guard of sixty-eight men for the capital at Richmond together with a night watch for each of its wards."[112] In addition, the state's "slave patrol laws became very stringent" and the model for legislation that was "copied elsewhere in the South."[113]

Then there was the issue of guns.[114] Whites understood that firearms were the only thing that stood between them and Black people's freedom. Monroe had made that clear when he moved the armory. And when William C. C. Claiborne, the newly appointed territorial governor of Louisiana, was headed to his post, he asked President Jefferson for thousands of muskets "since the negroes in the Island of Orleans are very numerous, and the number of free mulattoes is also considerable." He confided that "these people may be disposed to be riotous" once they learn that the rights they had under the Spanish will be eviscerated under the Americans.[115]

States thus legislated even greater controls on who could have a gun and under what circumstances. The enslaved were already banned from possession, but legislatures were determined to be even more explicit. It wasn't just gun ownership but the "sale or delivery of firearms to slaves [that] was forbidden in Florida, Georgia, Louisiana, and North Carolina."[116] South Carolina and Louisiana added that no slave could even use a firearm unless it was with the expressed permission of whites "to hunt within the boundaries of the owner's plantation."[117]

Free Blacks' access to guns was another problem altogether. In 1806, Virginia required them to have a license to carry firearms.[118] In Louisiana, one of the key targets was the free Black militia that had thrived under Spanish and then French rule. After the territory was purchased by the United States, whites demanded that all free Blacks be disarmed. In 1804, the new municipal council in New Orleans "began a campaign to exclude free blacks from any position in which they were required to bear arms." Not only was the Black militia targeted, but so were "the old black slave-catching crews," which the council now wanted replaced with a "white constabulary."[119]

Governor Claiborne heard the incessant demands to "crack down on politically assertive free men of color and to disband their militia."[120] Yet while initially amenable to the idea, especially because of the supposed "danger" involved in having so many free Blacks in New Orleans, the governor soon came to realize that this was no "motley" crew. The Black militia was well trained and professional, with a long, proud military tradition going back to the 1730s. This, he quickly surmised, was a group that could shore up the territory's ineffective and woefully stretched defenses. Except there was that one nagging detail—they weren't white.[121]

Claiborne understood that Black men as troops were often "employed as a desperate measure . . . in times of crisis."[122] For the governor, this felt like a crisis. Droves of refugees were pouring in from Saint Domingue. Avaricious planters were smuggling African-descended slaves into the Orleans Territory and snatching land from the indigenous people, and neither gave any indication that they would quietly accept the theft of their lives or their land. Meanwhile, Spain was fomenting slave revolts, promising freedom to those who ran away to Spanish-held lands in what is now Texas and challenging the validity of the borders that France and the United States had negotiated in the Louisiana Purchase.[123] Then there was the supposed militia. Its members were spread out over far too many plantations and too many miles to be effective, given the depth of the challenges the territory faced. And worse yet, the leadership was lacking as well. Several officers, Claiborne found, were "very young men holding rank above their years," and others were so "unpopular as officers" that the men were reluctant to serve under them, "if at all." Finally, there was the inability of this fighting force to even be able to communicate with one another. "Make a tour throughout that city [New Orleans] and in every street you will encounter native Americans [from the United States], native Louisianians, Frenchmen, Spaniards, Englishmen, Germans, Italians, etc., etc. Let a company of Militia be assembled and there is no one language in which the word of command can be given that will be intelligible to all."[124]

Faced with all these problems, Claiborne hoped to pull off the ultimate balancing act. He planned to mollify the plantation owners while still keeping the Black militia intact. His solution was to put the leadership of the troops in supposedly safer, more reliable hands as he "appointed white officers to oversee the black militia."[125]

The New Orleans legislative council was not mollified. In fact, its members were outraged. They excoriated and humiliated Claiborne in the press.[126] They sent a complaint directly to President Jefferson demanding the governor's removal. And in 1805, in "one of their first acts," they revised the militia law to write the Black militia right out of existence. That law ensured that public firearms were no longer available to the most organized, battle-tested group in the territory. And just as with the Militia Acts of 1792, only white males, regardless of how disorganized and dysfunctional their militia, could serve in this capacity. This was just the opening salvo. Legislation passed from 1806 to 1808 fastened the weight of subjugation tighter around the feet of the enslaved, while it curtailed, scuttled, and gutted the limited rights of free Blacks and "sounded the death knell for people of color's claim to citizenship."[127] One law, for example, made it a crime punishable by imprisonment for a free person of color to "presume to conceive themselves equal to the whites; . . . [refuse] to yield to them in every occasion, and . . . speak to or answer them disrespectfully."[128]

Louisiana was ratcheting up the restrictions because it was smuggling in and importing enslaved African-descended people as fast as the burgeoning sugar and cotton plantations could chew them up. As historian Daniel Rasmussen notes, "Nowhere in America was slavery as exploitative, or were profits as high, as in the cane fields of Louisiana. Slaves worked longer hours, faced more brutal punishments, and lived shorter lives than any other slave society in North America."[129] Those conditions fed into the brutality of iron collars, facemasks, cowhide whips, and even a Black child held as a pet to fetch food off the master's floor.[130] Louisiana proudly epitomized "the horrors of an archaic labor system with the rapacious efficiencies of capitalism."[131]

Not surprisingly, it was also the site of the largest slave rebellion in North America.

ON JANUARY 8, 1811, on what was known as the German Coast of Louisiana, a group of enslaved people led by Charles Deslondes gathered in the rain and began their thirty-six-mile liberation trek to New Orleans.[132] They knew it was all or nothing. Failed uprisings, like the one a few years earlier in Pointe Coupée, had a horrific, gory ending—"planters hanged twenty-three slaves, decapitated them, and nailed their heads to posts." And that uprising was stopped before it ever began.[133] Deslondes and his throng of insurgents, which would eventually grow between 150 to 500 strong, were undaunted and ready. Or so they thought.

The first stop was the plantation of Manuel Andry, who led one of the militia groups. By the time they were done with their axes, Andry was gravely wounded and his son dead, the ammunition and weapons that had been stockpiled for the planters' militia were raided, and Deslondes and other leaders had donned the uniforms kept in the basement. The insurgents' officers were immediately given the surprisingly few muskets found on Andry's property. The "troops" carried farm tools as weapons. Together, they set out to rally more slaves to the cause and destroy as many plantations and planters in the process.

As Deslondes's army of the enslaved moved along the levee, with drums beating and chants of "On to Orleans!" joyously exclaimed, plantation after plantation burned. Whites fled in a panic, rushing to New Orleans for safety. All except François Trépagnier, a slave owner whose contempt for Black people knew no bounds. He was going to stand and fight. Then he saw the rebellion coming right at him—"divided into companies, each under an officer, black men in militia uniforms advanc[ing] toward his plantation." He thought his double-barreled shotgun would scare them. He was wrong. As his plantation went up in flames, one of the leaders, Kook, began hacking Trépagnier to death. Legend has it that the child whom the slaver had kept as a dog also swung the ax "exacting final vengeance."[134]

By this time, the wounded Andry had sounded the alarm and worked to gather a group to stop Deslondes's forces.[135] As panicked whites poured into New Orleans, one carriage after the next piled with whatever possessions they could grab before the slave rebellion got to them, Claiborne knew that what passed for a militia in the territory would never stop what was coming.[136] A reckoning. Vengeance. Saint Domingue.[137] He called on General Wade Hampton, whose U.S. troops were away from the city keeping the Spanish at bay, to come immediately, and Claiborne reached out to the disinherited Black militia.[138]

This was a crisis. The crisis he had feared all along. At least five plantations along the German Coast were in flames, and rumors circulated that Deslondes's forces, which had already killed whites, were gaining numbers as they moved downriver closer to New Orleans. They were only about twelve miles away. Claiborne understood the moment. Whites were in serious trouble. The drive for untold profits built on the back of vast unpaid labor meant that by "1810, slaves constituted more than 75 percent of the total population, and close to 90 percent of households owned slaves."[139] In short, whites were outnumbered and they desperately needed free Black men armed and ready to fight. He also understood, though, that even while the plantations were going up in flames and the enslaved were marching to New Orleans, armed Black men, even when defending a slaveocracy, terrified whites. Claiborne made an executive decision. He banned sales of "weapons and munitions to any person of color" while he simultaneously called in the Black militia, asked them to stop the slave revolt that was headed to New Orleans and to swallow their pride, treat the fears of the plantation owners as legitimate, and accept white officers to lead Black troops. Even though the free Blacks' "relationship with Claiborne and the territorial legislature was tension-ridden at best," they agreed.[140]

The odds were already against the insurgents. The initial part of the plan collapsed because Andry's weapons depot was "nearly empty."[141] Thus, only one-fourth of the rebels were armed with muskets. And, to compound the problem, they did not have the right kind of ammunition for their weapons even as they prepared to take on the combined forces of 460 U.S. troops, the Black militia, vigilantes, Andry's militia, and the U.S. Navy.[142] This was not going to be the Battle of Teutoburg Forest, where a mighty foe was bested and stopped. Instead, not "a single white man died in the action; only a few [were] wounded."[143] On the other hand, the insurgents "were routed, killed, wounded, and dispersed . . . Sixty-six were shot or executed on the spot, seventeen were later reported missing and 'are supposed generally to be dead in the woods.'"[144]

Thus, while leniency, forgiveness, and pardons defined the conclusion of the Whiskey Rebellion, getting "slaughtered without a pretense of justice" was the gruesome ending to the 1811 Slave Rebellion.[145] For Deslondes, the "dogs got to him first." Wounded and shredded by canines, he was then dragged back into the cane fields to be made an example of. The "militiamen chopped off Charles's hands, broke his thighs, shot him dead, and then roasted his remains on a pile of straw."[146]

Many of the other insurgents, including Kook, weren't spared; they were tried before a tribunal comprised mostly of the plantation owners whose homes were burned. There was never any doubt of the outcome. "First," one observer noted, the militia "cut off their ears, hands, and legs; then the head is severed from the body and stuck upon a pole passed through his mouth and carried through the city by two of his black brethren. After this was done, his head was stuck up at the upper gate of the city."[147] The severed heads and dismembered corpses were then lined along the road of the German Coast "as an example to the remaining slaves of what rebellion would mean."[148]

Claiborne breathed a sigh of relief. A replay of Saint Domingue had just been averted, and for that, he was thankful. The governor noted, in particular, the role of the Black militia in saving New Orleans. He praised those men for their "patriotism and bravery." To the secretary of state, he extolled their "zeal for public safety" and how they performed their duties "with great exactitude and propriety." Another man, Charles Perret, wrote to the city's main French-language newspaper also praising the Black militia. He "singled out seven free men of color 'who in [his] own presence, helped to defeat the enemy with indefatigable zeal and intrepid courage.'"[149]

Nonetheless, despite a Black militia being instrumental in crushing a rebellion of enslaved Black people, no amount of zeal, patriotism, effectiveness, or courage could fully overcome white fears of Black men with guns. Thus, as the territory entered statehood in 1812, Louisiana's "policies . . . were slightly different than those of the Territory of Orleans, but no less discriminatory." The state's constitution was unequivocal: "Suffrage was limited to white males," and the militia would be composed of the "free white men of this State, [who] shall be armed and disciplined for its defence."[150]

THE WAR OF 1812 did little to change this dynamic. In many ways the war with Britain was just a replay of the dynamics in the American Revolutionary War. There was a racial war within a war. And the United

States was fighting both simultaneously. As before, the British had promised freedom to the enslaved in exchange for rising up against American forces. President Madison "called the British use of fugitive American slaves to raid the Chesapeake and to organize them into military units 'the worst the Enemy may be able to effect against us.'"[151] But that was just the beginning of the problem. Because of the aversion to a large standing army, U.S. forces were "small" and certainly not ready to take on a major military power. Moreover, "New England virtually boycotted the war, and the militia"—which the federal government had "placed greater reliance on," instead of a traditional army—was reluctant "to fight outside their own states."[152] Even staying close to home, the militias were stretched to the breaking point trying to repel an invasion, quell slave insurrections, and capture fugitive slaves. The dilemma was unwittingly laid out by the governor of Maryland, who ordered the militia to take on the British but also take down "the blacks who it appears . . . have created considerable disquietude in many sections of the state." Lieutenant Charles Grandison of the Georgia militia clearly understood who the dual enemies were: "I feel as much desire to catch a party of English . . . as . . . to catch a gang of run-away negros."[153]

For all the bravado, the states' militias were usually paper tigers when it came to an invasion, and the "net result was a series of early military disasters."[154] The British, for example, had just blown through the Maryland militia en route to burning down the White House and sending President James Madison and his cabinet fleeing to Virginia.[155] Some contemporaries derided the militias as "very little better than an infuriated mob" and "beneath contempt."[156]

As the British moved to attack New Orleans, Claiborne recognized, just as he had with the 1811 slave rebellion, that Louisiana's militia was not up to the task. He pleaded with the legislature to relent and recommission the Black militia.[157] A virtual armada was coming, and "free black soldiers were a military necessity."[158] The legislature finally conceded the point when it agreed to "consider the use of troops of color" as part of a strengthened militia bill. But there were numerous caveats and conditions—criteria that were not applied to white men.[159] This militia would "be chosen from among the Creoles, and from among such as shall have paid a State tax." Members also had to own extensive property, and, even with all that, they were to be commanded by white officers.[160] Whereas Blacks had often thought of and used military service to gain citizenship rights, that was not going to happen. They were now supposed to "serve their country," pay taxes, and put their bodies and lives on the line; but they could not vote, they could not be officers in command of troops, and, as Claiborne had ordered during the 1811 uprising, they had even been banned from purchasing firearms.[161]

This was an inauspicious beginning for the battle to control the key port of New Orleans and, as a consequence, the Mississippi River. Claiborne warned General Andrew Jackson that the free Black militia was less than eager to participate when there was nothing in it for them. Jackson, whose job it was to stop the British, was not deterred. He not only promised equal pay with whites and the respect that any soldier should receive; he then requested two additional battalions of Black militia to reinforce his troops. At that, even Claiborne balked. He explained a mindset that had thwarted him at almost every turn. "They [the legislators] think, that in putting arms into the hands of men of Colour, we only add to the force of the Enemy." That framework revealed that this wasn't even about the trepidation South Carolina had at the suggestion of arming the enslaved during the War of Independence. Arming free Blacks was apparently equally jarring and unnerving because Black people, in general, were "the Enemy."

Nevertheless, Andrew Jackson, a slave owner whose focus for now was on using whatever and whomever was available to defeat the British, continued to push in the face of this resistance. The legislature made it clear that the only way it would agree to two additional battalions of Black soldiers was if the general would "guarantee . . . they would leave Louisiana . . . after the British threat had passed."[162] It was only the presence of British warships on the horizon that convinced the legislature to finally concede. But, once again, the condition was that the additional Black troops had to be commanded by a white officer and "include only those males who possessed three hundred dollars in real property."[163]

Shortly before the decisive Battle of New Orleans, where Jackson's three thousand troops, six hundred of whom were free Blacks, took on eight thousand British and won, the general said "to the colored soldiers: 'I expected much from you, for I was not uninformed of those qualities which must render you so formidable to an invading foe . . . But you surpass my hopes.'"[164] Yet, that praise meant nothing. At war's end, the ideological and narrative power of "a white man's republic defended by white arms" held. In Louisiana, General Jackson sent this elite group of men in the Black militia out into the swamplands as a labor battalion to do the work that white militiamen refused to do.[165] Similarly, "Afro-American soldiers who risked their lives for the United States" in battles from Lake Erie to Mississippi "were rewarded with a summary dismissal from armed service because of their race."[166]

FROM THE LOUISIANA Territory's very inception as an American domain, Thomas Jefferson was adamant that only "white inhabitants would be granted citizenship 'on the same footing with other citizens of the US.'"[167] The subsequent state constitution was also clear that this was about white male citizenship—the right to vote and the duty to serve in the militia. Blacks, on the other hand, were trapped in that netherworld of rightlessness. As the United States gained control of Louisiana, whites stripped the Black militia of its official standing, blocked access to the cache of publicly funded weapons, and, when compelled because of a slave revolt and then a British invasion to reconstitute the best-organized and -trained militia in the area, dismantled its command structure and required white officers. The Second Amendment's well-regulated militia simply could not countenance, include, or embrace Black men. Being part of the militia "reflect[ed] . . . the idea that citizens had a duty to participate in the governing of the country."[168] But as the free Black militia's existence demonstrated, citizenship was further and further out of reach. By 1830, in fact, an act by Louisiana's legislature "defined militia service as the duty of 'every white inhabitant,'" and in 1834 the Black militia was officially disbanded.[169]

It wasn't just about the right to a well-regulated militia. The "right to bear arms" was not a right at all. The ongoing push to further disarm Black people was relentless. Even when calling upon the Black militia to save New Orleans from Deslondes's slave revolt, Claiborne had banned all gun and ammunition sales to people of color, including free Blacks. In Virginia by 1832, "free Negroes [were] not to carry firelocks of any kind, under penalty of thirty-nine lashes."[170] Florida passed a law in 1833 that allowed white citizen patrols "to seize arms found in the homes of slaves and free blacks," and those caught trying to bear arms could be "summarily punished" with up to "thirty-nine strokes on the bare back" all "without benefit of a judicial tribunal."[171] A white abolitionist and newspaper editor in Baltimore "decried how the deprivations brought about by black laws were also denials of citizenship," including the affront that "a free negro cannot keep a gun."[172] And while the 1846 *Nunn* decision by the Georgia Supreme Court over-turned a law that banned handguns because the Second Amendment protected a "right of the whole people, old and young, men women and boys . . . to keep and bear arms of every description," that decision, despite its supposed expansiveness, did *not* invalidate an 1833 law that prohibited "any free persons of colour in this state, to own, use, or carry firearms of any description whatever." Georgia's 1833 law matched ones in Tennessee, Arkansas, and Florida, which also limited arms to "free white men."[173] Between 1842 and 1850, Texas "prohibited slaves from using firearms altogether." In 1852, Mississippi included free Blacks in its ban, which already included the enslaved.[174] North Carolina's statute required a yearly renewable license issued by the Court of Pleas for any "'free negro, mulatto, or free person of color' to 'wear or carry about his or her person, or keep in his or her house, any shotgun, musket, rifle, pistol, sword, dagger, or bowie knife.'"[175] Statute after statute barring ownership or even the use of weapons, unless approved by whites, made this right, even for free Blacks, race-contingent and conditional.[176]

DECADES LATER, W. E. B. Du Bois would ask, "How does it feel to be a problem?" The Negro problem.[177] Antebellum America certainly felt besieged by it.[178] Slave revolts, especially those by Denmark Vesey and Nat Turner, continued to roil the South. Despite the hard-core conse-quences of decapitated heads on poles, public hangings, and show trials, nothing seemed to work. The defiance remained strong. In his *Appeal*, David Walker boldly stated, "One good black man can put to death six white men. And I give it as a fact, let twelve black men get well armed for battle and they will kill and put to flight fifty whites."[179] During the six years before the Civil War, "there were reports of slave conspiracies and revolts in Maryland, Virginia, the Carolinas, Georgia, Florida, Arkansas, Alabama, Louisiana, Texas, Kentucky, Missouri, and Tennessee."[180]

America was also racked with repeated sectional crises. As U.S. territory expanded from sea to shining sea, the South insisted on slavery growing with it. The North resisted. And, in that resistance, Congress quickly became a virtual "field of blood" as Southern senators and representatives were determined to bully, beat, and bludgeon their opponents into submission.[181] One of those concessions, the Missouri Compromise, eventually led to the horrors of Bleeding Kansas, where slavery's proponents launched a war of terror to try to force the state to join the slaveocracy.[182] Then, President James Knox Polk annexed slaveholding Texas into the Union, precipitating a war with Mexico that would eventually exacerbate the rising sectional tensions.[183]

The intensifying ill will between the North and South was further fueled by the problem of runaway slaves. Despite a clause in the Constitution and the subsequent enabling legislation, the Fugitive Slave Act of 1793, Northern states crafted statutes that defied the law, "interfered with slave recapture and exposed manhunters to assault and kidnapping charges."[184] It was that initial ineffectiveness and state interference that had prevented someone as powerful as George Washington from recapturing his wife's runaway slave, Ona Judge, who fled the Executive Mansion on May 21, 1796, and thwarted Washington at every turn.[185] Even the Supreme Court's "bombshell" 1842 *Prigg* decision, that ruled states cannot impede the capture of a fugitive slave, did not end resistance to federal law. The North simply responded with a slew of new legislation "forbidding states to cooperate in the rendition of fugitives"; essentially saying, "Do your own dirty work. We won't help."[186] Henry Clay of Kentucky had had enough. He "stomped to the floor of the United States Senate in 1849 to rant that 'it posed insecurity to life itself for slave-owners to cross the Ohio River to recover fugitives.'"[187]

The South insisted that federal law was supreme and it was time for the North to act like it. With the barely veiled threat of secession hanging in the air, Southern congressmen blustered and bullied until they secured passage of the Fugitive Slave Act of 1850. This was a law with teeth and venom. Northern states could no longer abstain or refuse to help slave hunters capture those who escaped human bondage. If officials refused to provide support to, as Frederick Douglass called them, the "bloodhounds of American slavery," then the sanctuary state had to compensate the slave owner for the loss of property.[188] In short, the North was either going to pay by providing the manpower to track and hunt down those who refused to be enslaved or by opening up the state treasury and filling the coffers of plantation owners. Moreover, the law challenged the way Northern states viewed themselves. Although Blacks had enormous difficulties in places like New York, still, freedom, even if it was a veneer, was essential to the way states above the Mason-Dixon Line defined what had made them distinct and, yes, better than those below it.[189] The Fugitive Slave Act of 1850, however, now made Northern states active, complicit participants in upholding slavery, in denying freedom.[190] That reality did not sit well. Equally abhorrent, the Fugitive Slave Act gutted due process. Those who were caught by the slave hunters had no rights whatsoever to proclaim their freedom. Only the slave catchers and slave owners had any standing in court. And with a bounty on virtually every Black head, it made no difference to slavery's bloodhounds whom they manacled and dragged into human bondage. Thus, it wasn't just about re-enslavement of fugitives; it was about the wanton, encouraged enslavement of free Blacks, too.

The 1850 Fugitive Slave Act was supposed to be part of a sectional compromise that would keep the United States actually united. Instead, it was a law that was so hated that the seams in the American fabric began to visibly tear apart.[191]

The Fugitive Slave Act of 1850 convinced many in the North that genuine compromise with the South was impossible because it came at the expense of cherished values and governance. Meanwhile, it emboldened those in the South. They saw how even the revered Daniel Webster of Massachusetts bowed down and worked to wrangle enough votes to put the act through. Southerners were convinced that Slave Power, the disproportionate influence of the South in national legislation and affairs, would now rule unencumbered by Northern sensitives.

And it steeled the resolve of Blacks who knew that the moral suasion of abolitionism was no match against the evil that created the Fugitive Slave Act of 1850.[192] The brutal reality of turning the entire United States into a slave catchers' paradise meant that Blacks had very few places to run; they were going to have to stand and fight and defend themselves "with the surest and most deadly weapons, including bowie knives and revolvers."[193] Frederick Douglass clarified that the only way to make the Fugitive Slave Act dead law was to have "half a dozen or more dead kidnappers carried down South."[194] He recommended a "good revolver, a steady hand and a determination to shoot down any man attempting to kidnap."[195] Robert Purvis, a Quaker who had previously been an abolitionist adverse to violence, said, "Should any wretch enter my dwelling . . . to execute this law on me or mine, I'll seek his life and I'll shed his blood."[196]

That's exactly what happened in Christiana, Pennsylvania, in September 1851. Maryland slave owner Edward Gorsuch, along with his son Dickinson, nephew Joshua, and U.S. marshal Henry Kline and his posse, had landed on William Parker's doorstep to retrieve, as

Gorsuch said, "his property"—enslaved men who had run away and were hiding in the house. Parker, himself a fugitive slave, was defiant. It was common knowledge what happened to runaways. They were "'run down and attacked by dogs, dragged through the woods on a noose attached to a horse, beaten with sticks, cut with whips, stapled to the floor of a cabin while a mob gathered outside' eager for a lynching." The slave owners didn't "mind having them kind o' niggers tore a good deal . . . [because] it makes the rest more afraid to run away." That's what awaited the men who had fled Gorsuch's wheat farm in Maryland. Parker was having none of it. He scoffed at these "barbarous and inhuman monsters" using a vile law that had "converted the old State of Pennsylvania . . . into a hunting ground." Kline tried to cow Parker into submission. "I am the United States Marshal," he said, thinking that brandishing that authority would get the man to step aside to let the slave catchers into the house. Parker was not impressed. He told the lawman that if he came any closer, he "would break his neck."[197]

Edward Gorsuch was stunned by the defiance and Kline's inability to just make Parker comply. The slave owner threatened to go up the stairs and drag "his property" out of there. Parker coldly explained, "See here, old man, you can come up, but you can't go down again. Once up here, you are mine." Gorsuch then threatened to burn the house down with them in it. Parker's wife, Eliza, sensing the full scale of the danger, ran into the garret and blew the horn, which was the warning signal for the Black Self-Protection Society, a community self-defense committee, to grab whatever they could lay their hands on to fight, because the slave catchers were far too close and hunting. Two of Gorsuch's men, surmising that Eliza's trumpet blast was a call to arms, immediately climbed the tree outside the house, aimed their guns at her, and began shooting. As the bullets whizzed by, she ducked down and kept blowing, blowing, blowing.[198]

The Battle at Christiana had officially begun. By the time it was over, Kline, the U.S. marshal, had run for his life, terrified by the sight of eighty members of the self-defense committee armed with muskets, corn cutters, pitchforks, axes, clubs, and anything else they could use as a weapon coming right at the slave catchers. Gorsuch, however, refused to flee. "I will have my property, or go to hell," he bellowed. He fired at Parker. And missed. Before the slave owner could get off another round, Parker knocked the gun out of his hand. At that moment, one of the slaves Gorsuch had planned to haul back to Maryland, Samuel Thompson, began to pistol-whip the man until he was sprawled out in the mud. Lifeless and bloodied. Joshua and Dickinson Gorsuch didn't escape either. They both were severely wounded.[199]

As the Gorsuch men lay there dead or bleeding, Parker and the fugitive slaves knew they would immediately need to flee Christiana. They ended up hundreds of miles away on Frederick Douglass's doorstep in Rochester, New York. The firebrand abolitionist had heard what happened in Pennsylvania and knew that, with a white man dead at the hands of Black folk, law enforcement would not be too far behind. Douglass mobilized his network, found a steamer headed for Canada that night, and managed, with fifteen minutes to spare, to safely get all the fugitives aboard. Just before the gangplank was raised, a grateful Parker turned a prized possession over to his old friend Douglass: "the revolver that fell from the hand of Gorsuch when he died . . . as a token of gratitude and a memento of the battle for liberty at Christiana."[200]

While Parker and the others were safely on their way to Canada—where his wife, Eliza, would join him shortly—authorities had rounded up half those who "came to Parker's aid," including five whites, and charged them with treason.[201] Castner Hanway, a Quaker who had refused to help Kline, was ostensibly the first defendant. But it was really the Fugitive Slave Act of 1850 that was on trial.

In his opening statement, the prosecution acknowledged that many saw the law as "obnoxious," but it was the law, nonetheless, he said. And Hanway had been asked by an agent of the U.S. government to help uphold that law, and the defendant refused. That refusal, the prosecution contended, was treasonous.[202]

The defense attorney, Theodore Cuyler, mocked that idea. Treason, he said, is "levying war against the United States." And, he continued, the prosecution is asking the jury to believe that a Quaker, "mounted on a sorrel nag," supposedly led a mob "armed with corn-cutters, clubs, and a few muskets" to wage war against the United States. It was only, he relayed dripping with sarcasm, through the grace of "God that our Union has survived the shock." What this case was really about, he circled around to, was that "a band of miscreants . . . professional kidnappers" had terrified the Black community in Pennsylvania by committing a "series of lawless and diabolical outrages." Hanway, however, was no miscreant. He was no kidnapper, which is exactly what Kline wanted the Quaker to become. Cuyler made the point: Fugitive Slave Act or no, "you cannot make active slave catchers of any respectable men in Pennsylvania, even by threat of the gallows."[203] Cuyler had painted a stark picture of the Fugitive Slave Act as lawless, diabolical, and something that no decent, respectable person would get near even when faced with execution.

On the stand, Kline, the U.S. marshal, guided by the prosecutor, then walked through what happened that day in September. How he had a warrant, how he asked Hanway to help execute this warrant to retrieve Edward Gorsuch's runaway slaves, and how there were twenty to thirty Black people armed "with their guns loaded" and coming to stop him, the U.S. marshal. Hanway's response, Kline continued, was that "the colored people had a right to defend themselves." The prosecutor asked Kline to repeat what he'd just said. He did. "Colored people had a right to defend themselves." Adding that when he explained the Fugitive Slave Act, the mandate to help, and the penalties for not doing so, Hanway's response was "he did not care for any act of Congress or any other law."[204] At that, the prosecutor was sure that he had extracted all he needed to gain a conviction. The defendant knew the law, "obnoxious" as it may be, and he refused to obey it.

The judge, in his instructions to the jury, however, didn't talk much about treason. Instead, he focused on the hellscape that the Fugitive Slave Act had created for Black people. They were, he said, just trying "to protect one another from what they termed kidnappers." Slave catchers, the judge told the jury, had invaded homes and snatched people away, and it didn't matter if they were "a free man or a slave." This "odious" business, spurred by the greed of rewards, had driven Blacks to "resist . . . aggressions." But, he continued, there is "no evidence of a conspiracy . . . to levy war against the United States." This wasn't about treason; this was about a law that compelled Blacks to defend themselves. With those instructions, the jury found Hanway not guilty. In fact, after that clear repudiation of the Fugitive Slave Act, no one was ever convicted for Edward Gorsuch's death or the wounding of his son and nephew.[205]

CHRISTIANA SEEMED TO signal that Blacks had the right to self-defense, but it actually signaled something much more complex. That right was heavily dependent on a confluence of interests where Blacks and whites were in agreement on the enemy. For example, when two Blacks and two whites burst into a courtroom in Boston in 1851 to free a fugitive slave and get him safely to Canada, they, like Castner Hanway, were found "not guilty" of violating a law that angered many in the North.[206] The joint anger at the Fugitive Slave Act was an outlier, however, that gave the illusion of a right to self-defense for Black people. The bitter truth was articulated in 1831 by Attorney General Roger Taney in a legal opinion to an official in South Carolina. Taney wrote that free Blacks "are permitted to be citizens by the sufferance of the white population and hold whatever rights they enjoy at their mercy."[207] This understanding of rights as predicated on whiteness and white benevolence affected even those who weren't Black but appeared to have a Black-driven agenda. Elijah Lovejoy, a white abolitionist in Illinois, had his printing press destroyed multiple times by angry white mobs. In 1837, they came to burn it down again. He'd had enough. He got his gun, but the mob got to him first and shot him dead. His assailants, although they were the aggressors, potential arsonists, and actual murderers, were found "not guilty." Lovejoy, while just trying to protect himself and his property, clearly did not have the right to self-defense. Worse yet, some of his allies in the abolitionist movement blamed him for his own death, surmising that "the mob would not have killed Lovejoy if he had not taken up arms."[208]

This phenomenon, played out on a larger scale in an 1841 attack on a Black neighborhood in Cincinnati, Ohio, reflects how ephemeral and white-dependent the right to self-defense for Black people is. The melee in Cincinnati also, as with Lovejoy's in Illinois, reveals the irrelevance of being armed or unarmed, because the key variable in the way that the Second Amendment operates is not guns but anti-Blackness.

In late summer 1841, a series of altercations between a handful of whites and Blacks, heavily influenced by ubiquitous rumors of Black men assaulting an unidentified white woman on a city sidewalk, led to a full-on riot where white mobs converged on the Black community to burn it down and kill as many as possible. Blacks, however, had armed themselves, and as the mob of nearly 1,500 descended on their neighborhood, the self-defense squad took up positions and began firing. The mob fell back. Then, enraged at the temerity of Black people for being armed and for refusing to just die, the white mob attempted another assault. Again, a volley of gunfire repelled the attackers. Now beyond enraged, the "crowd returned . . . bringing with it a six-pound cannon, and the battle ensued." Finally, city authorities intervened. But their solution was not to round up the mob leaders and cannon haulers; instead, police disarmed the Black community, hoping that would calm the fears and nerves of whites. It didn't. Disarmament left Blacks "naked to whatever indignities private parties might heap upon them and dependent on a government either unable or unwilling to protect their rights." The slaughter began. Historian Carter G. Woodson describes a "cowardly" assault as if by "savages" hunting defenseless prey.[209]

THE CARNAGE IN Cincinnati provides another insight into the irrelevance and the malevolence of the Second Amendment for Black people's right to self-defense. It didn't matter to officials that whites had stormed into the Black neighborhood to burn it down and kill whoever lived there. Instead, all the authorities saw were Black people with guns and identified that (and not the white mob hauling a cannon, intent on committing mass murder) as the problem. The right to self-defense, therefore, was and is no firewall to prevent the attempted annihilation of Black neighborhoods.

Meanwhile, confronted with the widespread bloodshed, the authorities' solution, unilateral disarmament, left Blacks in Cincinnati totally vulnerable to whatever violence and deprivation could and would rain down on them.[210] The Second Amendment was no shelter in this storm. Armed for self-defense or disarmed for self-preservation, whites were the arbiters of Black rights and Black safety. And if they deemed it necessary, the killing of free Blacks and the destruction of their communities were not far behind. Indeed, white mobs attacked Black communities in Providence (1831), New York (1834), Boston (1843), and Philadelphia (1849) with ferocious abandon.[211] Providence, for example, was a four-day assault on a Black neighborhood that authorities eventually tried to stop by having the militia fire blank cartridges at the white mob. That, of course, did not work. The mob kept coming. The governor had to call in 130 troops on the fourth day to actually battle whites on the streets of the city.[212]

As bad as it was for free Blacks, the enslaved had it even worse. The numerous slave codes that forbid the simple act of self-defense emphasized how those held in human bondage had no legal standing to protect themselves against white violence.[213] In 1855, just a few years after Christiana, an enslaved teenager, Celia, killed her master. She knew that she had to. Over the span of five years, since virtually the first day he bought her, he had raped her. Repeatedly. She told him to stop. Her demand to protect her own body, though, was irrelevant because Celia was his property and he was going to do to her what he wanted. He slithered in one night to take her again, and this time she bludgeoned him to death. She claimed self-defense. The state of Missouri said it was murder and sent her to the gallows.[214]

SAINT DOMINGUE, GABRIEL'S Rebellion, and the 1811 slave revolt, as well as Denmark Vesey and Nat Turner, affirmed and reified the foundational fear of Black people. That fear required white safety above all else, and the solution was to continue to whittle away at whatever concept of rights and access to weaponry that Black people—enslaved or free—had. A series of laws and actions thus established that Black people did not have the right to bear arms, the right to a well-regulated militia, or the right to self-defense. Gun control laws, to be clear, were everywhere in antebellum America. Indeed, "the South was the gun control center of the United States as local governments tried to lessen the violence among whites that seemed to dominate the region."[215] But the laws targeted at Black people that banned or severely limited access to weapons, carried racialized criteria and punishments. Even a court ruling that overturned a handgun ban in Georgia did not invalidate a law prohibiting Blacks from possessing any type of firearm.

In some ways so much of the turmoil in antebellum America was about the still-ambiguous legal status of free Blacks, who refused to abide in the "halfway" land of denizen. If some were citizens, perhaps, that could begin to break the stranglehold and the fear. And so, Blacks kept pushing.[216] The answer was supposed to be settled by a landmark Supreme Court decision in 1857 that would stretch Taney's initial "at-the-mercy" of whites' articulation of citizenship to America's breaking point.

The question of Blacks' citizenship rights had already cascaded through laws about naturalization and the militia into excluding them from carrying the mail, designating that only whites could be elected to public office in Washington, D.C., and denying a U.S. passport to Blacks because, as Attorney General William Wirt wrote in 1821, free Negroes "cannot be regarded, when beyond the jurisdiction of the Government, as entitled to the full rights of citizens."[217]

In 1857, Chief Justice Taney was ready to definitively address whether they were citizens and had any rights when they were *in* the jurisdiction of the U.S. government. The question before the court was, Could someone who was enslaved gain freedom and, thus, citizenship rights by living in a "free soil" state like Illinois and Wisconsin as Dred

Scott had done?[218] President James Buchanan, who behind the scenes helped engineer the decision, wanted the type of rock-solid ruling that would defuse the sectional crisis and stop the drive toward civil war.[219] Taney tried to deliver. The chief justice's opinion in *Dred Scott v. Sandford* (1857) asserted in a 7–2 decision that Blacks, including free Blacks, had never been considered citizens of the United States. Not in the founding documents. Not in the initial discussions and laws of Congress such as the 1790 Naturalization Act or the 1792 Militia Acts. Nor by the attorney general and the secretary of state, who refused to issue passports to Blacks because they "were not citizens of the United States."[220] If Blacks were citizens, he wrote, they would have the right to "enter every other state whenever they pleased . . . hold meetings on political affairs, or, worse to 'keep and carry arms wherever they went.' "[221] But because they are not now, have never been, and never will be citizens, he asserted, they don't have any rights "that a white man is bound to respect."[222]

Buchanan hoped that this clarification would quell the sectional divide. It didn't. Instead, the *Dred Scott* decision heightened the crisis that was evident with the Fugitive Slave Act of 1850. Abolitionists mobilized. Slaveholders mobilized. And the United States hurtled toward the Civil War, which, in the end, left over six hundred thousand dead, more than four hundred thousand wounded, and four million enslaved people now freed.[223]

The end of chattel slavery should have made the difference. Even citizenship should have made the difference. But it didn't. Because as the years after the Civil War would make clear, "the core of white supremacy was not chattel slavery, but antiblackness."[224] And that is the foundational root of the Second Amendment.

*Three*

# The Right to Kill Negroes

Freedom was right there, hanging by the barrel of a gun and ink on a piece of paper. For nearly five hundred thousand free Blacks and four million people who were no longer enslaved, this could have been the moment when they stepped fully into the protection and rights of American citizenship.[1] But that was not going to be. It couldn't be, with the Second Amendment a flashpoint as Black people asserted their right to bear arms, the right to a well-regulated militia, and the right to self-defense—and America responded with its right "to kill Negroes."[2]

That pathway to fractured citizenship was built by the battered but defiant Confederacy, President Andrew Johnson's unvarnished hatred of Black people, and the equivocation of the North about the rights and place of African Americans. The result was a nation half-heartedly trying to "build an egalitarian society on the ashes of slavery."[3] And those ashes, when mixed with the rivers of blood from Black people who thought citizenship would come through military service, who believed that they had the right to self-defense, and who hoped, after the Civil War, that they were now Americans, hardened into nearly impenetrable barriers.

ANDREW JOHNSON, WHO ascended to the presidency after Lincoln's assassination, was instrumental in sabotaging efforts to craft a political and legal environment in which the formerly enslaved and free Blacks could live fully. He pardoned many leaders of the Confederacy, welcomed those unrepentant rebels into their old positions in state government, and did not wince as they drafted new constitutions, such as Louisiana's, that boldly stated, "We hold this to be a Government of white people, made and to be perpetuated for the exclusive benefit of the white race." And perhaps even more important, the state's new Constitution affirmed the founding principle "that people of African descent cannot be considered as citizens of the United States."[4]

Johnson was also unfazed, as his emissary Carl Schurz reported in late 1865, on the miles and miles of recently butchered Black bodies hanging from trees, lying in ditches, and clogging roadways. Dismembered limbs strewn everywhere. Severed ears dotting the landscape. Burning and decomposing flesh making it almost impossible to breathe. While Schurz was clearly rattled by the way "murder stalks . . . and revels in undisputed carnage" in the South, Johnson had no qualms whatsoever about this "slow-motion genocide."[5]

The president was also unconcerned about the rise of Black Codes promulgated by those new-old governments in the defeated South. These laws were "an astonishing affront to emancipation" and were designed to regain control of Black people's labor and lives.[6] The Black Codes required African Americans, under the threat of criminal penalties including being auctioned off to work on a plantation, to sign unbreakable annual labor contracts. The law also banned the freed-people from any other jobs except as agricultural workers and domestics, unless with written approval by a judge or the mayor of the town. Blacks still weren't allowed to testify in court against whites, which meant there were no consequences or legal remedies for the rampant, unchecked violence that had led to thousands of African Americans being lynched after the Civil War.[7]

And to ensure that Black people, who had tasted freedom, would be defenseless against this seismic push back into a state of neo-servitude and subjugation, they were also, just as in the days of slavery, banned from owning weapons. Florida's legislation, for example, forbid "Negroes, mulattos, or other persons of color from possessing guns, ammunition or blade weapons" without getting the approval of whites in authority. For those caught with a weapon, the punishment was a public whipping up to "39 stripes."[8] Similarly, Alabama, Mississippi, and South Carolina made it "illegal to sell give or rent firearms or ammunition of any description 'to any freedman, free Negro or mulatto.'"[9] In Louisiana, Blacks couldn't even carry a weapon.[10]

African Americans countered by petitioning, insisting, and demanding that they now had Second Amendment rights. The bulletin of the African Methodist Episcopal Church explained that the "freedmen . . . have as good a right to keep firearms as any other citizens." A Black newspaper in Georgia went one further and laid out that not only did the formerly enslaved have the right to bear arms under the Second Amendment, but that no one had the right to strip them of their guns simply because they were Black, thereby "placing them at the mercy of others."[11]

But that simply wasn't so. That amendment was not designed to help them. Its inclusion in the Constitution was to ensure a role for militias to control the enslaved. The defeat of the Confederacy, despite all the elegiac language about "a new birth of freedom," had not changed the meaning or the goal of the Second.[12] The anti-Blackness that under-girded slavery, that had made it possible, and that sustained it for centuries still remained strong and unrepentant in post–Civil War America.[13] And the hard-fought-for change in the legal status of Black people could not scramble the DNA, the operating principles of anti-Blackness.

As the terror and butchery Schurz described rained down on the freedpeople, as controlling the labor of the once enslaved became the leitmotif of the post-antebellum regimes, and as states, local governments, and "petty plantation tyrants" demanded Black disarmament, it appeared that African Americans, despite their protestations of the right to bear arms, had "little chance of self-defense."[14] But they did not give up. While petitioning federal agents for help, Blacks tried to hold on to their guns, knowing the horrific penalties that awaited them for doing so but also well aware of the consequences of relinquishing the only thing that stood between them and the barbarism of re-enslave-ment by another name.[15]

Yet for all that courage, they knew they were outgunned and needed support. Their petitions to Congress and other federal officials asking for help were full of pain and dread, with just a shred of hope. "In a November 1865 letter to Major General Steadman of the Union Army, 125 freedmen in Columbus, Georgia, begged federal troops to stay in the city: 'We wish to inform you that if the Federal Soldiers are withdrawn from us, we will be left in a most gloomy and helpless condition. A number of Freedmen have already been killed in this section of country; and . . . we have every reason to fear that others will share a similar fate.'" They pleaded with the federal government "not to leave [them] to the tender mercy of [their] enemies—unprotected."[16]

Black soldiers, in particular, heard the call and intervened. Lincoln had originally forbidden African American enlistment in the Union Army, hoping to not antagonize the border states into joining their Southern kinfolk in waging war against the United States.[17] But the impending reality that victory might take years and that every able-bodied man was needed to fight, coupled with the unrelenting pressure from Blacks to join in this struggle against the most powerful slaveholding society in the world, led Lincoln to relent. With the 1862 Militia Act and the subsequent Emancipation Proclamation, African Americans had once again joined the ranks of the military and would eventually make up 10 percent of U.S. forces.[18] Frederick Douglass understood early on what this meant. He keenly observed, "Once you let the black man get upon his person the brass letters, 'U.S.,' let him get an eagle on his button, and a musket on his shoulder and bullets in his pocket, and there is no power on Earth which can deny that he has earned the right to citizenship in the United States."[19]

African American soldiers were determined to fully embrace that citizenship and, in doing so, protect the freedpeople who were being Black Coded and butchered back into slavery.[20] The soldiers' mission to protect the nation's most vulnerable against the violence of traitors did not go unnoticed. Nor was it appreciated.

Black soldiers' determination to quell the savagery that had engulfed the old Confederacy was met with an unalloyed sense of outrage by many white Southerners. The very existence of Black troops was simply "galling" and "infuriating." But that air of intense pique was heightened now as they served as an occupying army in a barely defeated land. A prominent man in Louisiana saw African American troops, "who comprised most of the occupation forces [as] . . . arrogant and overbearing, and their presence," he was certain, "encouraged freedpeople to break their contracts, quit the plantations, rob and steal, and congregate in the towns in a state of idleness. 'Their very presence demoralizes the negroes for all purposes of useful industry,'" he asserted.[21] A white woman in Nashville recalled in horror the sight of a "brigade of *negroes* uniformed and equipped [that] paraded our streets to day. Oh how humiliating," she exclaimed. Beyond humiliating, however, was the frightening possibility, she continued, that these "niggers" were being trained "in our midst to kill and destroy" whites.[22]

Her sentiment was echoed in refrain after refrain, complaint after complaint. While many white residents in the defeated Confederacy acknowledged that there was violence and bloodshed throughout the South, the rejoinder was that this was a problem beyond the ability of Black soldiers to solve. The overall sense was that "blacks were not respectable soldiers capable of keeping order—they were a degraded mob hell-bent on race war and anarchy."[23] From there it was just a small step to the bête noire of Saint Domingue. Black men, with military skills and guns, some Southerners claimed, were "hoping to initiate a Haitian-style race war."[24] In South Carolina, "the impression prevailed that a war of extermination was about to begin . . . that the blacks had risen with arms . . . and that the white people were in danger."[25]

From every corner of Louisiana, and from every state in the former Confederacy, whites justified strong measures by citing the threat of organized violence by the freedmen, which threat the presence of Black soldiers, they claimed, was exacerbating. "The colored troops manifest great malignity toward the white population . . . [and] are instigating the former slaves of the country to deeds of insurrection and Massacre." As 1865 drew to a close, rumors abounded that Blacks would rise up during the Christmas holidays, murder the whites, and seize their lands. In Caddo and Bossier Parishes, to the north of Natchitoches, militia companies scoured the plantations in search of firearms in the hands of freedmen. Forcibly entering Black homes, they confiscated any weapons they discovered.[26]

The presence of Black troops was destabilizing, especially because the aura of authority and power they carried directly contradicted the stereotypes of African Americans as "shaggy, slovenly creatures . . . not far removed from the primitive days of savagery."[27] Then there were those other African Americans who may not have been actual soldiers, a North Carolinian noted, but who carried themselves as if they were and had only one goal: "a general massacre of the white population." He complained, "Nearly every Negro is armed not only with a gun [long gun], but a revolver," and, worse, there are meetings "of a thousand or two Negroes every other Sunday, with Officers and Drilling." He concluded, that this was "a serious matter."[28]

White Southerners, thus, explained to federal officials that the violence, the chaos, and the turmoil that defined the Old Confederacy immediately after the Civil War were not about the refusal to accept defeat, the inability to acknowledge that those whom they once enslaved were now marching in military uniforms with arms through the streets, or the fact that African Americans resisted mightily implementation of the Black Codes. The real source of the problem, whites explained, was the presence of Black troops. Just "the sight of Negro troops stirred the bosoms of our soldiers with courageous madness," the Southerners explained.[29] If only "they could be removed," one man pleaded with Andrew Johnson, "we would have peace and good order at once and thereby put down much prejudice against the negro."[30]

This was both a perversion of the truth and a perverse truth. The "ending of prejudice against the negro" was not going to happen simply because Black troops would be removed. In fact, soldiers, Black and white, had had to intervene on multiple occasions to stop the locals from trying to kill or disarm the freedpeople.[31] In other words, the presence or lack of presence of Black troops was not the catalyst for repeated attempts to commit mass murder. The "peace" that the unreconstructed rebels wanted, instead, was Blacks' quiet subjugation, a willingness to be owned in a post-slavery society. An acquiescence to white supremacy.[32] What they got was defiance. "They come into town on Sabbath Days," complained one Mississippi planter, "parading Colts, navy sixes, and large knives, and with an air of defiance to God, man and the law."[33] It was societally blasphemous. The racial line between citizens and noncitizens was one that far too many whites, even in Congress, did not want breached. Yet Blacks kept trying. Democrats in Washington, D.C., "repeatedly identified American nationality with 'the Caucasian race,' insisted that the government 'was made for white men,' and objected to extending the 'advantages' of American citizenship to 'the Negroes, the coolies, and the Indians.'"[34]

"Peace," on those terms, was not attainable. So while many Southern whites offered a perversion of the truth, putting the onus and responsibility for the violence on African American soldiers, the perverse truth was that, because of anti-Blackness, the very existence of African American troops was the affront to white supremacists, the abomination. And the assumption that Black soldiers bred defiance and a sense of citizenship in African American civilians was equally appalling and unacceptable. "Mississippi minister Samuel Agnew exhibited the worry of many Southerners, writing in late 1865 that blacks . . . were now demanding that they had 'equal rights with a white man to bear arms.'"[35]

Andrew Johnson, a Democrat and a former slave owner from Tennessee, bristled at the thought. His presidency was bound up in ensuring that the guiding principles of *Dred Scott* remained untouched. Slavery, of course, was abolished, but that most certainly did not mean that the freedpeople had rights, certainly none that the U.S.

government was going to uphold.[36] He had told Frederick Douglass as much in a heated exchange at the White House. Douglass demanded Black suffrage and that African Americans had "their rights as citizens" and must have their "equality before the law" respected and enforced. Johnson could not believe it. He raged about being lectured to by the likes of Frederick Douglass, a man whom the president considered "just like any nigger . . . [who] would sooner cut a white man's throat than not." How could someone like that, Johnson bellowed, have the audacity to "talk about abstract ideas of liberty" without admitting that if Black people actually had that kind of freedom, it would surely start a "race war"? What Blacks really needed, the president continued, was not voting rights or rights equal to those of white men, but to be sent out of the United States and colonized in some far-off land.[37]

Clearly, there was no protection for Black people emanating from the White House. Rather, by mid-1866, Johnson saw to it that Black troops were removed from the interior of the South and sent to outposts on the coast. Then, by January 1867, the expulsion was complete and there were no African American soldiers stationed in the Old Confederacy.[38]

THE RADICAL REPUBLICANS in Congress had a different vision of what post–Civil War America could be. Even before the war ended, they had already drafted and passed the Thirteenth Amendment, which abolished slavery and was ratified in December 1865.[39] Then, seeing the recalcitrance of the Southern governments and the widespread blood-letting, it was obvious how untenable it was to suggest that the only right Blacks had was the right not to be enslaved. Even a Democrat, Congressman William Holman from Indiana, remarked that freedom from slavery was a "miserable idea of freedom."[40]

Congress agreed and passed the 1866 Civil Rights Act, which for the first time laid out the foundational principle of born-in-the-USA citizenship. In other words, no longer was whiteness the gateway to becoming a citizen of the United States. Just being born in America was enough. Johnson, of course, vetoed the bill. But Congress, for the first time in American history, overrode a presidential veto and, as it would turn out, would have to do so again and again. There was the Freedmen's Bureau Bill of 1866, which provided schools and labor contract support for all those left homeless or impoverished by the war, Blacks as well as whites. The Black part was too much for Johnson. He vetoed it; Congress overrode him. Then there was the Reconstruction Act of 1867, which enraged Johnson and the rebels in the South by providing the right to vote for Black men. The Reconstruction Act, however, also divided the Old Confederacy into five military districts with U.S. troops stationed in this defeated but unconquered land as an occupying army. Like singing an old refrain, Johnson vetoed; Congress overrode him, again.

These new laws, however, were not going to be enough. "Freedmen's Bureau agents reported over and again about violence against ex-slaves, including whippings, ritualistic torture, and murders."[41] Congress, therefore, followed up with an amendment, the Fourteenth, that would make birthright citizenship, equal protection under the law, and due process part of the U.S. Constitution. Just as important, however, was the legislative understanding that the Fourteenth would incorporate the first eight amendments of the Bill of Rights, including the Second, and, make those protections not only applicable against federal encroachment but protected under state law, as well.[42]

Ratified in 1868, the amendment still wasn't enough. Black men's voting rights "hung by a thread" as violence and intimidation threatened to cut off their access to the ballot box.[43] One Freedmen's Bureau official noted, "No Union man or Negro who attempts to take any active part in politics, or the improvement of his race is safe a single day; and nearly all sleep upon their arms at night, and carry concealed weapons during the day."[44] And it still wasn't enough, either. Whites slaughtered African Americans for trying to protect the right to vote in Camilla, Georgia; New Orleans and Opelousas, Louisiana; and Memphis, Tennessee.[45] Louisiana, in fact, had an "all-out 'nigger-hunt' complete with bloodhounds" and more than one thousand dead within the span of a few months.[46] Just a little to the west, African Americans tried to flee Texas "as if from death" because whites were determined to keep Black people "in perfect terror of their lives."[47]

The Radical Republicans, whose strength was waning in Congress, as its leadership began to die off and the rest of the nation tired of the ongoing turmoil in the South, made one last major push to build a fire-wall of democracy that would protect Black Americans, withstand the violence of white domestic terrorism, and not be dependent on Congress, the White House, or any other entity for the freedpeople to live fully. In 1870, the Fifteenth Amendment, which articulated a "right to vote" and made clear that it could not be "abridged on account of race, color, or previous condition of servitude," was ratified. Congress then passed the Third Enforcement Act, which made the domestic terrorism that defined the Ku Klux Klan and its progeny a federal offense. In those two moves—the right to vote and a federal law against domestic terrorism—the edifice to protect Black citizenship was apparently in place.

Yet it proved virtually impotent when confronted by the Klan and anti-Blackness. In the KKK stronghold of South Carolina in 1871, five hundred masked men attacked the local jail in Union County and killed African Americans whose primary offense was shooting at whites in self-defense.[48] "In York County, nearly the entire white male population joined the Klan and committed at least eleven murders and hundreds of whippings."[49] In Aberdeen, Mississippi, "armed riders drove freedmen from their homes and warned that they would be killed if they appeared to cast ballots." Black men who dared exercise their right to vote were met at the polls "by whites equipped with rifles and a six-pounder cannon."[50]

As the violence raged, Republican governors had few options. Those beautiful words on paper that Congress had worked so hard to ratify simply did not appear to be working. One African American asked, "Did not the 14th Article . . . say that no person shall be deprived of life nor property without due process of law? It said all person have equal protection of the laws but I say we colored men don't get it at all . . . it is wrong."[51]

What was missing was enforcement. Black soldiers had already been moved out of the South. The fear of a standing army had led to the few remaining white troops being unable to do much but just be there. Indeed, with "about 15 miles per soldier, the army was spread thin."[52] The only option really available was the state militias, often composed of Black men, who had been recruited under Republican governments. Yet many of those elected officials "feared the arming of a black militia would inaugurate all-out racial warfare."[53] In fact, the Democrats, the party of the unreconstructed rebels, "actually welcomed the prospect of fighting a black militia, convinced 'we will wipe them from the face of the earth.'"[54]

Colfax, Louisiana, underscored that point. The political violence in the state was already brutal, sadistic, and commonplace. The Democrats had shown nothing but disgust for Republicans, their supporters, and the votes that put the party of Lincoln into elected positions. In short, the Democrats did not believe in democracy. They believed, instead, that terror would bleed the Republicans into submission.[55]

A contested election in 1873, a slaughter whose trail of blood would end up all the way on the U.S. Supreme Court's docket, led to a ruling that made it clear that, for African Americans, *Dred Scott*, not the Fourteenth Amendment, was the law of this land.

In Grant Parish, a Black Republican, William Ward, was worried that the armed wing of the Democrats, the Klan, was going to overturn the results of the recent election, storm the government seat in Colfax, oust the elected officials, and stage a coup. Ward called upon the Black militia to defend this election, urged them to protect democracy. And they responded. They were "dog-bone set to fight for an idea, no matter the risk."[56] The men built a barricade around the courthouse, which was the symbol and the site of government power in Colfax, took their weapons, took their positions, and hoped they were ready. They weren't.

One of the Klansmen, Dave Paul, explained to his force of 165 men what was at stake as they planned the assault on the courthouse. "Boys, this is a struggle for white supremacy." He knew that the attack was fundamentally illegal, that those Black men were defending what everyone (but the Democrats) considered to be a duly-elected government, and that the possible consequences of the attack were daunting. The Klansman warned that those who survived the battle at Colfax "will probably be prosecuted for treason, and the punishment for treason is death."[57] Only twenty-five men dropped out.

On Easter Sunday, April 13, 1873, as the Klan approached the courthouse, what should have been easy military strategy for the Black militia—an initial fierce engagement, then retreating and using the positions in the building to pick off the invaders—didn't quite work. The barricades weren't high enough to slow down the Klan, and the Black forces didn't have enough weaponry and ammunition to repel the advance. Instead, only one-half to two-thirds of the men holed up in the courthouse had guns. And even then, they didn't have enough bullets to lay down a field of fire. They had to pick. Choose. Conserve. The coup makers took advantage and forced a Black man they had kidnapped to climb the courthouse and set fire to the roof. While the building was ablaze, the Klansmen aimed and fired their cannons. Flames and explosives were now consuming the courthouse.

Sensing inevitable victory, the key Klan leader, Christopher Columbus Nash, demanded that the Black men surrender their weapons. If they did, Nash promised he would allow them to leave unharmed. No one in that building believed it. Every African American knew that if they "laid down their arms, they would be at the mercy of these killers." Yet as fire consumed the seat of democracy in Colfax, the flames and the smoke became too much for the Black men to endure. And for the KKK, the thrill of killing African Americans, particularly those who thought they had some kind of militia, soldier, or citizen status, was just too tempting as they stumbled out of the raging fires. "If you ever wanted to see dead niggers," one of the murderers bragged to a man he had brought to the scene, "this is your chance."[58]

When federal authorities finally arrived, there was simply death. Buzzards, dogs, and insects feasting on what was left of the Black militia. Brains splattered all over the ground. Faces missing. Bullets that had made Swiss cheese of men's backs, especially those who had surrendered. Bodies upon bodies upon bodies that had clearly under-gone unspeakable torture all on the battleground of democracy.[59] It was no secret who did it. There were boasts, even. A "'veritable army' of 'old time Ku Klux Klan'" led by a judge, Alphonse Cazabat, and a sheriff, Christopher Columbus Nash, had killed at least one hundred—and the estimates go up to three hundred African Americans—sixty after they had already surrendered.[60]

Politically war-torn Louisiana wasn't about to do anything about this massacre. The U.S. Department of Justice, therefore, stepped in and charged eight terrorists with violating a federal law, the Enforcement Act, which Congress had passed specifically to stop the Klan and similar violent white supremacist organizations. This should have been easy. As the Klansman Dave Paul noted, what they did in Colfax is what gets you hung from the highest gallows. Yet when their convictions reached the U.S. Supreme Court, the justices ruled in *United States v. Cruikshank* (1876) that the Enforcement Act applied only to state action, not to private groups such as the Klan. Thus, according to the court, all the government's charges related to how these men "conspired" to deprive people of African descent of their right to assemble, their right to vote, and their right to bear arms had no basis in any federal law. Because it wasn't the State of Louisiana that slaughtered Black people in Colfax, African Americans' rights weren't violated. In short, the Supreme Court ruled that the Constitution was no refuge. As the court's *Cruikshank* decision made clear, even if a sheriff and a judge lead a band of terrorists to attack forces called by the government to protect the results of an election, when the protectors are of African descent, they did not have the right to a well-regulated militia, the right to bear arms, or the right to self-defense. There was no law that could protect them. The Second Amendment didn't apply, nor did the Fourteenth.[61]

President Ulysses S. Grant was outraged. The killings were bad enough. What the court did, however, was nearly unforgivable. For all the Southern talk about "civilization" and "Christianity," he railed, Colfax was nothing but "bloodthirstiness and barbarity." Yet now, with the Enforcement Act shredded, "no way can be found . . . to punish the perpetrators of this bloody and monstrous crime." The Supreme Court's 5–4 decision not only meant that the "Colfax murderers . . . walked off

scot-free," but the ruling also sent "a powerful message to white supremacists that they could slay blacks without any penalty."[62]

The Hamburg Massacre in South Carolina in 1876, just a year after
the *Cruikshank* decision, reaffirmed the lawlessness of the law. On
July 4, a group of Black militiamen paraded down the town's main
street celebrating the centennial of the nation's independence. A white
farmer, who came up behind them in his carriage, was furious that
these African Americans, in uniform no less, were obstructing "my
road." He swore out a complaint and had the officer in charge of the
Black militia arrested, brought before a judge, and ordered to stand
trial. The Black militiamen came to support their officer. When they
arrived, so did "a large number of armed whites." Sensing trouble,
ex–Confederate general Matthew C. Butler, who was one of the most
powerful and respected men in Hamburg, demanded unilateral disarmament. He ordered African Americans in the militia to drop their
weapons. Butler didn't issue that same command to the mob of armed
white men, however. The Black militiamen refused. Flat-out refused.[63]

Whites in Hamburg had been complaining for a while about these
men. Black men. In uniforms. With guns. Who acted like they had
authority. Who acted like they no longer had to obey white men. It was
"an insult [such] as no white people upon earth had ever to put up with
before."[64] That these men would dare show up at the courthouse, armed,
to ensure that their commanding officer wasn't lynched, was, at this
point, enraging. Just too much. Whites attacked. Black men in the
militia fought back, but the size of the mob was growing, and the men,
therefore, retreated, taking refuge in the nearby armory. Butler, meanwhile, had left the scene, only to return with hundreds of "reinforcements" and a cannon. As the explosives from the artillery shells hit the
armory, shook the building, and blew out the windows, pouring more
oxygen into the flames, a fiery, hellish death seemed to be how this story

would end. The Black men tried desperately to flee. But the moment they left the building, they were butchered, "gunned down in cold blood."[65]

There were others whom the white mob had captured. They would use their captives to enact a ritual of community-building for whites and danger-signaling for African Americans—to show that refusal to bow down to white supremacy, to accept the reign of anti-Blackness, had fatal consequences. The killers set up a "dead-ring," a place of pride to publicly execute the Black militiamen. The murderers, with each hanging, exclaimed: "By God! We will carry South Carolina now. About the time we kill four or five hundred men we will scare the rest."[66]

When word of the massacre reached President Grant, rage and sadness combined because he realized something horrible. Truly horrible. "Hamburg, as cruel, bloodthirsty, wanton, unprovoked, and as uncalled for as it was," he said, "is only a repetition" of Mississippi, Louisiana, and all these Southern states. The common thread among them, Grant solemnly acknowledged, was not civilization, not Christianity, but "the right to Kill negroes . . . without fear of punishment, and without loss of caste or reputation."[67] Simply the right to kill Black people.

RECONSTRUCTION AND THE constitutional amendments were, in the end, no match for the bullets, terror, cannon fire, and anti-Blackness that made African Americans in uniform not only repugnant and reviled but targets to be murdered. The hatred, of course, was not reserved for Black soldiers or militiamen but extended to African Americans with political success or ambitions; those who, against all odds, owned land—and those who thought they had rights as American citizens.[68]

The bullets, of course, did their damage. But so, too, did the U.S. Supreme Court, which, in a series of devastating decisions including *Cruikshank*, "tore down the edifice of Reconstruction law, brick by brick."[69] The court blasted a hole straight through the Fourteenth's due process and equal protection clause with the Slaughterhouse Cases (1873), *Cumming v. Richmond* (1899), and *Giles v. Harris* (1903). It mocked the Fifteenth with *Minor v. Happersett* (1874), *United States v. Reese* (1875), and *Williams v. Mississippi* (1898). And it derided the Thirteenth's "badges of servitude" with its humanity-defying decision in *Plessy v. Ferguson* (1896), which provided the legal basis and cover for Jim Crow.[70]

These Supreme Court decisions looked, felt, and smelled like betrayal. And that betrayal of the promise of the Civil War would only get more entrenched as Jim Crow—racially segregated inequality enforced through violence and the law—took hold in the United States. Frederick Douglass—after having escaped slavery, fought with all that he had for abolition, pushed for Black citizenship through military service, and worked with members of Congress to pass key legislation— knew that things had reached the point, after years of domestic terrorism, Northern retreat, and Supreme Court decisions, that "he could not fully trust his own country."[71] It was like being relegated to somewhere between slave and citizen. Historian Nan Elizabeth Woodruff poignantly wrote, "Black people had learned since the end of Reconstruction that what the federal government gave with one hand, it could take with another."[72]

African Americans were on their own. One man succinctly explained it to Congress: "You know the law does not protect me."[73] So Blacks stayed armed. "As they had since emancipation, both men and women carried guns and practiced armed self-defense."[74] But the very temerity of their attempt at self-defense only further provoked the wrath of whites "and resulted in more violence and the intervention of the state."[75] Unarmed, African Americans were vulnerable. Very vulnerable. They knew, however, that it was not the presence of weapons or lack of weapons that put crosshairs on their lives; it was their Blackness. Though "often outgunned and outnumbered," an African American man explained, "we have made up our minds to go down fighting for the race."[76]

And it was going to be a fight. Jim Crow ushered in a carnival of violence—lynching, spectacle lynching—where hundreds of whites joyously watched a human being tortured by, in one case, "jamming a red-hot poker into . . . [the] eyes . . . and using a clothes iron to burn off . . . genitals." These joyous community rituals of Black pain and death were often "the biggest thing since Ringling Brothers Circus came to town," said one white man.[77] And the circus of death kept coming. On average, there were a thousand lynchings for each of the next three decades—from the 1890s through the war "to make the world safe for democracy," the deaths just kept coming.[78]

Blacks were fighting against mobs while the police just stepped aside and looked on. They also had to confront the consistent threat of being slaughtered outright, especially as they dealt with batteries of machine guns brought in by the U.S. Army. Massacre-level state violence continued to reveal that the Second was not designed to provide protection for African Americans' citizenship. In fact, in 1906 the Supreme Court accepted the implicit suggestion that American-born whites were the only real "citizens."[79] African Americans, however, were just Black. And from "scientific studies," movies, books, plays, music, and sensationalized newspaper accounts of crime-infested neighborhoods, inherent criminality, and uncontrolled libidos, "the cumulative impression was of a world made precarious by Negroes."[80] Whites, thus, had a near paranoid sense of being "besieged, even though no one [was] at the gates."[81]

In Atlanta in the fall of 1906, local newspapers, law enforcement, and politicians' toxic anti-Blackness stoked that fear, fed that rage, and turned the city into a war zone. Four major papers in the city ran months of front-page stories with ghastly details of African American men harassing, sexually assaulting, and raping white women. No city street was safe. No park was carefree. No home secure. All were made unsafe by the presence of Blackness. Although the stories of Black men gone wild, replete with eroticized descriptions of hands and lips and torn bodices, were false or overdramatized for shock effect, the stories sold papers. Circulation doubled at the *Atlanta Evening News*. Tensions in the city kept rising with each new tale of African American debauchery, sadism, rape, and defilement of white virginal purity. The *Georgian* editorial page made it clear: "If the negro were no longer a part of our population, the women of the South would be freed from their state of siege . . . But under the black shadow of the fiendish passion of these ebony devils our women are as completely slaves as if they were in bondage to a conquering foe."[82]

Gubernatorial candidates and rival newspapermen Clark Howell and Hoke Smith, backed by another demagogue, Tom Watson, "did everything in their power to fan the flames of race hatred." They vowed to cleanse the state of "Negro domination," campaigned on the slogan that African Americans must be kept "in their place"—a subjugated, servile "place of inferiority"—so that no white person would ever have to be subjected to the looming, pervasive danger that Black people posed to society.[83]

Then it happened. An African American man actually attacked a white woman, choked her, dragged her into the woods. When she came to, she identified an itinerant laborer, Frank Carmichael, as her assailant. It didn't take long; the lynch mob got him. "In less than two seconds . . . six bullets were tearing their way through his heart," the *Journal* reported, "and he fell dying amid a solemn shout from a half a hundred avengers."[84]

After that, there were more and more claims of rape and sexual assault. At least twelve. Many of those appeared to be that an African American man looked at a white woman. Glanced her way. Peered at her salaciously.[85] Two of the charges, however, were true. Painfully true.[86] Each, nonetheless, was reported with the lewd, rage-inducing details conjuring up the imagery that Black barbarism was not simply at the gates but had climbed the walls, stolen the key, unlocked the gate, and let the thieving, raping horde into the city.[87]

By September 22, 1906, white men had had enough. "Are we Southern white men going to stand for this?" shouted one of the avengers exhorting a crowd to act. "No. Let's kill all the Negroes so our women will be safe." With that, the angry crowd quickly turned into a lynch mob.[88] It was the new "nigger-hunt"—not in the woods of Mississippi or the swamps of Louisiana, but in the streets and neighborhoods of Atlanta. One man said his boss warned him to go home because "we are going to kill niggers tonight!"[89]

In a frenzied crime spree, Black businesses were trashed, looted, and destroyed. Black people were pulled off trolley cars and pummeled, shot, and stabbed. African Americans trying to get to work in the city's hotels were chased down like "quarry." The mob "surged through Atlanta's downtown . . . shouting 'Kill them!' 'Lynch them!' 'Kill every damn nigger in sight!'" The carnage was overwhelming as "barbershops, restaurants, and hotel lobbies 'bore pools of blood,' while traces of 'brains were still to be found in places sheltered from the rain.'" And the response of the police was both edifying and horrifying. The speaker of the Georgia House of Representatives confessed that "practically nothing was done to stop the mob." Law enforcement just watched. Or they didn't answer the phone at the station. Not surprisingly, police even told African Americans, "We are not able to protect you."[90]

The sense of vulnerability was palpable. One Black man noted, "The city was in the clutches of a set of fiends, hunting and shooting down Negroes indiscriminately."[91] While being unable to protect African Americans, however, police (and the state militia) made a big show of disarming Black people. One of those arrested for carrying a concealed weapon would come to know the fatal cost of thinking he had the right to self-defense. The mob stormed the jail, got a rope, ignored his pleas for "mercy" as they dragged him into a wooded area, and lynched a Black man for daring to believe he needed protection from whites who were killing African Americans at will.[92]

The mob was not sated. With its appetite whetted by the carnage inflicted on African Americans where they worked, dined, got their hair cut, or played pool and drank, the mob then set out for where they lived. This was going to be a pogrom. In those other venues throughout the city, Blacks had to be chased. At home, especially in those "make-shift wooden shanties," they would be such easy, stationary targets.[93]

Whites, "carrying torches and firearms," were ready to "clean out the niggers." There was going to be a world-class bonfire as the Black working-class community, known as Darktown, "one of the roughest neighborhoods" in Atlanta, was burnt to the ground.[94] What the mob ran into that night, however, was a change of plans.

Quietly, methodically African Americans had been amassing arms and ammunition "during the tense weeks before" the mob had descended on Black people downtown. All the newspaper headlines and gruesome stories were an omen of the death and destruction that was headed Darktown's way. Blacks also had no faith that the police or militia would ever protect them. They knew better. Instead, they would protect themselves.

There was a general understanding that mobs kill because they can. Because there are no consequences, at least, not from the authorities. Given that cold, harsh reality, a Black man laid out the rationale for survival: "The duty of the Negro, therefore, . . . is to make it as perilous as possible for the mob . . . The only thing which these cowards respect . . . is force, brute force." In other words, the only way "to deal with a mob . . . is to shoot it to death; riddle it with bullets or dynamite it."[95]

As the torch-bearing, gun-toting whites approached Darktown, African Americans blew out the streetlights and opened fire. Stunned, the mob fell back. Whites regrouped, as if the hail of bullets was a fluke. It wasn't. As they surged toward the hardscrabble Black part of town, again African Americans, protecting their lives, their homes, their communities, opened fire.[96] The point, again, was to make it as "perilous as possible for the mob."[97] Message finally received. African Americans did what the police would not. And Darktown's "defensive success blocked the advancement of whites farther eastward into an area heavily populated by blacks."[98]

The mob was chastened, but reassembled and headed for Brownsville, where the Black middle class and elite lived—the doctors, the business owners, the professors—and where Clark College and Gammon Theological Seminary were. These African American physicians, teachers, and shopkeepers just felt like a much easier target. Rumors soon began to circulate in the city, however, that just as in Darktown, African Americans in Brownsville were also heavily armed. Of course they were. One faculty member spoke of having "two big revolvers" with the mob's name on them. A student wrote to his mother that "last night was one of the most scarey [*sic*] nights . . . the streets were wild with the mob all day . . . and some came out here at night . . . I slept with my gun under my bed."[99] Tensions were high, and when a group of armed white men came too close to Brownsville, bullets started flying. It wasn't the mob breaching the perimeter, however. These were plainclothes policemen, and one was now dead, four others injured. In this gun battle, Brownsville's sentries also suffered casualties.[100] But the pain was just beginning.

Black people. Armed. Shooting back. Simply because a white mob had gone on a multiday killing spree? Not in Georgia. The state retaliated. The militia, reinforced with "three infantry companies, the Governor's Horse Guard, a machine gun, and 10,000 rounds of ammunition," launched an invasion of Brownsville.[101] As in the old antebellum days of the slave patrol, Georgia's twentieth-century version used violence and terror to break into and ransack African Americans' homes in a hunt for weapons. The state militia chanted: "We are rough, we are tough, we kill niggers and never get enough!" Troops shot and beat Blacks while ripping their homes to shreds. Hundreds of African Americans were arrested and their guns confiscated.[102]

Disarmament, coupled with the electoral consequences of the hate-filled gubernatorial election that stripped most Blacks of their voting rights, made clear that "the Negro in the South is in peril of the white man. And it isn't an imaginary, it is a real peril."[103] For defending themselves, African Americans were lynched, beaten, tortured, shot, and jailed. One former resident of the city asked, "How would you feel if you saw a governor, a mayor, a sheriff, whom you could not oppose at the polls, encourage by deed or word or both, a mob of 'best' and worst citizens to slaughter your people in the streets and in their own homes, and in their places of business?"[104]

They not only encouraged the slaughter; they also committed the sin of omission. The lynching, beating, torturing, and shooting of Black people saw no real intervention by authorities. Over the course of a five-day bloodletting spree, "police arrested only forty whites, or less than 1 percent of the mob's members."[105] Yet when Blacks who had been hunted for days mistakenly fired on plainclothes officers, the response by the state was an overwhelming, awe-inducing, machine-gun-toting show of force. One prominent Black activist, T. Thomas Fortune, was outraged. "It makes my blood boil," he wrote. How are Black people disarmed "in a situation like that of Atlanta" when it could only result in "contempt and massacre of the race[?]"[106] Yet in the twisted irony and logic of the Second Amendment, the same result occurred when Black people were armed. While Darktown had successfully repelled the invaders, Brownsville faced not only the planned attack of the mob but the real assault from the state, too, and in the process, Black people were stripped of their weapons. An African American physician, William F. Penn, therefore, wanted to know, "How shall we protect our lives and property? . . . Tell us what your standards are for coloured men. What are the requirements under which we may live and be protected?"[107] The answer was horrifically simple: There was no protection.

EVEN BLACK SOLDIERS, stationed in the United States, were not safe. The 167 troops of the First Battalion, Twenty-Fifth Infantry (Colored) were scheduled to replace the white soldiers in Brownsville, Texas, who were rotating out to another fort. When the mayor received word in the summer of 1906 that African Americans were coming, he was apoplectic. His constituents were not going to accept "nigger soldiers." The townsfolk were angry and worried that these "Black heathens will rape, rob, and murder us in our beds." Whites in the dusty Texas town were determined that they would "get rid of the niggers some way."[108]

When the Black troops arrived, they were not seen as heroes who had been "willing to sacrifice their lives for their country" as they put it all on the line in recent wars.[109] Instead, they were the enemy. The sworn enemy. In Brownsville, African American troops were thus "denied access to local bars, shoved off sidewalks, beaten, and warned that their brains might be blown out." There was also the ever-present charge of rape. A white woman claimed that one of the soldiers, a "'large' Negro," tried to assault her. She had no description except his "khaki pants," but that was more than enough. The white commander of the Black troops immediately ordered a lockdown. All men were to stay on base.[110]

Yet despite the lockdown, the very next night, on August 13, there was an attack. A barrage of bullets ripped through the town. Unrelentingly for ten minutes, spraying homes and storefronts. One white man died, another had his horse shot out from under him, and a police officer's arm was so damaged that it had to be amputated.[111] The battalion's commander, hearing the gunshots, thought that it was the fort that was under attack and immediately ordered a roll call. As the gunshots continued to strafe Brownsville, every last one of his soldiers was present and accounted for.[112]

The mayor, nonetheless, sent a telegram to President Theodore Roosevelt laying out the guilt of the Black troops, making clear there were at least twenty to thirty men who shot up the town, killed a man, and seriously wounded another. Equally important, he warned Roosevelt that if the president didn't remove these soldiers from Brownsville, an armed mob would.[113] The commanding officer, however, reported that his soldiers couldn't have done it; they had all been present on base and accounted for. But the men were Black. They were accused by whites of doing what Black men do. Commit acts of violence, especially when they get guns.

The army investigators quickly embraced and affirmed those stereotypes. They rationalized away the physical impossibility of the troops committing these crimes, surmising, instead, that some of them had disobeyed their commanding officer, left the fort, shot up the town, and then "sprinted back as soon as they heard the bugle and snuck into line in time to holler 'Present' when the roster was read."[114] Although no one in town could identify the shooters and, even more important, shots were still heard during the roll call, the investigators were certain African American soldiers did this.

The mayor then showed up with "evidence" that proved the guilt of these unwanted troops. He had the casings from the expended bullets. With this proof in hand, the interrogations began in earnest. They ended in frustration. All the Black men said they were innocent. Not only were they innocent, but they had no idea who shot up Brownsville. They certainly knew it wasn't them. The denials and the "wooden, stolid look" on their faces angered the investigator, who grew up in Greenville, South Carolina, and knew Black guilt when he saw it. That collective stoicism could mean only one thing, collective guilt. A "conspiracy to obstruct justice."[115]

President Roosevelt was furious. He ordered his secretary of war, William Howard Taft, to dishonorably discharge every last single man—all 167 of them. If they wanted to protect the 20 or so of them who killed a man, a white man, who wounded a police officer and shot a horse, even, then all 167 would have to pay. No army pensions. No chance of a government job. Dishonorable discharge would haunt them throughout the rest of their lives. And, no, Roosevelt insisted, there would not be any courts-martial. They were getting booted straight out of the army. Either they tell the truth or they're gone. But, because there was nothing to tell, their fates were sealed.[116]

Roosevelt summoned Booker T. Washington, the most powerful African American in the United States, to the White House. Washington thought their conversation would center on the Atlanta riot and the violence that rained down on Black people and, perhaps, Brownsville, which he expected Roosevelt, who had developed a reputation as "friend of the Negro," would be sympathetic about. Instead, he was stunned as the president laid out a very sordid tale of drink-induced murder at Brownsville. Washington was even more shocked that 167 Black soldiers were going to get dishonorably discharged without a trial. A few days later when Washington followed up, he tried to dissuade Roosevelt from going through with this sledgehammer of a dismissal, suggesting that he had additional information that might prove useful. The president was curt: "You can not have any information to give me privately to which I could pay heed, my dear Mr. Washington."[117]

Washington tried to salvage what he could in order to maintain both his and Roosevelt's reputations and to boost the morale of the Black community, which had been gutted by the wholesale dismissal. He asked Secretary of War Taft to replace the dismissed soldiers with another battalion of Black troops. He also, after hearing that the army was going to expand the number of artillery regiments, suggested that creating Black artillery units would be ideal.[118]

Both were fantasies. Black troops were not going back into Brownsville. The townsfolk had done a masterful job of "getting rid of the niggers some way" by framing the soldiers. It turned out that the so-called evidence, the shell casings, was actually previously fired in Nebraska when the troops were stationed there, gathered up by the army to save money, and deposited in a container on the front porch of Fort Brown, readily available to military and civilians alike. In addition, an inspection of the troops' weapons at the time of the shooting gave every indication "that their rifles did not appear to have been fired."[119] The troops' Blackness was their guilt. Being Black men in uniform was their hubris. And that they were African American soldiers with guns was their crime.

That's why Booker T. Washington's other recommendation, a Black artillery unit in 1906, was a pipe dream. Sergeant Major Presly Holliday, an African American soldier who had first proffered the idea that made its way to Washington, remarked on the "white racial assumption" that "colored men can not be found with sufficient intelligence to make good artillerymen. I believe," he continued, "this theory is given out officially at the War Department." But it was more than that. As historian Louis R. Harlan wrote, "Behind the reluctance of white leaders to create black artillery units was not so much a doubt of their intelligence as an unspoken fear of black possession of the big guns."[120]

IN AUGUST 1914, WHAT began with an assassination of an archduke in Europe led to a war that would topple four empires, see the rise of Vladimir Lenin and the Bolsheviks in Russia, raise the international stature of the United States, and hurl America into a domestic bloodbath called Red Summer.[121] The American Civil War had already given some indication of what happens when the industrialization of death meets the horrors of battle. The suffering and the body count were simply unheard of.[122] The Great War, as World War I was then called, upped the ante and demonstrated how full mechanization of the instruments of death could lead to a million killed in one battle and more than three-quarters of a million in another.[123] What the generals had hoped would be a quick war, delivered with a decisive blow, turned into a war of attrition where the objective was no longer to move the battle-lines forward and capture territory but to bleed the other side into submission by killing more and more and more until their society couldn't sustain further losses.

When the United States finally entered the war in spring 1917, Britain, France, and Russia were relieved that help was on the way. The war had devolved into a blood-soaked, mustard-gassed stalemate. The United States had not only the industrial might but the manpower to tip the scales and act as a massive counterweight to German dominance. American entry, however, came with all kinds of rhetorical flourishes, war aims, and racial baggage. President Woodrow Wilson did not officially ally with Britain, France, and Russia but became, instead, an "associated power" to keep America's distance from what he saw as the Old World order of secret treaties, land grabs, and the lack of self-determination, where people were denied the right to choose their own leaders.[124] He called U.S. entry into the conflagration necessary because this would be a "war to make the world safe for democracy."[125] The autocrats and empires were relics of the past, he scoffed.[126] American democracy was the present and the future.

Yet for all the soaring language, the United States was a nation locked into a prison of anti-Blackness absolutely unsafe for democracy and also for African Americans. When the war began, there was great concern about what it would mean to have a sizable number of Black men in the armed forces.[127] The undersized U.S. military was simply not large enough to take on the fighting needs of the hell erupting in Europe. Congress, therefore, passed the Selective Service Act of 1917, which established a draft for all able-bodied men between the ages of twenty-one and thirty-one. Senator James "Big Chief" Vardaman of Mississippi, who had earlier bragged of his state's success in blocking access to the ballot box by eliminating the "nigger from politics," now "fought hard against conscripting African-Americans into the military," arguing "that it would be dangerous to racial harmony to arm African-Americans."[128] Vardaman's skewed definition of "racial harmony" was akin to that of Southern whites during Reconstruction who wanted the Black troops removed so there would be racial peace. The real concern was not harmony or peace but rather that "Southern whites did not want blacks to become trained in using weapons."[129]

And then came the uprising in Houston in August 1917, which did nothing to allay those fears. In fact, it heightened them: "Many white Americans were not prepared to accept large numbers of black males in one place, especially if they were armed."[130] Black soldiers in the Third Battalion, Twenty-Fourth Infantry Regiment had fought for the United States in Cuba, the Philippines, and Mexico but—because whites feared that this war, the war to make the world safe for democracy, would give African Americans an inflated sense of their status, especially if they engaged in combat—these soldiers were assigned to guard duty at a post in Houston. That sense of collective demotion for a proud fighting force was exacerbated by their knowledge of what happens to Black soldiers and Black people in Texas. There was, of course, Brownsville. Followed by near uprisings in 1911 and 1916 in San Antonio between African American soldiers and whites over Jim Crow and the debasement that came with it. The men of the Twenty-Fourth also had knowledge of the lynchings in Temple, Texas, in 1915 and the especially gruesome one in Waco the next year, where Jesse Washington was dismembered, strangled, and roasted alive. Then there was Galveston in 1917. The fighting force of the Twenty-Fourth knew that it was headed into hostile territory.[131]

Shortly after they arrived in Houston, they clashed with a system that did not see them as soldiers in the U.S. Army but as "just niggers." White contractors who needed to get on base refused to show ID. Refused to "obey a nigger." When the troops went into the city, white civilians' attitude was "that a nigger is a nigger and that his status is not effected [*sic*] by the uniform he wears." And then there were the police. They were the worst. The cops routinely terrorized the Black community. Beatings and false arrests were common. And the soldiers took umbrage at it, saw themselves as protectors, as they had been during the days of Reconstruction. On multiple occasions when a soldier or two witnessed the brutality and demanded that the officers stop, the police would respond by slugging and pistol-whipping the "uppity" military men. And those men in uniform were equally clear: "We ain't no niggers."[132]

Their commanding officer tried to defuse the situation and allay the concerns of the police by stripping the soldiers of their firearms. These Black men, who had fought in multiple wars and were relegated to guard duty, would now become soldiers without weapons. This was supposedly a "peace." What the men of the Twenty-Fourth understood, however, was that the U.S. Army had sold them out and they could rely only on themselves for justice.[133]

That realization crystallized on August 23, 1917. On that hot summer day, police chased a man into the home of a Black woman, Mrs. Sarah Travers. While she wasn't the object of their manhunt, she was the one whom they dragged out of her house "half naked." With neighbors everywhere, a grown woman barely clothed and exposed. The humiliation was too much. Private Alonzo Edwards of the Twenty-Fourth offered to pay whatever her fine was so that she could get back in the house with some dignity. The cops beat him savagely for that. Then they arrested him. When Corporal Charles Baltimore, an MP, went to the station to check on Edwards, police beat him, too. Then chased and repeatedly shot at him.[134]

When word reached the soldiers of the Twenty-Fourth that the police had, once again, attacked their brethren, but this time—as the rumors spiraled and spiraled with each telling—not just "shot at" but actually "shot" Corporal Baltimore, whatever barriers the commanding officer thought he had put between the stockpile of ammunition and the soldiers of the Twenty-Fourth ceased to exist. The troops grabbed their rifles and exclaimed, "To hell with going to France . . . Get to work right here." Between seventy-five and one hundred men gathered in military formation and set off to avenge not only the attacks on Corporal Baltimore and Private Edwards, but all the beatings and all the times they'd been called "a nigger." By the time they were done, "four soldiers lay dead as well as fifteen whites, four of whom were police officers. (A fifth officer died later.)"[135]

Military justice was swift. Nineteen of the soldiers were executed immediately after the trial and fifty-four were sentenced to prison. There would be no clemency here. Indeed, a Black editor who wrote of them as "martyrs" was charged and convicted under the Espionage Act. Nevertheless, the sentiment in the African American community was that it was a noble death these soldiers now faced. A letter to the *San Antonio Inquirer* stated, "We would rather see you shot by the highest tribunal of the United States Army because you dared protect a Negro Woman from the insult of a southern brute in the form of a policeman than to have you forced to go to Europe to fight for a liberty you can not enjoy." Another was equally resolute. It was much more honorable to protect a Black woman "than to have you die . . . in the trenches of Europe, fighting to make the world safe for a democracy that you can't enjoy."[136]

BLACK MEN IN the military fought for and served the United States, yet they were defined "as domestic enemies."[137] The soldiers of the Twenty-Fourth highlighted what was seen as the problem. Secretary of War Newton Baker explained to the chair of the House Judiciary Committee that the revolt by the troops in Houston "had revealed that 'these elements of our population did not have the necessary capacity for the high service of military duty, the respect for constituted authority, and the due appreciation of the obligations of a soldier.'" Guns, in the hands of African Americans who believed they had rights, could only lead to trouble. When the exigencies of war finally forced the United States to draft 380,000 Black troops and send 42,000 of them as combat units over to France, the *New Republic* openly worried that when the soldiers returned, "Will [the Negro] accept the facts of white supremacy with the same spirit as formerly?"[138]

The question was both fantasy and dogma to a nation simultaneously frightened of Black people but desperately in need of their presence to provide whites with labor, racial status, and a cultural touchstone to mark what was "civilized" and what was "primitive" or "savage." African Americans never bought into the paradigm, however, and challenged both the "facts" of white supremacy and that they had ever blithely accepted their subjugation. The Stono Rebellion, Gabriel's uprising, Charles Deslondes's march to New Orleans, Denmark Vesey, Nat Turner, Cincinnati, Christiana, Colfax, Atlanta, and Houston did not suggest some spirit of acquiescence. Those uprisings and defenses of self and community indicated, instead, a quest for freedom.

The Great War would be, said the grand master of the Negro Masons in Texas, our "second emancipation."[139] And in 1918, Black troops in France felt it, even in the hellish trenches on the French battlefield. They felt it. Came closer than they ever had before to experiencing it. That taste of freedom only stoked their refusal to accept the fractured citizenship America offered when they came home.[140] President Woodrow Wilson, an arch-segregationist, knew that trouble was brewing. "Black

American soldiers were being treated as equals by the French, he worried, and 'it has gone to their heads.'"[141]

RED SUMMER, AN orgy of lynching, terror, and racial pogroms, was the nearly nationwide concerted effort in 1919 to beat and burn the very idea of equality right out of African Americans.[142] It had to be done, one man in Mississippi explained, because the government "drafted blacks into the army, making them equal to whites." And they weren't. They would never be.[143] The Great War, for far too many whites, had changed nothing. "If the black man will stay where he belongs, act like a Negro should act, talk like a Negro should talk, and study like a Negro should study," a Louisiana paper editorialized, "there will be very few riots, fights, or clashes." Stay in your place was the message. The subordinate, "racial harmony," subjugated place. South Carolina congressman James F. Byrnes was emphatic: "This is a white man's country, and it will always remain a white man's country."[144]

The bloodbath of Red Summer was the culmination of the quest for African American freedom in "a white man's country." The National Association for the Advancement of Colored People (NAACP) documented "at least 25 major riots and mob actions . . . and at least 52 black people were lynched. Many victims [were] burned to death" between April and November 1919.[145]

In this latest version of a "nigger hunt," African Americans, once again, defended their homes, their communities, and their lives. In Washington, D.C., when the police refused for days to stop gangs of white sailors from stabbing, beating, and shooting African Americans, Black veterans got their guns.[146] The "Negroes stood in a practically solid line, armed and waiting for attack. Armed white men in automobiles attempted to rush this line, and the discharges of small arms were like a battlefield."[147] African Americans knew, just knew, that they "must abandon the hope of any protection from government" and were, "therefore, left no other alternative but a resort to self-protection."[148]

But Blacks with guns comes with a heavy cost.

In Knoxville, Tennessee, whites went on a rampage determined to avenge the death of a white woman after her alleged killer, a Black man, was secreted out to Chattanooga by the sheriff. Wild with rage, they broke into the local hardware store; stole rifles, pistols, and ammunition; and set out to destroy the Black community. African Americans set up barricades, including overturning a gravel truck and spreading oil on the street to slow down the horde. Black people aimed their rifles, hoping to do what they could—especially after the stores banned ammunition sales to African Americans—and prepared for war. Black people defending themselves against a slaughter, however, only further enraged the mob. Some members of the horde ran to authorities, lied, said that African Americans had killed a couple of their group and that the fine people of Knoxville needed reinforcements. Tennessee was determined to give it and responded with the state militia and two machine guns. With the cry "Let them have it!" the troops began to fire wildly for minutes on end into the Bowery district, where African Americans worked and lived. Blacks retreated deeper into the neighborhood. The machine guns and troops moved forward and unloaded another lethal blast. Although it had been the white mob that broke into the jail, beat the sheriff, and ransacked his home looking to lynch a Black man accused of rape and murder, the state's lethal power was fully directed at African Americans engaged in community self-defense. None of this was lost on Black people in Knoxville. One man noted, "And once again it has been made but too apparent that not only have the authorities no intention of protecting the Negro in his rights but that when he beats back the wanton aggression of white mobs these are usually reinforced, aided and abetted by the white militia and regulars called out to preserve 'law and order.'"[149]

IN ELAINE, ARKANSAS, African Americans would get baptized in the blood of that state's version of "law and order" because they dared to join a labor union to try to stop the theft of their wages, and because they knew "the whites . . . are going to kill us"—and they tried to prevent that by putting guards outside the church where they were meeting.[150]

World War I had caused the price of cotton to skyrocket. What had been a barely-make-it-through-rock-bottom commodity that left the sharecroppers in Elaine flat broke and heavily in debt had become the source of a windfall. Except only the white landowners benefited. Sharecropping required the farmers to buy all their goods throughout the year—food, seeds, tools, etc.—from the landowner on credit. Once the crop was harvested, the farmer was paid, minus whatever he and his family owed from the goods previously purchased. But there was a catch. Several of them, in fact. The landowner kept the books listing the price of each item, what was purchased, and how much was bought on credit. Stray bags of very expensive flour, thus, showed up quite regularly on the accounts. Sharecroppers were often charged for things they never ordered and never received. And yet they had no recourse; the charges were just sitting there on the bill as if they reflected a real debt and had to be paid. As a result, sharecroppers generally owed more than they had earned and were left deeper in debt, and forced to stay to work the following year for a dishonest landowner.[151]

The greed and the corruption were ripe in Elaine, Arkansas. As the price of cotton soared from seven cents a pound in 1914 to thirty cents a pound in 1918, the landowners were awash in money, but the sharecroppers' financial situation did not improve at all. In fact, because the landowners calculated the price of cotton picked at the prewar rate, and the goods purchased on credit at current day prices (or higher), the sharecroppers were losing up to $1,250 a year (the equivalent of nearly $19,000 in 2020). "No padding of accounts nor inflation of prices," journalist Ida B. Wells-Barnett remarked, could absorb that much money and look even quasi-legitimate.[152] The Black sharecroppers knew it. This was beyond mere theft. At one of the plantations, despite record-high rates for cotton and excellent production, "none of the sixty-eight tenants received a settlement in 1918."[153]

The sharecroppers began to organize. They heard about a labor union that could help—Progressive Farmers and Household Union. They started meeting, working out ways to withhold their cotton the next year until they were adequately and appropriately compensated. The last time Black sharecroppers had tried that was in the 1890s, and "white posses had gunned down two of the men and lynched nine more."[154] The men and women in Elaine knew this history, knew what could await them, and still they went forward. Organizing. Meeting. Joining the union. Signing their death warrants.

Rumors began to circulate in town, especially among the planter elite, that Blacks were joining a union, that they were going to upset the racial harmony in Arkansas by demanding to be paid.[155] The planters soon discovered that the sharecroppers were holding their union meetings in a church in Hoop Spur, still in Phillips County but a few miles from town. They sent an armed surveillance party of three to find out what was going on and do what needed to be done to "break . . . up the meeting."[156]

On October 1, 1919, about two hundred sharecroppers—men, women, and children—were in the church. They were listening to what the union could do for them, about the possibility of having a former

U.S. attorney with the Department of Justice, who was now in Arkansas in private practice, sue those planters for wage theft. They got to hear about being able to live freer. There were a few guards posted outside, to make sure that the sharecroppers weren't ambushed. Then one of the Black men on the church porch spotted it. A car, sitting up the road with the lights out. Two of the sharecropper sentries went to check. Suddenly, there was gunfire. Round after round of gunfire. Those in the church ducked for cover as bullets shattered the windows and started whizzing through the air around them.

By the time the shooting was over, one white man, a special agent of the Missouri Pacific Railroad who was in the car, was dead; another white man, a deputy sheriff, was wounded; and the Black trusty from the local jail, Kid Collins, who was with them, had scurried away to alert the authorities.[157] Those in the church scrambled out of that bullet-ridden sacred space to safety. Whites, they were convinced, had found out about their meeting and tried to kill them.

When the sheriff arrived at Hoop Spur and saw a dead white man, word of the killing and the Black "insurrection" spread throughout Arkansas and into neighboring Mississippi. African Americans, the story went, were amassing an arsenal of "high-powered rifles," launching a "Race War," and plotting to kill all the white people in Elaine.[158] The dead white man was proof. His death was just the beginning, however, of a vast, communist-driven, Bolshevik-inspired extermination plan. This was like an apocalyptic warning. Posses from all around, including Mississippi, rode into Elaine fully armed and ready to bring these killers to justice. Whether that came at the end of a bullet, a match, or a rope didn't matter.

It was killing season. Blacks around Elaine, Arkansas, were hunted like "wild beasts" by the lynch mob posses.[159] There was a "white heat of fury at the thought of African Americans arming themselves and having the temerity to fight."[160] That fury fueled the ensuing massacre. One white man saw "twenty-eight black people killed, their bodies then thrown into a pit and burned." Another sixteen were "hanging from a bridge." But, he was clear, "not a single one of the victims" was part of the shooting at Hoop Spur.[161] They just were Black. That was their crime.

As the mob's merciless hunt continued, African Americans were driven from their homes, hiding in their backyards, trying to keep still in the canebrake, trying to hush their children so that the mob wouldn't get them, hoping that the hunters would pass. Many were not successful. And failure was often gruesome. There were toes and ears missing from piles of corpses. One of the hunters bragged that he saw "five or six blacks come out unarmed, holding up their hands and some of them running and trying to get away. They were shot down and killed by members of the posse." Some Blacks who had guns, when fleeing to their next hiding spot, would shoot wildly, to back off the horde. Twice, however, the stray bullets hit their mark. Two more white men died.[162]

With white men dying and a story of Black killers who now had a taste of white blood and were hungry for more, Arkansas governor Charles Hillman Brough demanded that troops from the U.S. Army base Camp Pike join in the hunt. But this was not in the governor's scope of authority; only the secretary of war had the ability to call up the military for duty. When Arkansas's two U.S. senators weighed in, however, 583 soldiers, with the governor at the head, and a twelve-gun machine-gun battalion, "a rolling killing machine" fresh from the war in France, were on their way—an eight-hour journey—to do battle with Black insurgents.[163]

When the army arrived, the troops brought a precision and fire-power to the killing that the mob, which had already done so much damage, couldn't even begin to match. The posse members told the commanding officer that there were at least 150 Blacks, veterans, trained killers, hiding out in the woods among the canebrake. The soldiers fanned out in military precision and "immediately laid down a field of fire" across the tall vegetation. The machine guns chopped down the tall, thick foliage that had been a nearly impenetrable hiding place and, in the process, cut down all those human beings who just wanted to get paid for their labor. The governor bragged, "They took machine guns out there and let 'em have it." After one field was cleared, the troops moved to the next. Machine-gunning "everything that showed up." Then the next. Machine-gunning "them down like rabbits."[164]

Then the troops moved to a house-to-house search where they seized "about 400 guns and 200 pistols" and reportedly "killed many unarmed blacks." One journalist, haunted by the days upon days of mass murder, wrote that the army, "in concert with the posses, went on a 'march of death,' leaving behind 'a path strewn with orphans and widows.'"[165] Over the course of five days, up to 856 African Americans were killed and the "stench of dead bodies could be smelled for two miles," while the "killing fields of Phillips County stretched nearly 50 miles."[166]

Throughout all the carnage, some African Americans were able to just surrender. The soldiers herded them into a school building and detained them while the army continued its mop-up operations. The time safely away from the barrel of a machine gun, however, was not safe at all. The next phase was to gain confessions about how these men "planned to kill every white person they saw."[167] Their torture-fueled confessions were straight out of the Marquis de Sade's handbook. They began at the schoolhouse with gasoline poured over Black men's bodies and a lit match not too far behind. And ended at the prison in Helena, Arkansas, with beatings to the point of near unconsciousness, followed by being strapped in the electric chair with enough jolts to deliver a horrific preview of the future.[168] The subsequent trials, with all-white jury deliberations that ranged from four to nine minutes, condemned twelve of the men to death. Sixty-seven other African American men were sentenced to serve one to twenty-one years in prison.[169] No whites were indicted.

Once the army had completed its job, the planters welcomed the new "peace." Blacks had been disarmed. They were banned from purchasing weapons and ammunition, even as Elaine's white powerbrokers requested a massive restocking of rifles and thirty thousand rounds of ammunition from the federal government. There would also be no union to fight for their labor rights, and African Americans understood there was cotton to be picked. Stripped of their weapons, they were vulnerable. But armed, they were as well. They were a threat. A supposed insurrectionist threat justified not only a state-sponsored lynch mob but days of machine-gun fire, followed by "prostituting" the criminal justice system to make it all seem legitimate.[170]

EMANCIPATION AND RECONSTRUCTION had not led to the promised land. Instead, Blacks were ushered into the killing fields. African Americans' military uniforms angered. Their self-defense enraged. Their right to bear arms triggered. Their claims to citizenship lynched.

*Four*

# How Can I Be Unarmed When My Blackness Is the Weapon That You Fear?

"What the goddam hell you niggers doing with them goddam guns?" he bellowed. "Who in the goddam hell you niggers think you are?"[1]

This was no Southern sheriff barking invectives. Or even a hooded Klansman angry about that centuries-long Trouble: Negroes with Guns. Instead, it was an Oakland, California, police officer raging at African Americans years after the Civil Rights Movement had already wrung citizenship victories from the United States. Those legislative hallmarks of Black citizenship, the Civil Rights Act (1964) and the Voting Rights Act (1965), no matter how impressive, still did not have the power to overcome the anti-Blackness embedded in the Second Amendment.

That confrontation on the streets of Oakland made clear that Black people and the right to bear arms, even after African Americans had come into some semblance of full citizenship, was still anathema. The two men yelled at by the police, Huey Newton and Bobby Seale, had not broken the law.[2] In fact, they were well versed in the California Criminal Code and could recite the Second Amendment's text "verbatim."[3] But that was irrelevant. What would become clear in this era was that the law did not mean what it appeared to say. "What made northern racial barriers so frustrating," historian Thomas J. Sugrue wrote, "was that they were sometimes as hard and fast as they were in the South—but, . . . The rules of racial engagement in the North were seldom posted. And," he continued, "a countervailing set of rules . . . promised blacks that the strong arm of the law would be on their side."[4] It wasn't. Laws protecting Second Amendment rights, such as stand your ground, open carry, and even the "castle doctrine," which gives residents the right to defend their home if there's an intruder, just crumpled under the weight of anti-Blackness. The confrontation in Oakland thus also signaled the role of the police in upholding the underlying centuries-old rationale for the Second—a well-regulated militia to keep Black people in a state of rightlessness.

IN 1956 AND 1957 alone, the NAACP had brought six criminal cases and ten civil suits against the Los Angeles Police Department (LAPD) for subjecting the Black community to "exceptional levels of brutality."[5] The LAPD's disdain was obvious. "Officers on the force called their nightsticks 'nigger-knockers.' "[6] One man recalled, "You just had to be black and moving to be shot by the police."[7] "Between January 1962 and July 1965, Los Angeles law enforcement officers (mostly police, but also sheriff's deputies, highway patrol personnel, and others) killed at least sixty-five people. Of the sixty-five homicides by police that the Los Angeles coroner's office investigated during this period, sixty-four were ruled justifiable homicides." That included nearly thirty who were shot in the back, twenty-five who were unarmed, twenty-three who were being tracked for a nonviolent crime, and four who weren't suspected of anything at the time the police gunned them down.[8]

State-sponsored violence, however, was not isolated to the LAPD. In the 1950s, there was an investigation into the Oakland Police Department, where "over fifty witnesses testified before legislators and an audience of hundreds of West Oakland residents on a 'range of brutalities contradicted only by the police themselves.'"[9] The hearings uncovered that a Black musician "was beaten severely" when officers learned his wife was white. A young African American woman "had been jailed . . . arbitrarily and subjected to three days of venereal tests that later proved negative." Then there was "the tragic case of Andrew L. Hines who was fatally shot in custody after police picked him up on 'suspicion of loitering.'"[10]

Thus, the way the Oakland police engaged Newton and Seale was not unique. Coarseness, crudeness, and contempt were standard operating procedure for those on the force. What was different, however, was the response. Huey Newton and Bobby Seale, co-founders of the Black Panther Party for Self-Defense, "like many blacks in Oakland saw the police as oppressive," as the enemy of the African American community.[11] The two men believed that if they could demonstrate the verve, the sheer audacity to "police the police," it would serve as a mobilizing and organizing action as powerful as the Montgomery Bus Boycott. Thus, when that patrol officer stopped Newton and Seale, called them "niggers," and demanded they "get out of the goddam car and bring them goddam guns out of there," it was as providential (and planned) as Rosa Parks on the bus. It proved an opportune moment, especially because a crowd had gathered, to recruit members based on a new freedom strategy.[12]

Rather than the Civil Rights Movement's emphasis on nonviolence and being willing, as Martin Luther King Jr. said, to "wear you down by our capacity to suffer," the Panthers offered overt militance.[13] Newton raged at the officer. He was beyond defiant. The Panthers' co-founder was aggressive and assertive; he had so stunned the officer with not only his visible disdain for the police but also his full knowledge and clear understanding of the right to bear arms and the Fourteenth Amendment's due process clause and its implications for the seizure of private property, including guns, that the cop and the other officers who came to the scene simply got back in their patrol cars and drove away.[14] That lack of fear, that willingness to beat the police at their own game of aggression, that knowledge of the law and how it could be wielded to mystify and stymie the police, led Bobby Seale to define Huey P. Newton as "the baddest motherfucker in the world."[15]

Then there was the way the Panthers, working with the family, stepped in to investigate the police killing of a young Black man, Denzil Dowell, whom the Oakland P.D. had called a "burglar" but the community called a friend, neighbor, and son. That willingness to challenge the official police story of a "justified homicide" brought more and more adherents to the organization.

Dowell's death was highly suspicious. The police officer who pulled the trigger had previously vowed to kill him well before the shooting. The store Dowell was supposedly burglarizing showed no signs of forced entry. The pool of blood was not under his body on the road but yards away. The police claimed Dowell fled and when ordered to stop, that he jumped multiple fences to get away. But that was physically impossible. Dowell had a bad hip and a limp and could not run, much less leap over fences. Finally, it appeared that the only way that the bullet holes in his shirt could have matched up with the ones on his body was if Dowell had his hands up, surrendering, complying, rendered harmless; now dead.[16] Seale and Newton, at a street corner meeting with well over one hundred in attendance, made sure the community knew what their investigation had uncovered. One FBI informant relayed that he "had never seen Black men command the respect of the people the way that Huey Newton and Bobby Seale" had that day.[17]

As the membership expanded, the Panthers issued a manifesto in May 1967, the Ten-Point Program, that laid out the demands of Black Americans, one of which was "We want an immediate end to police brutality and murder of Black people."[18] The Panthers asserted:

> We believe we can end police brutality in our Black community by organizing Black self defense groups that are dedicated to defending our Black community from racist police oppression and brutality. The Second Amendment of the Constitution of the United States gives us a right to bear arms. We therefore believe that all Black people should arm themselves for self defense.[19]

In articulating this vision for the Black Panthers, Seale and Newton drew inspiration from the work done in the Deep South. In the early 1960s, as white terror threatened to extinguish the lives and the work of members of the Congress of Racial Equality (CORE) in Bogalusa, Louisiana, "dubbed 'Klantown, USA'"; as the police made it abundantly clear that they would do nothing to stop the beatings, the shootings, and the violence; and as the federal government demurred and refused to intervene, a group of Black men stepped up and took on the role of defending the freedom workers. The Deacons for Defense and Justice were well organized and heavily armed, and they grounded their efforts in the mantra of self-defense. Never the aggressor. But when threatened, they would shoot back.[20] Transporting the strategy used below the Mason-Dixon Line by the Deacons for Defense to the West Coast, however, proved complicated. The civil rights activism in the Deep South had deliberately linked nonviolent destruction of Jim Crow to the protection of democracy, American values, and a plain sense of fairness. It was "no easy walk," but nonviolence created the space for enough whites to see the brutality and consequences of Jim Crow.[21] When the Deacons for Defense's guns did come out—for example, in Bogalusa, Louisiana—it was understood as an attempt to protect those American values and the lives of civil rights workers and, equally important, to level those weapons against the Klan, a group that had become a notorious societal pariah.[22]

On the other hand, the strategy of defending the Black community against police violence ran aground on three major shoals that delegitimized the tactic and, eventually, the Panthers. First, California did not carry the aura of backwardness and overt history of white supremacist violence that defined Mississippi or the Deep South. (Indeed, Nina Simone's civil rights protest song was not "California Goddam" but "Mississippi Goddam.") California was, in the national narrative, the land where dreams were made, not a place of racial nightmares. The South, on the other hand, was the horror show of Jim Crow and state-sanctioned lynching and brutality. The nation's propensity to define racism as Southern-only made the Panthers' demands in California illegible, if not incomprehensible, to the larger society.

Second, between 1965 and 1967 major riots erupted in Watts, Cleveland, Newark, and Detroit, and, although sparked by intolerable living conditions and police violence, those uprisings and the source of the uprisings remained unintelligible to many Americans. This inability to grapple with and recognize systemic inequality when there were no "colored only" signs led the public to define what they saw in the North and the West as just Black people's natural tendency toward theft (looting), arson, and violence. In a 1965 Gallup poll, 64 percent of whites in California believed that the uprising in Watts, an area of Los Angeles, was due to "lack of respect for law enforcement and outside agitators."[23] Moreover, 62 percent of whites nationwide believed that looters "should be shot."[24] California governor Ronald Reagan slammed the rebellions as the "riots of the lawbreakers and the mad dogs against the people."[25] Those riots and the political response to them fed the surge into the racialized policies of "law and order."[26]

Third, the target of the Panthers was not the Klan but the police. Although the KKK had become repugnant to the larger society, the police were respected—revered, even.[27] Armed Black men asserting their right to defend the African American community against the police conjured up a horrifying specter. In a report marked "Confidential," the Oakland Police Department reported to the state legislature that Seale and Newton's "prime objective is to arm the negro community to full capacity for the purpose of backing all plays by the negro community to act as a deterrent to . . . the Oakland Police Department and the San Francisco Police Department."[28] Another report, while omitting the police officer's racism and belligerence, recalled the incident when Newton shouted down and stood up to the cop who tried to take his legally owned gun. The report focused on the firearms and the reasons for them: "They were observed displaying a shotgun in their moving vehicle . . . one passenger was carrying a loaded .45 cal. automatic pistol in his belt, in open view." If the (legal) open display of weapons weren't egregious enough, the police relayed that one of the Panthers started "shouting in a loud voice to students [at Merritt Business College, where the police had pulled over the

car], . . . 'We are here to protect you against these white baby killers.'"
To illustrate how lethal the police were to Black people, "He made
continual reference to a burglar [Denzil Dowell] who had been shot"
in the back six times by the police and left in the road to die. "Students
were invited to attend the next meeting of the Black Panther Party to
'learn how to shoot the white Facist [sp.] Police.'"[29]

The local newspapers were equally alarmed. The Panthers didn't just
bear arms or carry weapons; "Oakland's Black Panthers Wear Guns,
Talk Revolution" ran a headline in the *San Francisco Examiner*. Even
more frightening—"It's All Legal," the headline warned.[30]

This was the frustration of the Oakland Police, too. When they
stopped the Panthers, hoping to get the leaders and the members on
some kind of violation, the guns were always up to code. The way the
weapons were carried—never concealed, always visible, and never
pointed at anyone directly—was perfectly lawful. Nor did they violate
basic regulations: for example, no sawed-off shotguns. The firearms
were also legally owned: "Serial numbers taken from subjects' guns
have thus far been clear."[31] As one police report noted, "It is clear that
members are well informed concerning the laws governing the ownership and carrying of weapons." This law-abiding behavior, however,
was not to be commended or celebrated. Instead, police determined
that the Black Panthers "represent . . . a threat to the peace of any
community in which they choose to appear." The Oakland Police
Department wanted to get rid of the Panthers, but "under presently
existing laws, the police are powerless to act."[32]

The department set out to make sure that that would no longer be
the case. The police persuaded conservative state representative David
Donald "Don" Mulford, whose district included parts of Berkeley and
Oakland as well as the affluent suburb of Piedmont, to strip the Panthers

of their guns.[33] Mulford, who resented Huey Newton's intrusion into the case and his depiction of Denzil Dowell's murder, was determined to "get" the Panthers "and put an end to their armed police patrols."[34]

As Mulford set out to craft California Assembly Bill (AB) 1591, legislation to ban the "carrying of loaded firearms in public," he received a major boost from an unexpected source, the National Rifle Association. Founded in 1871 by ex-Union soldiers to promote marksmanship, the NRA had "enjoyed a 'mom and apple pie' reputation for nearly a century." It had been, in many ways, an apolitical organization. That changed in the 1960s "when the NRA believed that individual gun rights were in jeopardy . . . [and] formally engaged in the political process."[35] Yet, the concern about protecting those individual gun rights did not include the rights of members of the Black Panthers, who, up to that point, had broken no firearms laws. Instead, the NRA enlisted its Western representative, E. F. "Tod" Sloan, who was based in Redwood City, California, to get involved in drafting language for Mulford's bill, clarifying what "loaded" meant, and editing portions that the assemblyman had submitted for review.[36]

Huey Newton knew that this law would "effectively outlaw . . . the Black Panther strategy." As a sign of defiance and to continue to build the reputation of the group, he decided to "send an armed delegation to the state capitol" while the bill was being debated.[37] The newspapers, Mulford, and other legislators would call it an "invasion." They described a band of armed Black men, with their "bandoleers of ammunition," storming into the legislative chambers, knocking down the elderly sergeant-of-arms, and throwing the "capitol into a swivet as they entered the west door."[38]

That dramatic rendering isn't quite accurate. When Bobby Seale and a group of twenty-nine other Panthers arrived at the Capitol building, after making the eighty-two-mile drive from Oakland to Sacramento, he wasn't quite sure where to go and had to ask directions to find where the legislators met. Reporters and cameramen saw a group of Black men and women, with all of that leather, the berets, and the guns, and ran to get the story. By the time they reached the assembly floor, where the public was not allowed to go during session, there was a swarm of journalists and photographers around Seale and the other members. "Several of the reporters barged into the assembly to get a better picture of the Panthers as they entered. Seale and about twelve of the Panther followed." The legislators recalled at the time just seeing the "gaggle of news and television cameramen in what seemed to be a stampede."[39] Indeed "only a few of the legislators were actually aware of the intrusion."[40] Mulford was certain, however, that the Panthers were trying to intimidate him, and that would compel the California assemblyman to strengthen the bill as he turned proposed misdemeanors into felonies.[41]

After the Capitol police removed the Panthers from the room and seized their weapons, Seale read a statement that AB 1591 was designed to keep "black people disarmed and powerless at the very same time that racist police agencies . . . are intensifying the terror, brutality, murder, and repression of black people."[42] Seale invoked the Second Amendment. One of the officers present noted, "The Black Panther group . . . knew how far they could go . . . The weapons were loaded although no shells were in their firing chambers . . . the weapons were being carried openly without any attempt at concealment [and] . . . They were quoting the Constitution verbatim about their right to bear arms."[43]

Mulford adamantly denied that the legislation was aimed at African Americans and offered assurances that "there are no racial overtones to this measure."[44] He publicly asserted that AB 1591 was designed to cover the Klan and the Minutemen. But Willie Brown, a Black assemblyman from San Francisco, noted that Mulford had been against similar legislation "until Negroes showed up in Oakland—his district—with arms and then he seeks restrictive legislation."[45] And Mulford's private correspondence demonstrated that the Black Panthers were the genesis for this bill and the target. He explained to Governor Ronald Reagan that the "Black Panther movement is creating a serious problem." And that AB 1591 was, therefore, "introduced at the request of the Oakland Police Department."[46] For his part, Reagan, through his legislative secretary, informed Mulford that a prominent district attorney "emphasizes the danger of the carrying of firearms by groups such as the Black Panthers and the need for control in this area." Reagan was, thus, "keenly concerned" and pledged to "sign it [AB 1591] when it reaches his desk."[47]

It was sure to pass. AB 1591 had police backing and, as Mulford bragged, "the support of the National Rifle Association and Governor Reagan," all underscored by the dangerous image of the Panthers brought on by the "invasion" of the state capitol.[48]

> Many white Americans couldn't get over their first impression of the Black Panthers. Coverage of the 1967 protest introduced them to the party, and the fear of black people exercising their rights in an empowered, intimidating fashion left its mark. To them the Black Panthers were little more than a group of thugs unified behind militaristic trappings and a leftist political ideology.[49]

Or, as Reagan remarked while signing the Mulford Act, this law would not affect the "honest citizen."[50]

In the backlash to the Civil Rights Movement, Black people brandishing their constitutional and legal rights could be neither "honest" nor "citizen[s]." Indeed, by 1966, "85 percent of whites were certain that 'the pace of civil rights was too fast.'"[51] Therefore, Seale's assertions simply could not resonate as valid when he told the press that the Panthers had come to the state capitol "to defend their constitutional right to bear arms, criticize . . .'racist Oakland police' and oppose . . . a bill outlawing the carrying of loaded weapons in public," which had not been defined as dangerous, until the Panthers did it.[52]

The *Sacramento Bee* vehemently denounced the Black Panthers as "misguided," and the newspaper was wholly unimpressed by their "battle cries . . . [of] constitutional rights! Constitutional rights!" If the Panthers wanted to hide behind the Second Amendment, the editorial chided, they should "learn more about the Constitution and Bill of Rights they used as their shields." What the Panthers have done, the newspaper concluded, was unconscionable. They "defiled the very documents they quoted."[53] The *Los Angeles Times* derided Seale's stance on the Second Amendment's right to bear arms too, calling it "completely farcical." The point of a well-regulated militia, the editorial continued, was "to protect against the emergence of just such groups in the future." The *LA Times* further asserted, "Even the National Rifle Assn., that most militant defender of the right to possess arms, should agree that incidents such as occurred in Sacramento and which may occur elsewhere, cannot be tolerated in modern society."[54]

What the NRA did agree on was the Mulford Act and its target. One NRA member, Stephen D'Arrigo Jr., explained that the Second Amendment allowed a group of armed citizens to be "deputized at times of emergency." This does not mean, he continued, "bands such as the Minute Men, Black Panthers . . . or any other such groups by whatever name."[55] Tod Sloan, the NRA's Western representative who'd helped craft the legislation, "said his organization has no opposition to Mulford's bill because it will not affect the law-abiding citizen, sportsman, hunter, or target shooters."[56] Ignoring, of course, that before the Mulford Act, the Panthers were law-abiding citizens, too. The new law was designed to ensure that they would not be.[57]

THERE WAS ANOTHER major gun law on the horizon, driven by the tumult of the 1960s, which fed into the sense of a world imperiled. Assassinations, riots, and demonstrations against the war in Vietnam suggested that the American dream, reflected in the rise of the suburbs and relative affluence, was not going to survive the decade. Many felt the "futility of trying to stop the massive flow that is America going down the drain."[58] The fact that "the homicide rate leaped by more than 50 percent, driven by fatal shootings," added to the sense of precarity.[59] The assassination of President John F. Kennedy and the news that his killer, Lee Harvey Oswald, had purchased the murder weapon through the mail from an ad in the NRA's magazine sent the first tremors of federal gun control legislation through the land in nearly thirty years, since the era of gangsters John Dillinger and Bonnie and Clyde. Kennedy's murder, however, wasn't enough to move the bill through Congress.[60] Then came the uprisings in 1965, 1966, and 1967 that "wiped out whole neighborhoods" and that led to hundreds of casualties and millions of dollars in property losses.[61] For many whites, "it seemed that the guerrilla warfare of the Vietcong had found its way onto the streets of America."[62] Rumors of sniper fire pinning down police and firefighters evoked the worst fears about Negroes with Guns.[63] An affirmation of those fears came through in a "federal report on the riots [that] put at least part of the blame on the easy availability of guns. In the years just before 1967, the number of handguns registered in Michigan had increased by 128 percent. Newark had seen a 300 percent increase in permit applications in the preceding two years alone." The report concluded that gun control was essential to bring about "domestic peace and tranquility."[64] Chicago's mayor, Richard J. Daley, railed at President Lyndon Johnson in July 1966, "You've got people out there, especially the nonwhites, . . . buying guns right and left. You got guns and rifles and pistols and everything else," he said, stewing. "There's no registration. There isn't a damn thing" but "lawlessness and disorder."[65]

Still federal gun control legislation stalled. The NRA was key as it laid out for its 800,000 members a picture of a lawless apocalypse that required an armed citizenry for self-defense: "There is little indication that congressional sponsors . . . have given any thought to the fate of citizens who may be trapped and beleaguered by howling mobs that brush aside the police."[66] It would take Martin Luther King Jr.'s assassination and another wave of uprisings in April 1968, punctuated by Robert Kennedy's murder just two months later, to finally move the Gun Control Act out of Congress and onto the president's desk for signing. The NRA, however—by working through powerful Southern senators Strom Thurmond of South Carolina and James O. Eastland of Mississippi, who were both "hostile as hell" to the Gun Control Act and were "mutilating the bill as it is"—ensured that two of the key elements that President Lyndon Johnson wanted would not make it into the final bill.[67] One was a federal registry of firearms and the other was a federal licensing requirement for gun owners. With those two provisions stripped from the bill, all the NRA's the "sky-is-falling warnings about the government taking away gun rights" transformed into "legislation they could 'live with.'"[68] The Gun Control Act of 1968 restricted "mail-order sale of rifles, shotguns, and ammunition," banned "dangerous" people—"felons, fugitives, dishonorably discharged from the military" as well as the mentally ill, addicts, and minors—"from purchasing or possessing guns," and blocked a certain type of weapon, cheap, poorly built guns, the Saturday night specials, "so named by Detroit police for their association with urban crime, which spiked on weekends," from being sold. The NRA explained to its members, with little to no irony, that when it came to Saturday night special handguns, the organization "does not necessarily approve of everything that goes 'Bang!'"[69] As the debates over the Gun Control Act unfolded, it became clear that "having a gun was a white prerogative."[70] One advocate for the Gun Control Act, thus, incisively noted that the new federal law "was passed not to control guns but to control blacks."[71]

Protecting law-abiding citizens from "mad dogs" and "thugs" became nothing short of a political gold mine.[72] "The subtext was that African Americans were dangerous, that poverty combined with inept upbringing and untamed rage were all coming to the surface in the successes of the Civil Rights movement."[73] Indeed, in 1967, Richard Nixon wrote in *Reader's Digest* that the uprisings in the wake of the movement revealed some "racial animosities . . . But riots were also the most virulent symptoms to date of another, and in some ways graver, national disorder—the decline in respect for public authority and the rule of law in America. Far from being a great society, ours is becoming a lawless society."[74]

This positioning, known as the Southern Strategy, which used dog-whistle synonyms for the n-word to define anti-Blackness, was a way for those seeking elected office to identify whites as honest, hard-working Americans besieged by Black people, who were freeloaders and threats to society.[75] Nixon's presidential campaign, for example, ran an ad that "carefully avoided using pictures of African Americans while at the same time showing cities burning, grainy images of protestors out in the streets, blood flowing, chaos shaking the very foundations of society," followed by silence and bold lettering telling the viewers to vote as if their very lives depended upon it. After viewing the ad, Nixon exclaimed that "the commercial 'hits it right on the nose . . . It's all about law and order and the damn Negro–Puerto Rican groups out there."[76] Politicians thus proved their "tough on crime" mettle by passing laws that were to signify their commitment to "law and order" (even when the crime rates had plummeted). Policymakers and their constituents denigrated public expenditures for schools, jobs, housing, and health care as the quixotic plans of "bleeding heart" liberals who were "coddling criminals" and who had "irresponsibly squandered taxpayer money on ineffective social programs to control crime."[77] As President Reagan dismissively said in 1987, "In the sixties we waged a war on poverty, and poverty won."[78] Instead, since 1971, the one-trillion-dollar government investment was now being funneled into policing and prisons.[79] That depth of expenditure required a nation in a perpetual state of fear. The media was key. "While the murder rate in the United States fell by 20% from 1990-1998, the numbers of stories about murder (excluding O.J. Simpson) on the network news *increased* by 600 percent." The message was clear: "Be afraid, be very afraid!"[80] That fear focused on African Americans and their supposedly documented and inherent propensity for violent crime.[81] That pervasive anti-Blackness, even after the Civil Rights Movement, turned the Second Amendment's laws for protection—the castle doctrine, stand your ground, and open carry—against African Americans.

IT WAS EARLY in the morning, close to Thanksgiving 2006, when ninety-two-year-old Kathryn Johnston, a Black woman, heard the clanking of burglar bars being pried off the door in her Atlanta home. Fearing the worst, Johnston grabbed her "rusty revolver" to defend herself and the place where she had lived for nearly seventeen years. When three men "kicked that door down," she pulled the trigger. Her one shot was answered with a hail of bullets, thirty-nine of them. Five of which hit the elderly woman. Johnston fell to the floor of her beloved home bleeding, mortally wounded. The men, narcotics officers in the Atlanta Police Department, had a no-knock warrant to conduct a drug raid to find a dealer named "Sam" and his kilo of cocaine. Instead, they found a ninety-two-year-old woman scared for her life. After they "shot her down like a dog," they handcuffed the dying Johnston and scoured her home looking for drugs and the elusive Sam. Neither was there.[82]

Johnston's niece was furious. Her aunt's home was not a place where drugs were sold. Just "ask the neighbors!" she exclaimed.[83] The police department, however, insisted that the narcotics officers had the right house and that they were justified in gunning down a ninety-two-year-old woman in her home because she shot first.[84] Of course she did. The right to protect your home and life from an intruder is basic law, the castle doctrine. It was the wee hours of the morning. She lived alone. She heard the burglar bars clanking as they were being removed from her home in a high-crime area. She was fearful. A neighbor, another elderly woman, had recently been raped. Johnston had to wonder, was the same trauma going to happen to her? Then she witnessed the violent entry into her home. In short, what happened that morning—"tumultuous entry," the rightful fear that intruders were there to commit a felony, that someone was illegally entering who was not a relative—met all the criteria of the castle doctrine.[85] Except in this case, it didn't apply. Assistant Chief Alan Dreher said the police "were justified in shooting once they were fired upon."[86] He claimed they "had a legal warrant and 'knocked and announced' before they forced open the door."[87]

That wasn't true. It was a no-knock warrant, where police do not have to announce themselves before entering a residence, in order to prevent key evidence from being destroyed. The police had received this warrant, however, based on an extorted confession from a dealer whom the police had planted drugs on, in order to get him to reveal his supplier. Under threat of an interminable prison term for possessing bags of marijuana that weren't even his, he lied. The cornered dealer gave Johnston's address and told the narcotics officers that a kilo of cocaine and his supplier, "Sam," would be there. In short, the "police were able . . . to fabricate evidence and obtain an emergency, no-knock warrant based on an imaginary person."[88] As outrageous as this seems, the story held up for almost a month because the officers, Gregg Junnier, Jason Smith, and Arthur Tesler, planted marijuana and crack in Johnston's home, which undermined the neighbors' assertion that "they got the wrong house."[89]

With Sam never materializing, however, and no valid record of drug sales or arrests at Johnston's home, the narcotics officers tried to shore up their story. They reached out to a trusted informant to back their version that the house where they had fired thirty-nine bullets at a scared, elderly Black woman was actually a major center of drug activity. The informant, fearing for his life, given what the officers had already done to a ninety-two-year-old woman, chose, instead, to go to a major media outlet with his story. That's how the truth came to light. Prior to that time, enough doubt had lingered over Johnston that one woman, when asked about the killing, justified it: "She was 92 years old. I understand that, but she opened fire."[90] The castle doctrine, in the end, provided as much protection for a Black woman living alone as a "rusty revolver."

YEARS LATER, IN Louisville, Kentucky, the castle doctrine proved, once again, to be a house made of straw when anti-Blackness came pounding on the door with another no-knock warrant. On March 13,

2020, twenty-six-year-old Breonna Taylor, an emergency room tech-nician, was in her apartment with her boyfriend, Kenneth Walker. They had the television on, barely watching a movie, when they heard a horrible, frightening pounding on the door. Taylor was screaming "at the top of her lungs," "Who is it?!" No response. Just pounding. She and Walker got out of bed, and he grabbed his licensed gun, afraid it could be Taylor's ex-boyfriend, a drug dealer. They "were scared to death." Then the door "comes off its hinges. Like an explosion." Walker fired a shot. The response was fast and lethal. Thirty-two bullets rained down into that apartment, plowed into the walls, the kitchen, the ceiling, a clock, the windows, and five or six went into Taylor, one of which was the "kill shot." She collapsed in the hallway. Bleeding. She received no medical attention for at least twenty minutes.[91]

Kentucky attorney general Daniel Cameron concluded that because Walker had shot first, hitting one of the officers in the femoral artery, the killing of Taylor was "justified." In coming to that conclusion, Cameron misled the public about key elements in the case. He said that when the police came to Taylor's apartment to search for drugs or money, which her ex-boyfriend had supposedly stashed there, it "was not served as a no-knock warrant"—but as journalist Radley Balko countered, "It absolutely was. It says so right on the warrant."[92] The hocus-pocus of presenting it as a regular search warrant was necessary because a regular warrant meant the officers would have been required to announce themselves before entering. If the police had actually done that, Walker and Taylor would have had notification that it was law enforcement on the other side of the door.

Whether the police announced themselves or not, however, could not be fully verified because, in violation of the department's policy, not one of the seven officers in the raid had turned on his body camera. A canvass of eleven neighbors, however, revealed that no one had heard the police identify themselves. A second round of interviews brought the same result. Finally, when asked by investigators a third time, one of the neighbors changed his story and said he heard the announcement.[93] That is the thin reed on which the attorney general of Kentucky hung the label of "justified." Under Kentucky's statute, "law-enforcement officers are the only home invaders that residents aren't allowed to use deadly force against, but only if they clearly identify themselves as law enforcement."[94] Based on the newly remembered announcement, when officers entered the apartment, Walker supposedly knew law enforcement was coming through the front entry at 12:43 a.m. and picked up his Glock 9mm and fired at the police. The cops, therefore, "returned fired after having been fired upon."[95] That single piece of remembering dissolved the castle doctrine. Justified. Days of protest denounced that conclusion.

The Louisville Metropolitan Police Department (LMPD) was getting excoriated for a warrant that was so flawed, the judge who signed it believed the officer had lied about the details to obtain it. Police were being hammered for changing the times on the warrant to make it look as if officers had no knowledge that their key suspect, Taylor's ex-boyfriend, had already been arrested ten miles away, and, as a result, there was no need to go in hard with a battering ram on Taylor's apartment. Officers were being scolded for botching the basics of how to conduct a raid.[96] And so, the police decided to turn to an old playbook: "thugify" the victims, Taylor and Walker, and make the killing look like a reasonable response to Black criminality. The LMPD released to the press a tranche of photos marked "Partners in Crime" of the couple with the gun Walker used to "fire at police."[97] The response on social media was blistering. "I thought we all had the right to bear arms"; "He had the right to protect his home when those cops idiotically barged in without stating their presence as cops"; "And!?? It was a legally owned firearm";

"take this down"; "Leaps and bounds to further vilify Black people"; and "If it wasn't self defense why didn't the boyfriend get charged for shooting a cop . . . BECAUSE IT WAS SELF DEFENSE!"[98]

IN AUGUST 2010, it had certainly looked like self-defense, too. Except in a stand-your-ground state, it wasn't.[99] Marissa Alexander had previously suffered a beating so horrific by her then husband, Rico Gray, that she had to be hospitalized. In 2009, Alexander had to take out a restraining order against him. Nevertheless, when she was eight months pregnant, she ended up with a black eye.[100] Later, at home with her nine-day-old baby girl, she found Gray enraged after he came across text messages on her phone that suggested she was more than ready to move on to someone else. "If I can't have you," he screamed, "nobody going to have you!"[101] As many who have suffered domestic violence know, that phrase is often the trip wire to death.[102] Alexander broke free, ran to the garage, couldn't get out, then retrieved her gun from the car, and came back in the house. Gray, who admitted to abusing "all five of his babies' mamas except one," acknowledged that "during the tussle," with his nine-year-old and thirteen-year-old sons right there, he "was going towards her" when Alexander fired a warning shot to get him to back off; to not "put [his] hands on her anymore."[103]

This was in Florida, a stand-your-ground state. In fact, Florida was the first in America to have this law, which was written under the heavy influence of the NRA.[104] Marion Hammer, the powerhouse NRA lobbyist in Florida, said, "Through time, in this country, what I like to call bleeding-heart criminal coddlers, want you to give a criminal an even break, so that when you're attacked, you're supposed to turn around and run, rather than standing your ground and protecting yourself and your family and your property."[105] Not anymore. With stand-your-ground laws, the castle doctrine expanded beyond the home and emphasized that there is no requirement to retreat, no responsibility to leave the danger before engaging the perceived (as opposed to actual) threat. In an ever-fearful America, stand your ground "stems from a 'kill-or-be-killed'" outlook.[106]

Alexander, however, wasn't trying to kill Gray. She just wanted him to stop. A battered woman, fending off a man who had admitted to police he had threatened her, who had previously beaten her so badly she had to be hospitalized, would seem to fall under the stand-your-ground canopy. In fact, Alexander explained: "I didn't realize how serious it was until my first meeting with my attorney and he looked pretty spooked about the whole thing. And, I'm looking at him like 'Why? I had a restraining order against [my ex-husband] and a concealed-weapons license. What's the big deal? It's self defense.' And he was like: 'No, this is pretty serious.'"[107] The state attorney Angela Corey concurred, and vigorously pursued an aggravated assault with a deadly weapon charge, which carried a twenty-year prison sentence, against this Black woman.

Corey argued that when Alexander fired, it wasn't a warning shot, because the bullet didn't go into the ceiling; it went into the wall, about "adult-height." She noted that Gray's sons were there and could have been hurt. Corey insisted, as well, that when Alexander went into the garage and came back into the house with a gun, that erased any stand-your-ground claims. She could have "fled the scene," Corey claimed. "Although in 1999 the Florida Supreme Court ruled that a woman attacked by her husband in the home they share has no duty to flee," that ruling proved to be irrelevant.[108] Alexander "believed [that the way] the court viewed her defense, 'It was a crime from the jump,' adding the Stand Your Ground law 'was never considered.'"[109] The judge was clear: Florida's expanded self-defense law would not apply because Alexander "didn't appear afraid."[110] Her ex-husband's attorney noted what he considered to be a key fact: that Gray "was unarmed and she shot at him."[111] The jury took twelve minutes to deliberate and found her guilty; she was sentenced to twenty years in prison.[112]

In Alexander's case, Corey had clearly set the parameters of what constituted stand your ground—"because Alexander had to exit the house to retrieve the gun from her car in the garage, she was no longer in any imminent danger and thus not afforded immunity under Florida's stand-your-ground defense. Furthermore, Alexander's warning shot hit the wall, as opposed to the ceiling, and prosecutors insisted that this put Gray and his children in physical danger."[113]

Those stand-your-ground parameters—the possibility of not engaging, protection of a child's life, firing a weapon to warn not to kill—crumbled at the feet of a dead Black teenager, Trayvon Martin, just two years later. In February 2012, Martin was watching the NBA All-Star game, when, during halftime, he decided to go to the local convenience store to get a snack. On his way back home in the gated community, a self-styled neighborhood watch captain, George Zimmerman, spotted Martin and thought he saw something suspicious.[114] This wasn't unusual for Zimmerman, who had made numerous calls to 911 reporting "suspicious" African American males. Those "driving real slow looking at all the [vehicles] in the complex blaring music" and those who were "on foot . . . in a tank top and shorts . . . near the development's back entrance," as well as "two black teens in the same area," given that "[juveniles] are the subjs who have been [burglarizing] in this area," and a "black man in a leather jacket near one of the development's units." None of those calls panned out. Police came and found nothing.[115]

The next time Sanford Police came, however, they would find a dead child. Zimmerman had put a bullet in Trayvon's chest. The gunman claimed self-defense. Prior to the killing, Zimmerman told the 911 operator, "This guy looks like he's up to no good or he's on drugs or something, . . . and he's a black male . . . Something's wrong with him." Then, "Yup, he's coming to check me out, he's got something in his hands . . . I don't know what his deal is . . . These assholes, they always get away." After a discussion with 911 on his specific location, it was clear that Zimmerman had left his car and was now after Martin. "Shit," the gunman said, "he's running." The dispatcher queries, "Are you following him?" "Yep," came Zimmerman's reply. "Okay, we don't need you to do that," the 911 operator warned. The gunman ignored her. He took his loaded 9mm and stalked the unarmed teenager through the neighborhood. Trayvon Martin was on the phone with Rachel Jeantel, his childhood friend since the second grade. She heard him say, "Why are you following me?" She heard pushing and shoving, then the phone went dead. Trayvon Martin didn't answer her subsequent, urgent phone call. He couldn't. Zimmerman had shot the teenager in the heart.[116]

When the police arrived, they barely investigated. No homicide detective was brought to the scene.[117] Zimmerman wasn't given a drug or alcohol test, which is standard when there's a killing.[118] The chief of police, Bill Lee, admitted that he felt handcuffed by stand your ground and the liabilities that his department would incur for making an arrest. He also insisted that there simply wasn't enough evidence to contradict Zimmerman's claim that it was self-defense.[119] The attorney for Trayvon Martin's family was outraged. "When you add it up, it just doesn't make sense . . . Trayvon Martin, a kid, has a bag of Skittles. (Zimmerman) had a 9mm gun. Trayvon Martin didn't approach George Zimmerman, George Zimmerman approached Trayvon Martin. So how can he now assert self-defense?"[120]

The uproar led Angela Corey's office to get the case and prosecute Zimmerman. Yet the stand-your-ground parameters that her office had erected against Marissa Alexander were not holding up. An unarmed minor was killed by a man who had stalked the teenager through the neighborhood with a loaded weapon. When warned by the 911 operator, Zimmerman had the choice to not engage. Although the chief of police held that "911 directions . . . are not mandatory instructions," that still does not obviate the option available to the gunman to stay in the SUV and not trail a child in the darkened, rain-soaked night.[121]

Despite this, right-wing media, including Breitbart, Glenn Beck, Geraldo Rivera on *Fox and Friends*, and others, began the process to "thugify" Trayvon Martin and show that Zimmerman had every right to be afraid. They posted stories, with no evidence, that Martin was a juvenile delinquent, kicked out of school for drugs, and that he was a "gold-toothed" "thug wannabe." Rivera, remarking on the hoodie Martin wore, asserted, "You dress like a thug, people are going to treat you like a thug." The point, as columnist Zerlina Maxwell noted, was an "attempt to portray Zimmerman as a do-gooder neighborhood watchman, with no racial biases and black friends, who was attacked for no reason by dangerous thug Trayvon while he was just doing his job of patrolling his gated community with a nine millimeter." Martin, as a commenter at Breitbart wrote, was "just another black punk who got what he deserved."[122]

Journalist Leonard Pitts reflected on the thugification. He recalled: "One woman forwarded a chain email depicting a tough-looking, light-skinned African-American man with tattoos on his face. It was headlined: 'The Real Trayvon Martin,' which it wasn't. It was actually a then-32-year-old rapper who calls himself The Game. But the message was clear: Trayvon was a scary black man who deserved what he got."[123] One conservative writer ran with that point: "Martin was no 'child.' He was not yet a legal adult, but at 17 years of age he could, with a parent's permission, kill and die for the United States military. And

17 year olds, particularly when they are six feet tall, intoxicated on drugs, and physically fit, as was Martin, can and do kill and die in the streets of America."[124] The big, Black, scary, gangsta imagery of dying "in the streets," especially, for someone unarmed who was still a minor, had transformed Trayvon Martin "from a 5'8", 158 lbs. tall, 17-year-old," into a six-foot-tall, "pot-smoking, hoodie-wearing, jewelry stealing, aggressive thug, who had attacked a man who was older, less athletic, and vulnerable. The only equalizer was a 9mm."[125]

Although Zimmerman did not cite stand your ground during his trial, it affected the police investigation and the judge's instructions to the jury, which limited the scope of what the jurors could consider.[126] Judge Debra Nelson restricted the evidence to be deliberated upon to only the confrontation, and Zimmerman's fear, and not how that fateful encounter began with him stalking a child or even how the 9mm ended up at the site where the killing occurred.[127] With the jury instructions, the last parameter collapsed. Zimmerman could bring a gun to confront an unarmed teenager, claim he was fearful for his life, shoot the minor, and be found not guilty of second-degree murder.

The killing led Florida legislators, on both sides of the political aisle, to question the effects of this NRA-backed law, which the organization had called a "human right."[128] Before the verdict, Republican state senator Dennis Baxley, a co-sponsor of the legislation, told the *Miami Herald* that Zimmerman "has no protection under my law . . . There's nothing in this statute that authorizes you to pursue and confront people, particularly if law enforcement has told you to stay put." Democratic state senator Oscar Braynon similarly noted, "When the Legislature passed this in 2005, I don't think they planned for people who would . . . become vigilantes or be like some weird Batman who would go out and kill little kids like Trayvon."[129]

Whatever the expectations, the results of stand your ground were obvious. There was a battered Black woman who was armed but not protected by this law and, conversely, an unarmed African American teen with nothing but Skittles and iced tea who also was left unprotected by stand your ground. Alexander received a twenty-year sentence, Martin a death sentence. In America's anti-Black environment, there was no ground upon which their right to be unharmed could stand.

The *Tampa Bay Times* conducted an investigation and found that since stand your ground had been enacted in Florida, "nearly seventy percent of those who invoked it as a defense had gone free." Moreover, "there was a racial imbalance: a person was more likely to be found innocent if the victim was black."[130] This racial imbalance was affirmed by another study, which found that from 2005 to 2013, "juries were twice as likely to convict the perpetrator of a crime against a white person than against a person of color."[131]

JUST AS STAND your ground was an affirmation of the Second Amendment's right to self-defense, open carry laws were the companion piece for the right to bear arms—and proved to be equally lethal to Black Americans. The research project Mapping Police Violence has documented that between 2013 to 2019, with more than 1,900 deaths, Black Americans were killed by police "at three times the rate of white Americans . . . when adjusted for population." In addition, they were more likely than any other racial or ethnic group to be unarmed when killed by law enforcement.[132] Those data, coupled with the work of Stanford University researcher Jennifer Eberhardt, suggest that Black people are perceived as the universal threat.[133] Her team "conducted studies where police and others, cued with an image of a black person, quickly deciphered very blurred images often associated with crime, such as a gun. White people see an African American, and they're immediately looking for something illegal. They almost instantly see a threat."[134] As the studies on police killings of African Americans indicate, this is the case even when Blacks are unarmed. Thus, when African Americans openly carry a gun, although allowed by law, it raises exponentially the sense of danger about them and to them.

On August 5, 2014, John Crawford III, a twenty-two-year-old Black man, was in a Walmart in the Dayton, Ohio, area, shopping for the ingredients to make s'mores and talking on the phone to the mother of his two children, when he happened to spot a BB gun out of its packaging lying on the shelves in the toy department.[135] He picked it up as he continued to go through the store shopping and talking. A customer, April Ritchie, spied him and told her husband, Ronald Ritchie, that Crawford looked "very shady" because he wasn't making eye contact and seemed to not want to draw attention to himself. She felt "unsafe."[136] Ronald Ritchie agreed, followed Crawford throughout the Walmart, and called 911 reporting that "a gentleman [was] walking around with a gun in the store . . . he's like pointing it at people." He claimed Crawford was loading what appeared to be a rifle and "waving it back and forth."[137] Ritchie, who had previously shared with his friends an article from the Tea Party News Network that Barack Obama and his attorney general Eric Holder were "race hustlers," stayed on the phone describing a Black man who had begun pointing the gun "at, like, two children" and then reaffirmed that claim for the 911 operator.[138]

Spurred on by the fears of a couple afraid of a Black man in an open carry state, who was openly carrying a "rifle" in a store where guns are sold, police officer Sean Williams and Sergeant David Darkow believed they were rushing into something akin to an active-shooter situation.[139] From the description, they knew they were looking for a Black male wearing blue pants and a blue shirt who was "waving a rifle."[140] They scoured the store and set eyes on Crawford, who had his back to them while still on the phone.[141] One of the officers commanded, "Drop the weapon!" Crawford didn't. Perhaps because he was distracted by his phone conversation. Perhaps because the officers did not identify themselves as police. Perhaps because it was a BB gun and not, in his mind, a weapon. Nevertheless, Crawford's unintended noncompliance amplified the fear. In those fateful few seconds, Officer Williams recalled, "I felt at that moment that my life was in immediate danger, that Sergeant Darkow's life was in immediate danger, and that the lives of all the families, children and customers were in immediate danger. I then fired two rounds at the suspect."[142]

Open carry law is clear. As long as the gun owner is not posing a threat, the right to openly carry a firearm is inviolate. What is also clear from the release of the surveillance tape from Walmart was that John Crawford III was not a threat. "John was doing nothing wrong in Walmart, nothing more, nothing less than shopping," the Crawford family's attorney said.[143] When the FBI synced up the video with Ronald Ritchie's 911 call, it was obvious that he had described events to the emergency operator that had never happened. Crawford was not aiming the weapon at anyone, much less two children. There was no loading of the BB gun or aiming the muzzle at customers. There was no "waving the rifle around." Crawford generally kept it pointed toward the floor, and when he did bring the gun up, it was to point at some shelves, and there was no one around him at the time. The Ritchies, though, had conjured up the trifecta of threats: a Black man, with a rifle in Walmart, pointing the gun at children. The special prosecutor remarked that when it came to Ronald Ritchie, "If he's not there, then maybe we would not be here."[144] In short, because the couple felt "unsafe" about Crawford being in a store that sells guns, carrying what they thought was a gun, in an open carry state, the young father was put in the crosshairs of two police bullets. Unfazed by what he had done, Ritchie, who would not be charged with making a false 911 call, sounded like those in the wake of Trayvon Martin's killing, where the victim was blamed for his own death. Ritchie offered that Crawford "kind of deserved it . . . if you're dumb enough to point any kind of weapon at a police officer you get what's coming to you."[145]

That same callous sentiment surrounded the slaying by police of a twelve-year-old child in Cleveland, Ohio, just a few months after Crawford's death. There was the official statement of imminent threat and fear to justify the killing, and then there was the video that contradicted the story. But just as with Crawford, it did not matter. Tamir Rice had swapped with a friend a cell phone for a used toy gun, a replica of a Colt pistol that was missing its orange tip that signaled it wasn't real. He was in a pavilion at a community center playing with his new toy. A call came in to 911: There's "a guy in here with a pistol." The caller went on, adding that the weapon was "probably fake" and that it was wielded by "probably a juvenile." For some unknown reason, those last two bits of key information were not relayed to the officers dispatched to the pavilion.[146]

Officer Frank Garmback, who drove the patrol car, and Timothy Loehmann, a rookie to the Cleveland Police Department who had resigned from a much smaller, suburban department because his immaturity and complete meltdown on the firing range had him scheduled to be fired, rushed to the community center.[147] They decided to take a shortcut to get there faster. That choice, however, had them skid and pull up within a few yards of where Tamir was playing. By this time, he had tucked the toy in his waistband and put his head down on the table, when he heard the car pull up so close that "it made it difficult [for the police] to take cover, or to use verbal persuasion or other tactics suggested by the department's use-of-force policy." In other words, they had skidded their car within a distance that created an unsafe situation.[148] Within two seconds of the police car's arrival, Loehmann had exited and "shot Tamir in the abdomen from point-blank range."[149] Garmback called it in: "Shots fired, male down . . . Black male, maybe 20, black revolver, black handgun by him. Send E.M.S. this way, and a roadblock."[150]

The officers' rendition of the killing was a textbook threat assessment that could overrule Ohio's open carry law. The police said that there were people in the pavilion with Rice, thereby putting others in jeopardy. The officers relayed that they had ordered him three times to put his hands up. Instead, Rice, they claimed, walked toward them and put his hand in his waistband to pull out the gun. " 'He gave me no choice,' Loehmann told another officer moments after the shooting. 'He reached for the gun and there was nothing I could do.' "[151]

The video, however, told another story. Tamir Rice was alone in the pavilion—there was no one there for him to threaten. It would have been virtually impossible within two seconds for police to order him to put up his hands three distinct times and for him to not comply before Loehmann pulled the trigger.[152] In addition, in those two seconds, as the videotape shows, Rice was not reaching for his toy gun.[153]

Despite the fact that "the video shows some damning inconsistencies with the officers' initial statements," the prosecutor relied on the expert witness reports from a Colorado district attorney and an FBI agent that the killing of the twelve-year-old was justifiable. And Cuyahoga County prosecutor Timothy McGinty said that the case met the Supreme Court standard for use of force. Loehmann "had a reason to fear for his life," and "the law gives the benefit of the doubt to officers who must make split-second decisions."[154]

Meanwhile, McGinty and the media began to question the grief of Tamir Rice's parents, suggesting that their concerns were "economically motivated" and that the criminal history of the father and mother indicated the inevitable threat that the child presented to the police.[155] Many comments on a *New York Times* article about the officers not facing any charges vilified the parents and Tamir Rice and stressed the danger to society of Black people with guns: "Why do parents, especially black parents, still allow their children to play with toy guns? I think any parent that lets their children play with toy guns should be referred to child protective services." Another: "WHY is a 12-year old carrying a replica of a gun aiming at people? Where does his idea of fun and play come from? How about his parents who apparently failed to instill some ideas for healthy toy-choices in their son." And yet another: "This was a failure of parenting. No parent should allow a black teen out of their home waving a handgun around in public." The problem, one commenter observed, was Black societal violence: "See what kind of insanity is happening in our inner cities and how kids as young as 12 are killing innocents ."[156]

The aura of Black threat loomed. Like Trayvon Martin, Rice, too, aged dramatically from a minor into adulthood the moment they died. "As a recent study of police officers indicated, 'Black boys are seen as older and less innocent and that they prompt a less essential conception of childhood than do their White same-age peers.' Worse yet, the researchers' 'findings demonstrate that the Black/ape association,' which is a dehumanization process, 'predicted actual racial disparities in police violence toward children.'"[157] Moreover, "computerized police simulators show black and white officers are each more likely to open fire on an African American subject they believe is armed, compared to a white subject who is dressed and behaving identically."[158] Columnist Charles P. Pierce wrote, "At its heart, open carry is about open season on the people who scare you. It's certainly not about an absolute Second Amendment right that applies to black people as well as white."[159] The descriptors that often provide a cover of innocence—elderly, teenager, child, health care provider, mother—when applied to African Americans, were no match for the societal fear of Black people.

In the film *The Hate U Give*, an activist portrayed by Issa Rae encapsulates the problem: "It's impossible to be unarmed when your Blackness is the weapon that they fear."[160]

# Racism Lies Around like a Loaded Weapon

On August 25, 2020, Kyle Rittenhouse, a white seventeen-year-old, had his mother drive him from Illinois to Kenosha, Wisconsin, with his illegally acquired AR-15, to join "patriots" determined to put down protests about another Black man, Jacob Blake, who was shot seven times in the back by police and left paralyzed from the waist down.[1] Law enforcement, which was out in force, saw Rittenhouse carrying his rifle, and they were not afraid. Instead, they offered him a bottle of water on that summer night and conveyed how much "they appreciate" the armed counterprotesters out on the streets in Kenosha.[2] Shortly thereafter, Rittenhouse killed two men and severely wounded another. Law enforcement then ignored him as he approached "a handful of police vehicles with his hands in the air, after firing shots at multiple people, as if to surrender."[3] He made it all the way home, across state lines, before he was arrested. His attorneys claimed the teen "was acting as part of a 'well-regulated militia' under the Second Amendment" and that this was also a case of "self-defense."[4]

The Second Amendment claim was like catnip for the right wing in American politics.[5] Donald Trump's Department of Homeland Security crafted media talking points to praise Rittenhouse as someone who "took his rifle to the scene of the rioting to help defend small business owners."[6] It sounded so heroic. It dripped of old-fashioned, manufactured Americana like *Shane* or *High Noon*. *Red State* wrote, "Kyle Rittenhouse did nothing wrong . . . Law and order had completely broken down in Kenosha, Wisconsin. Decent hard-working people watched their lives' work turned to rubble and burned to the ground by mobs of crazed degenerates."[7] Fox News's Tucker Carlson evoked the spirit of the colonial militia stopping the Redcoats from rampaging when he asked, "How shocked are we that 17-year-olds with rifles decided they had to maintain order when no one else would?"[8] The heroism, bravery, and patriotism was worthy of emulation. Indeed, the "President like[d] a tweet that said the alleged shooter, Kyle Rittenhouse, was 'a good example of why I decided to vote for Trump.'"[9]

Nevertheless, for all the "law and order" backslapping, Rittenhouse was a minor who was illegally carrying the AR-15 in an open carry state, and he had killed two men and wounded another. Yet as the police, media, and elected officials made clear, Rittenhouse still had Second Amendment rights not available to Tamir Rice, who had been sitting alone in a pavilion with a toy gun.[10]

The dichotomy between the state's treatment of Rittenhouse and that of Rice cannot be understood by the standard Second Amendment debates over whether there is a right to a well-regulated militia or an individual right to bear arms. Regardless of how African Americans have engaged this right, it has been used against them. In other words, what is so striking about the Second Amendment is witnessing its inherent anti-Blackness centuries after its ratification. The well-regulated militia faced disarmament in early nineteenth-century

Louisiana; Supreme Court–sanctioned slaughter in 1873 Colfax; collective punishment in 1906 Brownsville, Texas; and courts-martial and executions in 1917 Houston. The right to bear arms has its own tally of casualties, from the laws banning the enslaved and free Blacks from possessing guns, to the *Dred Scott* decision, to Reconstruction-era Black Codes, to the Atlanta Riot of 1906, to John Crawford, Tamir Rice, and Philando Castile. Similarly, the right to self-defense was quashed in seventeenth-century Virginia, denied in Cincinnati in 1841, machine-gunned into oblivion in 1919 Elaine, Arkansas, and brutally denied to Trayvon Martin, Kathryn Johnston, and Breonna Taylor. The centuries-long arc of these violations indicates how they are impervious to the citizenship status of African Americans. From enslaved to post–Civil Rights Black Americans, the application of the Second Amendment, in whatever traditional interpretation, was not applicable.

Even the NRA mantra of "the only way to stop a bad guy with a gun is a good guy with a gun" could not stand up against anti-Blackness.[11] On November 11, 2018, Jemel Roberson, a security guard at a Chicago nightspot, pounced on and held at gunpoint a man who had started shooting at some customers. When the police arrived, they did not see the word "Security" written on Roberson's clothes; they did not hear the patrons warn that "he was a security guard." Instead, the officer saw a Black man holding a gun and "shot and killed the 26-year-old."[12]

Just a few weeks later in Alabama, gunfire erupted at a local shopping mall, with an eighteen-year-old and a twelve-year-old hit. Army veteran Emantic Bradford Jr.'s training kicked in. He pulled out his licensed-to-carry gun, in open carry Alabama, and began to move shoppers to safety. Police saw him, a Black man with a gun, immediately defined him as a "threat," and "within milliseconds" fired three shots from behind—one to the back of Bradford's head, the other to his neck, and another to his back. Any of these could have been the kill shot.[13] The twenty-one-year-old army veteran was dead.

Initially, after they had killed Bradford, the police chief applauded his officers: "Thank God, . . . they took out the threat." Then the police came to realize, after running ballistics test on the bullets from the two wounded shoppers, that they had let the actual shooter escape. But they tried to cover their mistake by tweeting that Bradford "may have been involved in some aspect of the crime"; he had, after all, "brandished a gun." Those last statements required further clarification after it became clear that Bradford had actually saved lives in the mall that day, that he did not "brandish," but simply that "Mr. Bradford held a gun in his hand."[14] *Rolling Stone*'s Jamil Smith decried this "lack of ability to imagine a black person as a hero"—as a good guy with a gun.[15] That myopia also impacts African Americans in law enforcement, who have been beaten "like Rodney King" and shot by their fellow white officers.[16] One, who had stopped a crime in progress only to be shot by another police officer who came to the scene, said to the cop who pulled the trigger, "Me being black with a gun, you never gave me a chance . . . You wouldn't have walked up to a white guy and just shot him like that."[17]

Trevor Noah, the host of *The Daily Show*, asked, after the killing of Bradford, "How does this shit keep happening? . . . The cops are called into a situation. They see a black person. And immediately they shoot." Noah then noted a key racial disparity that has played out in these scenarios. "How many times have we seen a shooter who is white and a man get talked down?" It happened in Aurora, Colorado, after the killer left twelve dead and wounded seventy others in a movie theater. Despite the carnage, the police took him alive. The same happened, Noah remarked, after a gunman murdered nine people in Bible study at a Charleston, South Carolina, church. That killer was also taken into custody unharmed.[18]

Because of this disparity, Noah surmised that "the Second Amendment is not intended for black people . . . The Second Amendment was not made for black folks."[19] But it was, just not the way it has traditionally been understood or elegized. That's why debating whether there is an individual or collective right to bear arms is asking the wrong question.[20] As unsettling as it may have been when the U.S. Supreme Court overturned long-standing jurisprudence to create an individual right to bear arms and make self-defense a constitutionally protected right in the *Heller* (2008) and *McDonald* (2010) decisions, that debate just washes over the racially disparate responses to the Second Amendment, as well as the anti-Black foundational roots for that disparity.[21] Or, as Supreme Court justice Robert H. Jackson noted in a case saturated with discrimination—Japanese internment during World War II—racism "lies about like a loaded weapon ready for the hand of any authority that can bring forward a plausible claim of an urgent need."[22]

A series of slave revolts in the 1600s and 1700s led to a number of laws in colonial America restricting Black people's access to weapons and meting out brutal punishment for possession or use of firearms. There was a concomitant creation of slave patrols, working hand in hand with militias, to keep the enslaved population under control and disarmed.

And while the mythmaking surrounding the Second heralds the bravery and effectiveness of individual citizens in the militia as a bulwark against tyranny and foreign invasions, the reality, however, was decidedly more mundane. The militia could not take on an invading army, not for any sustained, effective amount of time.

Gouverneur Morris, a signatory to the Constitution, knew this, as he called the militia an "expensive and inefficient force," which, as they learned during the Revolutionary War, could not be counted on to do much because "to rely on militia was to lean on a broken reed."[23] Not only Morris knew it; George Washington knew it, too. Nor, given Shays's Rebellion, could the militia be relied on to uphold the law.

Where the militia was reliable, however, was in putting down slave revolts, such as at Stono. That was of paramount importance. During the drafting of the Bill of Rights and ratification of the Constitution, the Southern distrust of Northern states' commitment to uphold slavery merged with the Anti-Federalists' heightened fear of a strong central government that would control the militia, and led to the extortionist hardball that had already inserted the three-fifths clause into the nation's founding document. Virginians Patrick Henry and George Mason had made clear to James Madison that the protection of slavery was the sine qua non for ratification of the U.S. Constitution. What Madison had already done with the fugitive slave clause, the extension of the Atlantic slave trade for twenty years, and the three-fifths clause was not enough. The concerns Henry and Mason raised about local control of the militia and how essential it was to put down slave revolts and protect plantation owners had to be addressed. The Second Amendment served that purpose. Thus, in the Bill of Rights, emerged an amendment rooted in fear of Black people, to deny them their rights, to keep them from tasting liberty. The Second became the Faustian bargain made to weaken Anti-Federalists' and Southern opposition to the Constitution.

That is why the current-day veneration of the Second Amendment, driven by the lobbying and publicity campaign of the NRA, is, frankly, akin to holding the three-fifths clause sacrosanct.[24] They both were designed to deny African Americans' humanity and rights while carrying the aura of constitutional legitimacy. They both damaged American democracy and called into question the basic founding principles of equality. The Second is lethal; steeped in anti-Blackness, it is the loaded weapon laying around just waiting for the hand of some authority to put it to use.

# ACKNOWLEDGMENTS

What a time to write a book. Especially this book. Death and violence haunted every word, every document, every life against the horrific backdrop of the present-day storming of capitols in Washington, D.C, Oregon, and Michigan, the numerous killings of Black people by police, and a pandemic that needlessly cost hundreds of thousands of lives. While the racial disparities in the nation's response to violence made the story that unfolds on these pages far too salient, Covid-19 compelled an isolation that was more intense than the usual solitary writing experience.

I am, therefore, immensely grateful for the village, virtual and otherwise, that supported, advised, encouraged, and helped get this book into the world. I thank my colleagues in the Department of African American Studies, who read an early draft chapter and provided wonderful insight. And, then, there were those who took an even deeper dive into the chapters, Dianne Stewart, Walter Rucker, Leslie Alexander, Leslie Harris, and Kali Gross: thank you, thank you, thank you. I know I talked and talked and talked about this book. Your advice, insights, recommendations, and clarification about relevant scholarship were just invaluable. My research assistants, Timothy Rainey II, Ayriel Coleman, and Meena Iyer, were able to uncover the documents, articles, and books that were on my long, long list. Even more impressive, however, is how all of you went above and beyond. You are appreciated. And Tim especially. You've been with me through *White Rage*, *One Person, No Vote*, and now *The Second*. Thank you, so much. Gabrielle Dudley, Erica Bruchko, and the late Pellom McDaniels III were just magnificent in curating and identifying the rich resources in the Stuart Rose and Woodruff Libraries at Emory.

My literary agent, Rob McQuilkin, saw the vision immediately and never wavered. Rob, you were present at the creation. And you were there through it all. Forever grateful for your brilliance, savviness, insight, and generosity. You're simply the best! My editor, Nancy Miller, whose deft, skilled hand and flexibility made the difference. I value you, your laughter, and your ability. Thank you. Tara Kennedy, publicist par excellence, last time my book tour was to the moon and back. They've landed on Mars now; I guess that's the new itinerary. Let's do this! Angela Mamaril, thank you for helping to keep me on time, on task, on target, and digitally legible. Not bad for a Luddite; thanks for bringing me into the twenty-first century. La Shanda Perryman, you consistently delivered what I needed most to keep the Emory side of my life moving forward and staying afloat. I know that it was no easy feat but you did it. Thank you. I also thank the Pozen Family Center for Human Rights at the University of Chicago and the John Simon Guggenheim Foundation for generous fellowships that supported a crucial leave necessary for this work.

First and foremost, my incredible family, whose love allows me to fly while staying firmly grounded. My brothers, Earl and Wendell (and we miss David something fierce). My sons, Aaron and Drew, you are my everything. Everything! My wonderful extended family, Lisa, Monica, Shirley, Lori, Maia, Rhea, Brooklyn, Shayla, Randall, Ryan, Regina, Erin, Uncle Sam, Aunt Barbara, and Aunt Lennie. Generational love. Generational strength.

# NOTES

INTRODUCTION: "WHY DID YOU SHOOT HIM, SIR?"

1.  Julio Jacobo and Enjoli Francis, "Cops May Have Thought Philando Castile Was a Robbery Suspect, Noting 'Wide-Set Nose,' Dispatch Audio Indicates," ABC News, July 11, 2016, http://abcnews.go.com/US /cops-thought-philando-castile-robbery-suspect-dispatch-audio/story ?id=40439957, accessed February 18, 2017.

2.  Jacobo and Francis, "Cops May Have Thought Philando Castile Was a Robbery Suspect, Noting 'Wide-Set Nose,' Dispatch Audio Indicates."

3.  Jacobo and Francis, "Cops May Have Thought Philando Castile Was a Robbery Suspect, Noting 'Wide-Set Nose,' Dispatch Audio Indicates."

4.  Catherine E. Shoichet, Joshua Berlinger, and Steve Almasy, "Alton Sterling Shooting: Second Video of Deadly Encounter Emerges," CNN, July 6, 2016, http://www.cnn.com/2016/07/06/us/baton-rouge-shooting -alton-sterling/index.html, accessed March 16, 2017.

5.  Gabrielle Bruney, "Here's the True Story of the Waco Siege, and Where Its Survivors Are Now," *Esquire*, May 10, 2020, https://www.esquire .com/entertainment/tv/a32428291/waco-true-story-survivors-now, accessed December 1, 2020; Jason Wilson, "Ruby Ridge, 1992: The Day the American Militia Movement Was Born, *The Guardian*, August 26, 2017, https://www.theguardian.com/us-news/2017/aug/26/ruby-ridge -1992-modern-american-militia-charlottesville, accessed December 1, 2020; Adam Shah, "Fox News Turns to LaPierre, Who Once Called

ATF Agents 'Jack-Booted Government Thugs,'" *Media Matters*, March 10, 2011, https://mediamatters.org/blog/2011/03/10/fox-news -turns-to-lapierre-who-once-called-atf/177439, accessed March 16, 2017.

6.　Patrice Taddonio, "Gunned Down: The Evolution of Wayne LaPierre," *Frontline*, PBS, January 6, 2015, http://www.pbs.org/wgbh/frontline /article/the-evolution-of-wayne-lapierre, accessed March 16, 2017.

7.　Josh Horwitz, "Is Cliven Bundy the New NRA Poster Child?," *Huffington Post*, April 23, 2014, http://www.huffingtonpost.com/josh -horwitz/is-cliven-bundy-the-new-n_b_5197066.html, accessed March 16, 2017.

8.　Lincoln Anthony Blades, "If the Bundys Were Black Would They be Free?," *Ebony*, October 28, 2016, http://www.ebony.com/news-views /cliven-bundy-white-privilege#axzz4bmHTpDT3, accessed March 19, 2017; Henry Decker, "5 Lowlights from the 2014 NRA Convention," *National Memo*, April 28, 2014, http://www.nationalmemo.com/5 -lowlights-2014-nra-convention/6, accessed March 16, 2017.

9.　Brian Fung, "The NRA's Internal Split over Philando Castile," *Washington Post*, July 9, 2016, https://www.washingtonpost.com/news /post-nation/wp/2016/07/09/the-nras-internal-revolt-over-philando -castile, accessed February 18, 2017; Lois Beckett, "NRA Comments on Philando Castile Shooting Without Using His Name: Gun Rights Organization Obliquely Refers to Shooting Death of Black Man Who Was Carrying Concealed Gun After Criticism from Racial Justice Advocates," *The Guardian*, July 8, 2016, https://www.theguardian.com /us-news/2016/jul/08/nra-response-philando-castile-police-shooting, accessed February 18, 2017.

10.　Peter Rugg and James Nye, "'The Most Revolting, Tone Deaf Statement I've Ever Seen': NRA Condemned After Its Astonishing Response to Sandy Hook Massacre Calling for Schools to Arm Themselves," *Daily Mail*, December 21, 2012, http://www.dailymail.co.uk/news/article

-2251762/NRA-condemned-astonishing-response-Sandy-Hook
-massacre-calling-schools-arm-themselves.html#ixzz4Z5RDQ18a,
accessed February 18, 2017; Hannah Levintova and Kate Sheppard,
"NRA Goes MIA . . . Yet Again," *Mother Jones*, December 18, 2012,
http://www.motherjones.com/mojo/2012/12/nra-response-newtown
-mass-shootings, accessed February 18, 2017; Brett LoGiurato,
"NRA's American Rifleman Tweets: 'Good Morning, Shooters. Happy
Friday! Weekend Plans?,'" *Business Insider*, July 20, 2012, http://www
.businessinsider.com/nra-twitter-colorado-theater-shooting-batman
-aurora-2012-7, accessed March 17, 2017; James Warrant, "The National
Rifle Association's Bizarre Colorado Response: The Gun-Rights Group's
Friday Night Webcast Barely Touched on the Colorado Shooting; Most
of the Show Was Devoted to Bashing the U.N. for Trying to Curb
Global Arms Sales," *Daily Beast*, July 22, 2012, http://www.thedailybeast
.com/articles/2012/07/22/the-national-rifle-association-s-bizarre
-colorado-response.html, accessed March 17, 2017; Patrik Jonsson, "As
NRA Meets, Great Gun Debate Intensifies America's Culture War:
Both Sides in the Debate Over Gun Policy Are Indulging in Stereotypes
and Name-Calling, Fueled by a Distrust Bred from Previous Culture
War Fights. As the NRA Convention Continues This Weekend, Are
Red and Blue America Really So Far Apart?," *Christian Science Monitor*,
May 4, 2013, https://www.csmonitor.com/USA/2013/0504/As-NRA
-meets-Great-Gun-Debate-intensifies-America-s-culture-war, accessed
March 17, 2017.

11. Hanna Kozlowska, "Where's the NRA? Americans Are Asking About
the Second Amendment Rights of Alton Sterling and Philando Castile,"
*Quartz*, July 8, 2016, https://qz.com/726004/wheres-the-nra-americans
-are-asking-about-the-second-amendment-rights-of-alton-sterling
-and-philando-castile, accessed March 17, 2017.

12. David A. Graham, "The Second Amendment's Second-Class Citizens:
Black Citizens of the United States Have Seldom Enjoyed the Same
Right to Bear Arms That Whites Do," *The Atlantic*, July 7, 2016,
https://www.theatlantic.com/politics/archive/2016/07/alton-ster

ling-philando-castile-2nd-amendment-guns/490301, accessed March 17, 2017.

13. Eugene Robinson, "In America, Gun Rights Are for Whites Only," *Washington Post*, September 22, 2016.

14. Mark Anthony Neal retweet, Lamont Lily (@LamontLilly), "Does 'open and carry' state only apply to white people?," Twitter, August 14, 2016, via Mark Anthony Neal, https://twitter.com/LamontLilly/status/7648 26899939942400?s=20, accessed September 20, 2016.

15. Ari Berman, *Give Us the Ballot: The Modern Struggle for Voting Rights in America* (New York: Farrar, Straus and Giroux, 2015); Manfred Berg, *The Ticket to Freedom: The NAACP and the Struggle for Black Political Integration* (Gainesville: University Press of Florida, 2005); Carol Anderson, *One Person, No Vote: How Voter Suppression Is Destroying Our Democracy* (New York: Bloomsbury, 2018, 2019).

16. For the Eighth Amendment, see Bryan Stevenson, *Just Mercy: A Story of Justice and Redemption* (New York: Spiegel and Grau, 2014); for the Fourth, Fifth, and Sixth Amendments, see Michelle Alexander, *The New Jim Crow: Mass Incarceration in the Age of Colorblindness* (New York: New Press, 2012).

17. Constitution Annotated, https://constitution.congress.gov/constitution/amendment-2, accessed December 2, 2020.

18. Les Adams, *The Second Amendment Primer: A Citizens' Guidebook to the History, Sources, and Authorities for the Constitutional Guarantee of the Right to Keep and Bear Arms* (Birmingham, AL: Palladium Press, 1996).

19. Paul Finkelman, "2nd Amendment Passed to Protect Slavery? No!," *The Root*, January 21, 2013, http://www.theroot.com/2nd-amendment-passed-to-protect-slavery-no-1790894965, accessed March 18, 2017.

20. Stephen P. Halbrook, *The Founders' Second Amendment: Origins of the Right to Bear Arms* (Chicago: Ivan R. Dee, 2008), 128, 142, 166, 168.

21. Finkelman, "2nd Amendment Passed to Protect Slavery? No!"

22. Robert J. Cottrol and Raymond T. Diamond, "The Second Amendment: Toward an Afro-Americanist Reconsideration," *Georgetown Law Journal* 80 (1991): 309–361.

23. *Lewis v. United States*, 445 U.S. 55 (1980); *District of Columbia et al. v. Heller*, 554 U.S. 570 (2008); *McDonald v. Chicago*, 561 U.S. 742 (2010).

24. *Powell v. Alabama*, 287 U.S. 45 (1932); *Batson v. Kentucky*, 476 U.S. 79 (1986); *McCleskey v. Kemp*, 481 U.S. 279 (1987); *Miller-El v. Cockrell*, 537 U.S. 322 (2003); ACLU, "Race and the Death Penalty," https://www.aclu.org/other/race-and-death-penalty, accessed March 19, 2017.

25. *Furman v. Georgia*, 408 U.S. 238 (1972); *Gregg v. Georgia*, 428 U.S. 153 (1976); *Baze v. Rees*, 553 U.S. 35 (2008); Death Penalty Information Center, "Race of Death Row Inmates Executed Since 1976," http://www.deathpenaltyinfo.org/race-death-row-inmates-executed-1976, accessed March 19, 2017; "Retire Big Yellow Mama," *Tuscaloosa News*, February 1, 2001, http://www.tuscaloosanews.com/news/20010201/retire-big-yellow-mama, accessed March 19, 2017.

26. *Lewis v. United States*, 445 U.S. 55 (1980); Kali N. Gross, *Colored Amazons: Crime, Violence, and Black Women in the City of Brotherly Love, 1880–1910* (Durham, NC: Duke University Press, 2006); Carl N. Suddler, *Presumed Criminal: Black Youth and the Justice System in Postwar New York* (New York: New York University Press, 2019); Naomi Murakawa, *The First Civil Right: How Liberals Built Prison America* (New York: Oxford University Press, 2014); Khalil G. Muhammad, *The Condemnation of Blackness: Race, Crime, and the Making of Modern Urban America* (Cambridge, MA: Harvard University Press, 2010); Todd R. Clear, *Imprisoning Communities: How Mass Incarceration Makes Disadvantaged Neighborhoods Worse* (New York: Oxford University Press, 2007).

27. *District of Columbia et al. v. Heller*, 554 U.S. 570 (2008); *McDonald v. Chicago*, 561 U.S. 742 (2010).

28. Mark Suppelsa, "Indiana Guns: Favorite of Chicago Gangbangers," WGNTV.com, September 3, 2014, http://wgntv.com/2014/09/03 /indiana-guns-favorite-of-chicago-gangbangers, accessed March 20, 2017; Perry Stein, "D.C.'s Summer Gun Violence: By the Numbers and Neighborhoods," *Washington Post*, August 6, 2015, https://www.wash ingtonpost.com/news/local/wp/2015/08/06/d-c-s-summer-gun-violence -by-the-numbers-and-neighborhoods, accessed March 20, 2017.

29. See, for example, Iyen Acosta, "*Doe v. Wilmington Housing Authority*: The Common Area Caveat as a Paradigmatic Balance Between Tenant Safety and Second Amendment Rights," *Catholic University Law Review* 62, no. 1113 (2013).

30. For the legal foundation of the right to self-defense, see Don B. Kates Jr., "The Second Amendment: A Dialogue," *Law and Contemporary Problems* 49, no. 1 (Winter 1986): 146–147n16; Jonathan Meltzer, "Open Carry for All: *Heller* and Our Nineteenth-Century Second Amendment," *Yale Law Journal* 123, no. 5 (March 2014): 1486–1530.

31. Joyce Tang, "Enslaved African Rebellions in Virginia," *Journal of Black Studies* 27, no. 5 (May 1997): 601; June Purcell Guild, *Black Laws of Virginia: A Summary of the Legislative Acts of Virginia concerning Negroes from Earliest Times to the Present* (New York: Negro Universities Press, 1936; Richmond: Whittet & Shepperson, 1969), 46.

32. U.S. Commission on Civil Rights, *Examining the Race Effects of Stand Your Ground Laws and Related Issues*, February 2020, 16.

33. U.S. Commission on Civil Rights, *Examining the Race Effects of Stand Your Ground Laws and Related Issues*, 16.

34. U.S. Commission on Civil Rights, *Examining the Race Effects of Stand Your Ground Laws and Related Issues*, 3.

35. "Second Amendment: A Citizen's Right," NRA, January 3, 2008, https://www.nraila.org/articles/20080103/second-amendment-a-citizen -s-right, accessed March 23, 2017.

CHAPTER ONE: "SHEEP WILL NEVER MAKE A REVOLUTION"

1. Gordon S. Wood, *The American Revolution: A History* (New York: Modern Library, 2002), 55; Ben Baack, "Forging a Nation State: The Continental Congress and the Financing of the War of American Independence," *Economic History Review* 54, no. 4 (November 2001): 639; Paul David Nelson, "British Conduct of the American Revolutionary War: A Review of Interpretations," *Journal of American History* 65, no. 3 (December 1978): 623.

2. John Ferling, *Almost a Miracle: The American Victory in the War of Independence* (New York: Oxford University Press, 2007), 29–33, 48–60; Rick Atkinson, *The British Are Coming: The War for America, Lexington to Princeton, 1775–1777* (New York: Henry Holt, 2019), 58–82, 92–115; Ben Baack, "Forging a Nation State," 641.

3. James Haw, "The Rutledges, the Continental Congress, and Independence," *South Carolina Historical Magazine* 94, no. 4 (October 1993): 241.

4. Edward B. Rugemer, "The Southern Response to British Abolitionism: The Maturation of Proslavery Apologetics," *Journal of Southern History* 70, no. 2 (May 2004): 226.

5. Peter H. Wood, *Black Majority: Negroes in Colonial South Carolina from 1670 Through the Stono Rebellion* (New York: Alfred A. Knopf, 1974), Kindle, Location 136.

6. James Madison, Edward J. Larson, and Michael P. Windship, *The Constitutional Convention* (New York: Modern Library, 2011), Kindle, Location 3396, 3400; quote found in Paul Finkelman, "Slavery in the United States: Persons or Property?," in *The Legal Understanding of Slavery: From the Historical to the Contemporary*, 115–116, https://scholarship.law.duke.edu/cgi/viewcontent.cgi?article=5386&context=faculty_scholarship, accessed October 19, 2019.

7. Joseph J. Ellis, *The Quartet: Orchestrating the Second American Revolution, 1783–1789* (New York: Vintage Books, 2016), 10.

8. David Waldstreicher, *Slavery's Constitution: From Revolution to Ratification* (New York: Hill and Wang, 2010), pbk. ed., 54.

9. John Hope Franklin and Loren Schweninger, *Runaway Slaves: Rebels on the Plantation* (New York: Oxford University Press, 1999), xiv–xv, 2–4.

10. Erica Armstrong Dunbar, *Never Caught: The Washingtons' Relentless Pursuit of Their Runaway Slave, Ona Judge* (New York: 37 Ink, 2017); Catherine Clinton, *Harriet Tubman: The Road to Freedom* (New York: Little, Brown, 2004); Andrew DelBanco, *The War Before the War: Fugitive Slaves and the Struggle for America's Soul from the Revolution to the Civil War* (New York: Penguin Press, 2018), 24–25.

11. Waldstreicher, *Slavery's Constitution*, 38; Thomas J. Davis, "Emancipation Rhetoric, Natural Rights, and Revolutionary New England: A Note on Four Black Petitions in Massachusetts, 1773–1777," *New England Quarterly* 62, no. 2 (June 1989): 256.

12. Herbert Aptheker, "American Negro Slave Revolts," *Science and Society* 1, no. 4 (Summer 1937): 512–538; Harvey Wish, "American Slave Insurrections Before 1861," *Journal of Negro History* 22, no. 3 (July 1937): 299–320; Joyce Tang, "Enslaved African Rebellions in Virginia," *Journal of Black Studies* 27, no. 5 (May 1997): 598–614.

13. George Fitzhugh, "The Universal Law of Slavery," *Africans in America*, PBS, https://www.pbs.org/wgbh/aia/part4/4h3141t.html, accessed January 30, 2020; Sally E. Hadden, *Slave Patrols: Law and Violence in Virginia and the Carolinas* (Cambridge, MA: Harvard University Press, 2003), pbk. ed., 135, 137.

14. Finkleman, "Slavery in the United States," 109.

15. Tang, "Enslaved African Rebellions in Virginia," 604.

16. Finkleman, "Slavery in the United States," 108; Tang, "Enslaved African Rebellions in Virginia," 600; Kelli Carter Jackson, *Force and Freedom: Black Abolitionists and the Politics of Violence* (Philadelphia: University of Pennsylvania Press, 2019), Kindle, Location 2352.

17. Wish, "American Slave Insurrections Before 1861," 307–308.

18. Tang, "Enslaved African Rebellions in Virginia," 601.

19. Benjamin Quarles, "The Colonial Militia and Negro Manpower," *Mississippi Valley Historical Review* 45, no. 4 (March 1959): 647.

20. Alejandro de la Fuente and Ariela J. Gross, *Becoming Free, Becoming Black: Race, Freedom, and Law in Cuba, Virginia, and Louisiana* (New York: Cambridge University Press, 2020), 74.

21. Nicholas J. Johnson, David B. Kopel, George A. Mocsary, and Michael P. O'Shea, *Firearms Law and the Second Amendment: Regulation, Rights, and Policy* (New York: Wolters Kluwer Law and Business, 2012), 103; Robert G. Parkinson, *The Common Cause: Creating Race and Nation in the American Revolution* (Chapel Hill: Omohundro Institute of Early American History and Culture and University of North Carolina Press, 2016), Kindle, Location 13416.

22. Edda L. Fields-Black, *Deep Roots: Rice Farmers in West Africa and the African Diaspora* (Bloomington: Indiana University Press, 2008); Norrece T. Jones, *Born a Child of Freedom, Yet a Slave: Mechanisms of Control and Strategies of Resistance in Antebellum South Carolina* (Hanover, NH: Wesleyan University Press, 1990); Wish, "American Slave Insurrections Before 1861," 307–308.

23. Jones, *Born a Child of Freedom, Yet a Slave*, 15.

24. Walter C. Rucker, *The River Flows On: Black Resistance, Culture, and Identity Formation in Early America* (Baton Rouge: Louisiana State University Press, 2006), Kindle, 95, 97.

25. Benjamin Quarles, review of *Black Majority: Negroes in Colonial South Carolina from 1670 Through the Stone Rebellion*, by Peter H. Wood, *Journal of Negro History* 60, no. 2 (April 1975): 332; Jones, *Born a Child of Freedom, Yet a Slave*, 6.

26. Perry L. Kyles, "Resistance and Collaboration: Political Strategies Within the Afro-Carolinian Slave Community, 1700–1750," *Journal of*

*African American History* 93, no. 4 (Fall 2008): 501; Hadden, *Slave Patrols*, 23.

27.  Hadden, *Slave Patrols*, 147.

28.  Rucker, *The River Flows On*, Kindle, 98–99.

29.  Wood, *Black Majority*, Location 6828, 6830.

30.  Creek is the name whites used to define the indigenous people who lived in what is now Florida, Alabama, and Georgia, because they lived near the waterways. Jack Healy, "For Oklahoma Tribe, Vindication at Long Last," *New York Times*, July 11, 2020, https://www.nytimes .com/2020/07/11/us/muscogee-creek-nation-oklahoma.html, accessed September 12, 2020.

31.  Quarles, "The Colonial Militia and Negro Manpower," 644.

32.  Hadden, *Slave Patrols*, 19, 21.

33.  Hadden, *Slave Patrols*, 106, 123.

34.  Wood, *Black Majority*, Location 6836, 6839–6840.

35.  Wood, *Black Majority*, Location 6847, 6859, 6861; Rucker, *The River Flows On*, 99.

36.  Jones, *Born a Child of Freedom, Yet a Slave*, 25.

37.  Rucker, *The River Flows On*, 99.

38.  Ryan A. Quintana, *Making a Slave State: Political Development in Early South Carolina* (Chapel Hill: University of North Carolina Press, 2018), 15–17. Some scholars, such as Peter Charles Hoffer in *Cry Liberty: The Great Stono River Slave Rebellion of 1739*, argue that the uprising was spontaneous, not planned.

39.  Carl T. Bogus, "The Hidden History of the Second Amendment," *UC Davis Law Review* 31, no. 2 (Winter 1998): 332.

40. John K. Thornton, "African Dimensions of the Stono Rebellion," *American Historical Review* 96, no. 4, 1102–1103; Thomas J. Little, review of *Stono: Documenting and Interpreting a Southern Slave Revolt*, ed. Mark M. Smith, *Journal of Southern History* 74, no. 1 (February 2008): 146.

41. Hadden, *Slave Patrols*, 23.

42. Huw David, review of *Calling Out Liberty: The Stono Slave Rebellion and the Universal Struggle for Human Rights*, by Jack Shuler, *South Carolina Historical Magazine* 112, no. 1–2 (January–April 2011): 85.

43. Jones, *Born a Child of Freedom, Yet a Slave*, 15; Rucker, *The River Flows On*, 101.

44. James G. Thomas, "Slave Revolts," in *The New Encyclopedia of Southern Culture* (Chapel Hill: University of North Carolina Press, 2006), 239.

45. Rucker, *The River Flows On*, 102.

46. Quarles, "The Colonial Militia and Negro Manpower," 650.

47. Rucker, *The River Flows On*, 100.

48. Transcription from David J. McCord, ed., *The Statutes at Large of South Carolina*, vol. 7, Containing the Acts Relating to Charleston, Courts, Slaves, and Rivers (Columbia, SC: A. S. Johnston, 1840), 397, https://digital.scetv.org/teachingAmerhistory/pdfs/Transciptionof1740SlaveCodes.pdf, accessed January 26, 2020; Rucker, *The River Flows On*, 103; David, review of *Calling Out Liberty*, 84.

49. James Lindgren and Justin L. Heather, "Counting Guns in Early America," *William and Mary Law Review* 43, no. 5 (2002): 1800, 1803–1804, 1806, 1817.

50. David McCullough, *American History: John Adams* (New York: Simon and Schuster, 2001), Kindle, Location 1962.

51. Wood, *The American Revolution*, 56–57.

52. Quarles, "The Colonial Militia and Negro Manpower," 645.

53. Quarles, "The Colonial Militia and Negro Manpower," 648.

54. *The Statutes at Large of Pennsylvania from 1682 to 1801*, vol. 2, *1700–1712* (Philadelphia: State Printer of Pennsylvania, 1896), 79; Matthew Mason, "Slavery and Politics to 1808," in *Slavery and Politics in the Early American Republic* (Chapel Hill: University of North Carolina Press, 2006), 11.

55. Johnson, Kopel, Mocsary, and O'Shea, *Firearms Law and the Second Amendment*, 101.

56. James T. Kloppenberg, *Toward Democracy: The Struggle for Self-Rule in European and American Thought* (New York: Oxford University Press, 2016), 261.

57. Mitch Kachun, *First Martyr of Liberty: Crispus Attucks in American Memory* (New York: Oxford University Press, 2017); Noel B. Poirier, "A Legacy of Integration: The African American Citizen-Soldier and the Continental Army," *Army History*, no. 56 (Fall 2002): 18.

58. Benjamin Quarles, *The Negro in the American Revolution* (Chapel Hill: Omohundro Institute of Early American History and Culture and the University of North Carolina Press, 2012), Kindle, 124.

59. Quarles, *The Negro in the American Revolution*, 17, 67.

60. Quarles, *The Negro in the American Revolution*, 52.

61. Ferling, *Almost a Miracle*, 196–197.

62. Ferling, *Almost a Miracle*, 164, 167.

63. Waldstreicher, *Slavery's Constitution*, 44–45.

64. W. B. Hartgrove, "The Negro Soldier in the American Revolution," *Journal of Negro History* 1, no. 2 (April 1916): 117.

65. Poirier, "A Legacy of Integration," 18–19, 22; Parkinson, *The Common Cause*, Location 9902, 9909.

66. Poirier, "A Legacy of Integration," 20; Quarles, *The Negro in the American Revolution*, 53–54, 56.

67. Poirier, "A Legacy of Integration," 20.

68. Ferling, *Almost a Miracle*, 185–186; Parkinson, *The Common Cause*, Location 9690, 9695.

69. Michael Waldman, *The Second Amendment: A Biography* (New York: Simon and Schuster, 2014), 16.

70. Parkinson, *The Common Cause*, Location 10688, 10691, 10699; John Buchanan, *The Road to Charleston: Nathanael Greene and the American Revolution* (Charlottesville: University of Virginia Press, 2019), Kindle, Location 198.

71. Parkinson, *The Common Cause*, Location 9741–9747; Buchanan, *The Road to Charleston*, Location 267.

72. Poirier, "A Legacy of Integration," 22; Parkinson, *The Common Cause*, Location 9865–9866, 9890–9901.

73. Quarles, *The Negro in the American Revolution*, 64.

74. Quarles, *The Negro in the American Revolution*, 64.

75. Quarles, *The Negro in the American Revolution*, 65.

76. Buchanan, *The Road to Charleston*, Location, 6309, 6343.

77. Parkinson, *The Common Cause*, Location 9984-9990, 11308-11310.

78. Andrew DelBanco, *The War Before the War: Fugitive Slaves and the Struggle for America's Soul from the Revolution to the Civil War* (New York: Penguin Press, 2018), Kindle, 73.

79. Parkinson, *The Common Cause*, Location 13688, 13690.

80. Parkinson, *The Common Cause*, Location 10670.

81. Quarles, *The Negro in the American Revolution*, 71, 79.

82. Parkinson, *The Common Cause*, Location 10031, 10038–10039, 10061, 10109; Waldstreicher, *Slavery's Constitution*, 57.

83. Declaration of Independence: A Transcription, National Archives, https://www.archives.gov/founding-docs/declaration-transcript, accessed February 5, 2020.

84. Jack Rakove, "The Legacy of the Articles of Confederation," *Publius* 12, no. 4 (Autumn 1982): 45; John Ferling, *Jefferson and Hamilton: The Rivalry That Forged a Nation* (New York: Bloomsbury, 2013), 179, 183–184.

85. Jill Lepore, *These Truths: A History of the United States* (New York: W. W. Norton, 2018), 114–116.

86. James Madison, Edward J. Larson, and Michael P. Winship, *The Constitutional Convention: A Narrative History from the Notes of James Madison* (New York: Modern Library, 2005), Kindle, Location 170, 205; Fergus M. Bordewich, *The First Congress: How James Madison, George Washington, and a Group of Extraordinary Men Invented the Government* (New York: Simon and Schuster, 2016), Kindle, Location 222–226; Waldstreicher, *Slavery's Constitution*, 69; Don Higginbotham, "The Federalized Militia Debate: A Neglected Aspect of Second Amendment Scholarship," *William and Mary Quarterly* 55, no. 1 (January 1998): 43; David O. Stewart, *The Summer of 1787: The Men Who Invented the Constitution* (New York: Simon and Schuster, 2007), 11–13. For the uprising in Massachusetts, see David P. Szatmary, *Shays' Rebellion: The Making of an Agrarian Insurrection* (Amherst: University of Massachusetts Press, 1980).

87. Mark V. Tushnet, *Out of Range: Why the Constitution Can't End the Battle over Guns* (New York: Oxford University Press, 2007), 51.

88. Bordewich, *The First Congress*, Location 239, 242; Paul Finkelman, "'A Well Regulated Militia': The Second Amendment in Historical Perspective," *Chicago-Kent Law Review* 76, no. 1 (October 2000), 211.

89. Kloppenberg, *Toward Democracy*, 387–388; Bordewich, *The First Congress*, Location 221.

90. Madison, Larson, and Winship, *The Constitutional Convention*, Location 3379; Kloppenberg, *Toward Democracy*, 407.

91. Waldstreicher, *Slavery's Constitution*, 3.

92. Michael J. Klarman, *The Framers' Coup: The Making of the United States Constitution* (New York: Oxford University Press, 2016), 263.

93. DelBanco, *The War Before the War*, 18. The end of slavery in the North had two major driving forces. One, competition with white wage laborers became untenable for the economic system. Two, the states had begun to put in place a vast carceral system to maintain control of their Black population. See Seth Rockman, *Scraping By: Wage Labor, Slavery, and Survival in Early Baltimore* (Baltimore, MD: The Johns Hopkins University Press, 2009); Leslie Patrick-Stamp, "Numbers That Are Not New: African Americans in the Country's First Prison, 1790–1835," *The Pennsylvania Magazine of History and Biography* 119, no. 1/2 (January–April 1995): 95–128.

94. Kloppenberg, *Toward Democracy*, 407; David McCullough, *American History: John Adams* (New York: Simon and Schuster, 2001), Kindle, Location 6287.

95. Bogus, "The Hidden History of the Second Amendment," 357, 233n.

96. Klarman, *The Framers' Coup*, 263; Kloppenberg, *Toward Democracy*, 387–388, 403.

97. Kloppenberg, *Toward Democracy*, 407.

98. Marvin R. Zahniser, *Charles Cotesworth Pinckney: Founding Father* (Chapel Hill: University of North Carolina Press, 1967), 89–91.

99. Stephanie E. Smallwood, *Saltwater Slavery: A Middle Passage from Africa to American Diaspora* (Cambridge, MA: Harvard University

Press, 2007); Klarman, *Framers' Coup*, 268; Madison, Larson, and Winship, *The Constitutional Convention*, Location 2706.

100. DelBanco, *The War Before the War*, 49.

101. Pauline Maier, *Ratification: The People Debate the Constitution, 1787–1788* (New York: Simon and Schuster, 2010), 284.

102. Klarman, *The Framers' Coup*, 268–269, 276–277; Lepore, *These Truths*, 116; Madison, Larson, and Winship, *The Constitutional Convention*, Location 1769, 1778, 1782.

103. Don Higginbotham, "The Federalized Militia Debate: A Neglected Aspect of Second Amendment Scholarship," *William and Mary Quarterly* 55, no. 1 (January 1998): 44.

104. Waldstreicher, *Slavery's Constitution*, 120.

105. Maier, *Ratification*, 283.

106. DelBanco, *The War Before the War*, 20; Klarman, *The Framers' Coup*, 291–294, 299, 302; Waldstreicher, *Slavery's Constitution*, 6.

107. Waldman, *The Second Amendment*, 37.

108. Waldman, *The Second Amendment*, 38

109. Waldman, *The Second Amendment*, 39.

110. Waldstreicher, *Slavery's Constitution*, 144.

111. Harlow Giles Unger, *Lion of Liberty: Patrick Henry and the Call to a New Nation* (Cambridge, MA: Da Capo Press, 2010), 229; Bogus, "The Hidden History of the Second Amendment," 353.

112. Waldstreicher, *Slavery's Constitution*, 145; Bogus, "The Hidden History of the Second Amendment," 354.

113. Waldman, *The Second Amendment*, 26–27, 32, 42, 46; Bogus, "The Hidden History of the Second Amendment," 357–358.

114. Bordewich, *The First Congress*, Location 267.

115. Joseph J. Ellis, *The Quartet: Orchestrating the Second American Revolution, 1783–1789* (New York: Vintage Books, 2016), 206.

116. Klarman, *The Framers' Coup*, 577–580; Finkelman, "'A Well Regulated Militia,'" 213.

117. Johnson, Kopel, Mocsary, and O'Shea, *Firearms Law and the Second Amendment*, 215; Bogus, "The Hidden History of the Second Amendment," 363.

118. Bogus, "The Hidden History of the Second Amendment," 363.

119. Bogus, "The Hidden History of the Second Amendment," 365.

120. Bogus, "The Hidden History of the Second Amendment," 350.

121. Klarman, *The Framers' Coup*, 594.

122. Lawrence Delbert Cress, "An Armed Community: The Origins and Meaning of the Right to Bear Arms," *Journal of American History* 71, no. 1 (June 1984): 25, 27, 28, 30; Bordewich, *The First Congress*, Location 2050.

123. John Gilbert McCurdy, *Quarters: The Accommodation of the British Army and the Coming of the American Revolution* (Ithaca, NY: Cornell University Press, 2019), 236–244.

124. Washington's Farewell Address 1796, Avalon Project, Lillian Goldman Law Library, Yale Law School, https://avalon.law.yale.edu/18th_century /washing.asp, accessed February 28, 2020; Michael J. Hogan, *A Cross of Iron: Harry S. Truman and the Origins of the National Security State, 1945–1954* (New York: Cambridge University Press, 1998).

125. Matthew Waxman, "Remembering the Whiskey Rebellion," *Lawfare*, September 25, 2018, https://www.lawfareblog.com/remembering-whiskey -rebellion, accessed September 29, 2018.

126. Bogus, "The Hidden History of the Second Amendment," 339.

127. Bogus, "The Hidden History of the Second Amendment," 340, 342, 345.

128. Mark M. Smith, "Remembering Mary, Shaping Revolt: Reconsidering the Stono Rebellion," *Journal of Southern History* 67, no. 3 (August 2001): 519; Bogus, "The Hidden History of the Second Amendment," 336.

129. Hadden, *Slave Patrols*, 144.

130. Thomas Cooper, *The Statutes at Large of South Carolina: Acts from 1716 to 1752* (Columbia, SC: A. S. Johnston, 1836–1873), 468.

131. Donnie D. Bellamy, "The Legal Status of Black Georgians During the Colonial and Revolutionary Eras," *Journal of Negro History* 74, nos. 1–4 (Winter–Autumn 1989): 6.

132. Bogus, "The Hidden History of the Second Amendment," 368.

133. Waldman, *The Second Amendment*, 58.

134. Waldman, *The Second Amendment*, 52.

135. Bordewich, *The First Congress*, Location 1913, 1929; Waldman, *The Second Amendment*, 58.

136. Waldman, *The Second Amendment*, 54–55.

137. Higginbotham, "The Federalized Militia Debate," 51n38; Robin L. Einhorn, "Patrick Henry's Case Against the Constitution: The Structural Problem with Slavery," *Journal of the Early Republic* 22, no. 4 (Winter 2002): 552, 556, 559.

138. Higginbotham, "The Federalized Militia Debate," 50.

139. Bordewich, *The First Congress*, Location 1944, 1950, 1971, 1976.

140. Bordewich, *The First Congress*, Location 1976, 2040, 2042; Tushnet, *Out of Range*, 51.

141. Bordewich, *The First Congress*, Location 2258, 2267.

142. Waldman, *The Second Amendment*, 63. His focus was on the standing army.

143. Higginbotham, "The Federalized Militia Debate," 50.

144. Bogus, "The Hidden History of the Second Amendment," 369, 371.

145. Johnson, Kopel, Mocsary, and O'Shea, *Firearms Law and the Second Amendment*, 218.

### CHAPTER TWO: KEEPING A FEROCIOUS MONSTER IN CHAINS

1. David Skillen Bogen, "The Maryland Context of Dred Scott: The Decline in the Legal Status of Maryland Free Blacks, 1776–1810," *American Journal of Legal History* 34, no. 4 (October 1990): 410.

2. Alejandro de la Fuente and Ariela J. Gross, *Becoming Free, Becoming Black: Race, Freedom and Law in Cuba, Virginia, and Louisiana* (New York: Cambridge University Press, 2020), 182.

3. Vernon Valentine Palmer, "The Customs of Slavery: The War Without Arms," *American Journal of Legal History* 48, no. 2 (April 2006): 177.

4. Mark Pitcavage, "Ropes of Sand: Territorial Militias, 1801–1812," *Journal of the Early Republic* 13, no. 4 (Winter 1993): 483.

5. For the legal foundation of the right to self-defense, see Don B. Kates Jr., "The Second Amendment: A Dialogue," *Law and Contemporary Problems* 49, no. 1 (Winter 1986): 146–147n16; Jonathan Meltzer, "Open Carry for All: *Heller* and Our Nineteenth-Century Second Amendment," *Yale Law Journal* 123, no. 5 (March 2014): 1486–1530.

6. Fergus M. Bordewich, *The First Congress: How James Madison, George Washington, and a Group of Extraordinary Men Invented the Government* (New York: Simon and Schuster, 2016), Kindle, Location, 3197, 3216, 3221, 3253, 3254, 3277, 3324, 3329; Jill Lepore, *These Truths: A History of the United States* (New York: W. W. Norton, 2018), 131, 135; Joanne B. Freeman, *The Field of Blood: Violence in Congress and the Road to Civil War* (New York: Farrar, Straus and Giroux, 2018), 70.

7. Joseph J. Ellis, *Founding Brothers: The Revolutionary Generation* (New York: Vintage Books, 2000), 137.

8. Bordewich, *The First Congress*, Location, 3322, 3327, 3328, 3337; James Madison to James Madison Sr., letter, September 8, 1783, James Madison Papers, Library of Congress, https://www.loc.gov/item/mjm012487, accessed April 14, 2020; Lepore, *These Truths*, 136–137.

9. Elizabeth F. Cohen, "The Political Economy of Immigrant Time: Rights, Citizenship, and Temporariness in the Post-1965 Era," *Polity* 47, no. 3 (July 2015): 342.

10. Bordewich, *The First Congress*, Location, 3174, 3179, 3190.

11. Cohen, "The Political Economy of Immigrant Time," 343.

12. Devon W. Carbado, "Yellow by Law," *California Law Review* 97, no. 3 (June 2009): 635n11; R.L.H Jr., "Aliens: Naturalization: Who Is a 'White' Person?," *California Law Review* 11, no. 5 (July 1923): 350.

13. Nationality Act of 1790, Immigration History, Immigration and Ethnic History Society, https://immigrationhistory.org/item/1790-nationality -act, accessed March 4, 2020.

14. Mae M. Ngai, "The Architecture of Race in American Immigration Law: A Reexamination of the Immigration Act of 1924," *Journal of American History* 86, no. 1 (June 1999): 71.

15. Martha S. Jones, *Birthright Citizens: A History of Race and Rights in Antebellum America* (New York: Cambridge University Press, 2018), Kindle, 25.

16. Erika Lee, *America for Americans: A History of Xenophobia in the United States* (New York: Basic Books, 2019), 36.

17. Parkinson, *The Common Cause*, Location 13737, 13740.

18. Benjamin Quarles, *The Negro in the American Revolution* (Chapel Hill: Omohundro Institute of Early American History and Culture and the

University of North Carolina Press, 2012), 62; Ira Berlin, *Slaves Without Masters: The Free Negro in the Antebellum South* (New York: New Press, 1974, 2007), 97; Carol Anderson, *White Rage: The Unspoken Truth of Our Racial Divide* (New York: Bloomsbury, 2016).

19.  Quarles, *The Negro in the Making of America*, 106; *Hudgins v. Wright*, 11 Va. (1 Hen. & Mun.) 134 (1806).

20.  Cohen, "The Political Economy of Immigrant Time," 343.

21.  Richard Allen quoted in David Walker, *Walker's Appeal: In Four Articles; Together with a Preamble, to the Coloured Citizens of the World, but in Particular, and Very Expressly, to Those of the United States of America* (Boston: self-published, 1829), 57, W. E. B. Du Bois's copy, found in Vault 2017 235, Stuart A. Rose Manuscript, Archives, and Rare Book Library, Emory University, Atlanta, Georgia. Emphasis in the original.

22.  Andrew K. Diemer, *The Politics of Black Citizenship: Free African Americans in the Mid-Atlantic Borderland, 1817–1863* (Athens: University of Georgia Press, 2016), 112–113.

23.  Ian Haney-López, *White by Law: The Legal Construction of Race* (New York: New York University Press, 2006); Quarles, *The Negro in the Making of America*, 112.

24.  Michael J. Klarman, *The Framers' Coup: The Making of the United States Constitution* (New York: Oxford University Press, 2016), 304.

25.  Douglas Egerton, *Gabriel's Rebellion: The Virginia Slave Conspiracies of 1800 and 1802* (Chapel Hill: University of North Carolina Press, 1993), Kindle, 15.

26.  Quarles, *The Negro in the Making of America*, 101, 105, 112.

27.  Kenneth M. Stampp, *The Peculiar Institution: Slavery in the Ante-Bellum South* (New York: Vintage Books, 1956), 215. Emphasis in the original.

28. Dunbar, *Never Caught*, 30–31, 64.

29. Edward Price, "The Black Voting Rights Issue in Pennsylvania, 1780–1900," *Pennsylvania Magazine of History and Biography* 100, no. 3 (July 1976): 356–365; Berlin, *Slaves Without Masters*, 45–49; Quarles, *The Negro in the Making of America*, 106–107, 112.

30. Robert J. Cottrol and Raymond T. Diamond, "The Second Amendment: Toward an Afro-Americanist Reconsideration," *Georgetown Law Journal* 80 (1991): 335.

31. Cottrol and Diamond, "The Second Amendment," 335.

32. Price, "The Black Voting Rights Issue in Pennsylvania," 359.

33. Quarles, *The Negro in the Making of America*, 112–113; Cottrol and Diamond, "The Second Amendment," 339n150.

34. David Skillen Bogen, "The Maryland Context of Dred Scott: The Decline in the Legal Status of Maryland Free Blacks, 1776–1810," *American Journal of Legal History* 34, no. 4 (October 1990): 388; Thomas N. Ingersoll, "Free Blacks in a Slave Society: New Orleans, 1718–1812," *William and Mary Quarterly* 48, no. 2 (April 1991): 197.

35. Litwack, "The Federal Government and the Free Negro, 1790–1860," *Journal of Negro History*, 43, no. 4 (October 1958), 274.

36. Janice L. Sumler-Edmond, "Free Black Life in Savannah," in *Slavery and Freedom in Savannah*, ed. Leslie M. Harris and Daina Ramey Berry (Athens: University of Georgia Press, 2014), 125–126.

37. Stampp, *The Peculiar Institution*, 216.

38. Quarles, *The Negro in the Making of America*, 107.

39. Berlin, *Slaves Without Masters*, 65–66.

40. Cottrol and Diamond, "The Second Amendment," 331.

41. Michael Waldman, *The Second Amendment: A Biography* (New York: Simon and Schuster, 2014), 65.

42. Herbert Aptheker, "American Negro Slave Revolts: Fifty Years Gone," *Science and Society*, 51, no. 1 (Spring 1987): 70.

43. Thomas, "Slave Revolts," 240; David Brion Davis, "Impact of the French and Haitian Revolutions," in *The Impact of the Haitian Revolution in the Atlantic World*, ed. David P. Geggus (Columbia: University of South Carolina Press, 2001), Kindle, Location, 442.

44. Lepore, *These Truths*, 142.

45. Wim Klooster, *Revolutions in the Atlantic World: A Comparative History* (New York: NYU Press, 2018), 91.

46. Johnhenry Gonzalez, *Maroon Nation: A History of Revolutionary Haiti* (New Haven, CT: Yale University Press 2019), 49–50.

47. Julius S. Scott, "Afro-American Sailors and the International Communication Network: The Case of Newport Bowers," in *African Americans and the Haitian Revolution: Selected Essays and Historical Documents*, ed. Maurice Jackson and Jacqueline Bacon (New York: Routledge, 2010), 29; Ternant to George Washington, letter, September 24, 1791, Founders Online, National Archives, https://founders.archives .gov/documents/Washington/05-09-02-0006, accessed April 17, 2020.

48. William Merkel, "To See Oneself as a Target of a Justified Revolution: Thomas Jefferson and Gabriel's Uprising," *American Nineteenth Century History* 4, no. 2 (Summer 2003): 4–5.

49. Charles Pinckney to George Washington, letter, September 20, 1791, https://founders.archives.gov/documents/Washington/05-08-02-0379, accessed April 17, 2020.

50. George Washington to John Vaughan, letter, December 27, 1791, https:// founders.archives.gov/documents/Washington/05-09-02-0212, accessed April 17, 2020.

51. Nathaniel Cutting to Thomas Jefferson, letter, December 28, 1791, https://founders.archives.gov/documents/Jefferson/01-22-02-0428, accessed April 17, 2020.

52. Davis, "Impact of the French and Haitian Revolutions," Kindle, Location 455, 511, 515.

53. Charles Forsdick and Christian Høgsbjerg, *Toussaint Louverture: A Black Jacobin in the Age of Revolutions* (London: Pluto Press, 2017), 105.

54. Philippe Girard, "'Liberté, Égalité, Esclavage': French Revolutionary Ideals and the Failure of the Leclerc Expedition to Saint-Domingue," *French Colonial History*, 6 (2005): 56.

55. Gordon S. Brown, *Toussaint's Clause: The Founding Fathers and the Haitian Revolution* (Jackson: University of Mississippi Press, 2005), Kindle, 4.

56. Klooster, *Revolutions in the Atlantic World*, 118.

57. Girard, "'Liberté, Égalité, Esclavage,'" 66.

58. Girard, "'Liberté, Égalité, Esclavage,'" 66.

59. Daniel Rasmussen, *American Uprising: The Untold Story of America's Largest Slave Revolt* (New York: HarperCollins, 2011), Kindle, 45.

60. DelBanco, *The War Before the War*, 195.

61. Kellie Carter Jackson, *Force and Freedom: Black Abolitionists and the Politics of Violence* (Philadelphia: University of Pennsylvania Press, 2019), Kindle, Location 302.

62. Lepore, *These Truths*, 143.

63. Gonzalez, *Maroon Nation*, 58.

64. Maurice Jackson, "The Rise of Abolition," in *The Atlantic World: 1450–2000*, ed. Toyin Falola and Kevin D. Roberts (Bloomington: Indiana University Press, 2008), 229. Emphasis in the original.

65. Girard, "'Liberté, Égalité, Esclavage,'" 56–57.

66. Brown, *Toussaint's Clause*, 3–4.

67. Sara C. Fanning, "The Roots of Early Black Nationalism: Northern African Americans' Invocations of Haiti in the Early Nineteenth Century," in Jackson and Bacon, *African Americans and the Haitian Revolution*, 40.

68. Nathaniel Cutting to Thomas Jefferson, letter, March 1, 1792, https://founders.archives.gov/documents/Jefferson/01-23-02-0165, accessed April 17, 2020; Nathaniel Cutting to Thomas Jefferson, letter, December 28, 1791, https://founders.archives.gov/documents/Jefferson/01-22-02-0428, accessed April 17, 2020.

69. Merkel, "To See Oneself as a Target of a Justified Revolution," 2.

70. Lepore, *These Truths*, 144.

71. Simon P. Newman, "American Political Culture and the French and Haitian Revolutions: Nathaniel Cutting and the Jeffersonian Republicans," in Geggus, *The Impact of the Haitian Revolution in the Atlantic World*, Kindle, Location 2650.

72. Scott, "Afro-American Sailors and the International Communication Network," 31.

73. Brown, *Toussaint's Clause*, 99–100; Robert Alderson, "Charleston's Rumored Slave Revolt of 1793," in Geggus, *The Impact of the Haitian Revolution in the Atlantic World*, Kindle, Location 3019.

74. Alejandro de la Fuente and Ariela J. Gross, *Becoming Free, Becoming Black: Race, Freedom and Law in Cuba, Virginia, and Louisiana* (New York: Cambridge University Press, 2020), Kindle, 123.

75. Jack D. L. Holmes, "The Abortive Slave Revolt at Pointe Coupée, Louisiana," *Louisiana History: The Journal of the Louisiana Historical Association* 11, no. 4 (Autumn 1970): 344.

76. Scott, "Afro-American Sailors and the International Communication Network," 30.

77. Brown, *Toussaint's Clause*, 101.

78. Egerton, *Gabriel's Rebellion*, 47.

79. Newman, "American Political Culture and the French and Haitian Revolutions," Location 2633.

80. Jeffrey J. Crow, "Slave Rebelliousness and Social Conflict in North Carolina, 1775 to 1802," *William and Mary Quarterly*, 37, no. 1 (January 1980): 80, 93–94.

81. Newman, "American Political Culture and the French and Haitian Revolutions," Kindle, Location 2658.

82. Brown, *Toussaint's Clause*, 101.

83. James Madison to Edmund Pendleton, letter, March 25, 1792, https://founders.archives.gov/documents/Madison/01-14-02-0235, accessed April 17, 2020.

84. Jeffrey R. Kerr-Ritchie, "Rehearsal for War: Black Militias in the Atlantic World," *Slavery and Abolition* 26, no. 1 (April 2005): 9.

85. Cynthia L. Krom and Stephanie Krom, "The Whiskey Tax of 1791 and the Consequent Insurrection: 'A Wicked and Happy Tumult,'" *Accounting Historians Journal*, 40, no. 2 (December 2013): 91, 92, 94–95, 97, 100–101.

86. Krom and Krom, "The Whiskey Tax of 1791 and the Consequent Insurrection," 91, 92, 94–95, 97; Thomas P. Slaughter, *The Whiskey Rebellion: Frontier Epilogue to the American Revolution* (New York: Oxford University Press, 1986), 180.

87. Richard H. Kohn, "The Washington Administration's Decision to Crush the Whiskey Rebellion," *Journal of American History* 59, no. 3 (December 1972): 567–584; Krom and Krom, "The Whiskey Tax of 1791 and the Consequent Insurrection," 105, 106–109; Slaughter, *The Whiskey Rebellion*, 178–181.

88. Krom and Krom, "The Whiskey Tax of 1791 and the Consequent Insurrection," 109; Slaughter, *The Whiskey Rebellion*, 219, 220.

89. Egerton, *Gabriel's Rebellion*, 20, 30.

90. Aptheker, "American Negro Slave Revolts," 520.

91. Egerton, *Gabriel's Rebellion*, 102.

92. Egerton, *Gabriel's Rebellion*, 46.

93. John Ferling, *Adams vs. Jefferson: The Tumultuous Election of 1800* (New York: Oxford University Press, 2004), 181–182.

94. Egerton, *Gabriel's Rebellion*, 49. For white women as slave owners, see Stephanie E. Jones-Rogers, *They Were Her Property: White Women as Slave Owners in the American South* (New Haven, CT: Yale University Press, 2019).

95. James Thomson Callender to Thomas Jefferson, letter, September 13, 1800, https://founders.archives.gov/documents/Jefferson/01-32-02 -0090, accessed April 22, 2020.

96. Egerton, *Gabriel's Rebellion*, 50, 64, 68; Michael L. Nicholls, "'Holy Insurrection': Spinning the News of Gabriel's Conspiracy," *Journal of Southern History*, 78, no. 1 (February 2012): 45.

97. Egerton, *Gabriel's Rebellion*, 67–68.

98. Egerton, *Gabriel's Rebellion*, 71; Guild, *Black Laws of Virginia*, 70.

99. James Monroe to Thomas Jefferson, letter, September 9, 1800, https://founders.archives.gov/documents/Jefferson/01-32-02-0086, accessed April 22, 2020.

100. Douglas R. Egerton, "Gabriel's Conspiracy and the Election of 1800," *Journal of Southern History* 56, no. 2 (May 1990), 207.

101. Aptheker, "American Negro Slave Revolts," 519.

102. James Monroe to Thomas Jefferson, letter, September 15, 1800, https://founders.archives.gov/documents/Jefferson/01-32-02-0094, accessed April 22, 2020.

103. Egerton, *Gabriel's Rebellion*, 74–77.

104. Maurice Jackson and Jacqueline Bacon, "Fever and Fret: The Haitian Revolution and African American Responses," in Jackson and Bacon, *African Americans and the Haitian Revolution*, 13.

105. James Monroe to Thomas Jefferson, letter, September 15, 1800, https://founders.archives.gov/documents/Jefferson/01-32-02-0094, accessed April 22, 2020; Wish, "American Slave Insurrections Before 1861," 311.

106. Egerton, "Gabriel's Conspiracy and the Election of 1800," 208.

107. Nicholls, "'Holy Insurrection,'" 45.

108. Nicholls, "'Holy Insurrection,'" 50.

109. Nicholls, "'Holy Insurrection,'" 45.

110. James Monroe to Thomas Jefferson, letter, September 15, 1800, https://founders.archives.gov/documents/Jefferson/01-32-02-0094, accessed April 22, 2020.

111. Aptheker, "American Negro Slave Revolts," 521.

112. Aptheker, "American Negro Slave Revolts," 521.

113. Wish, "American Slave Insurrections Before 1861," 312.

114. Fuente and Gross, *Becoming Free, Becoming Black*, 185.

115. Holmes, "The Abortive Slave Revolt at Pointe Coupée, Louisiana, 1795," 347; James E. Wainwright, "William Claiborne and New Orleans's Battalion of Color, 1803–1815: Race and the Limits of Federal Power in the Early Republic," *Louisiana History: The Journal of the Louisiana Historical Association* 57, no. 1 (Winter 2016): 13.

116. Cottrol and Diamond, "The Second Amendment," 336–337n129.

117. Cottrol and Diamond, "The Second Amendment," 337.

118. Fuente and Gross, *Becoming Free, Becoming Black*, 185.

119. Ingersoll, "Free Blacks in a Slave Society," 198.

120. Fuente and Gross, *Becoming Free, Becoming Black*, 123.

121. Wainwright, "William Claiborne and New Orleans's Battalion of Color," 9, 15; Christina Proenza-Coles, *American Founders: How People of African Descent Established Freedom in the New World*, foreword by Edward L. Ayers (Montgomery, AL: New South Books, 2018), 90.

122. Wainwright, "William Claiborne and New Orleans's Battalion of Color," 15.

123. James H. Dormon, "The Persistent Specter: Slave Rebellion in Territorial Louisiana," *Louisiana History: The Journal of the Louisiana Historical Association* 18, no. 4 (Autumn 1977): 391–393; Eric Herschthal, "Slaves, Spaniards, and Subversion in Early Louisiana: The Persistent Fears of Black Revolt and Spanish Collusion in Territorial Louisiana, 1803–1812," *Journal of the Early Republic* 36, no. 2 (Summer 2016): 283–287, 289.

124. Wainwright, "William Claiborne and New Orleans's Battalion of Color," 14.

125. Fuente and Gross, *Becoming Free, Becoming Black*, 123–124; Wainwright, "William Claiborne and New Orleans's Battalion of Color," 9, 15, 18.

126. Herschthal, "Slaves, Spaniards, and Subversion in Early Louisiana," 294.

127. Fuente and Gross, *Becoming Free, Becoming Black*, 125; Wainwright, "William Claiborne and New Orleans's Battalion of Color," 23, 27.

128. U.S. Congress, House, *Executive Documents*, 41st Cong. 2d sess., 1869–1870, vol. 13, no. 265: 349.

129. Rasmussen, *American Uprising*, 50.

130. Rasmussen, *American Uprising*, 18, 108.

131. Manisha Sinha, *The Slave's Cause: A History of Abolition* (New Haven, CT: Yale University Press, 2016), 3.

132. Thomas Marshall Thompson, "National Newspaper and Legislative Reactions to Louisiana's Deslondes Slave Revolt of 1811," *Louisiana History: The Journal of the Louisiana Historical Association* 33, no. 1 (Winter 1992): 7.

133. Rasmussen, *American Uprising*, 89.

134. Rasmussen, *American Uprising*, 108–109.

135. Nathan A. Buman, "Historiographic Examinations of the 1811 Slave Insurrection," *Louisiana History: The Journal of the Louisiana Historical Association* 53, no. 3 (Summer 2012): 324.

136. Wainwright, "William Claiborne and New Orleans's Battalion of Color," 34.

137. Robert L. Paquette, "'A Horde of Brigands?' The Great Louisiana Slave Revolt of 1811 Reconsidered," *Historical Reflections* 33, no. 1 (Spring 2009): 74.

138. Buman, "Historiographic Examinations of the 1811 Slave Insurrection," 330.

139. Rasmussen, *American Uprising*, 17.

140. Paquette, "'A Horde of Brigands?,'" 74; Wainwright, "William Claiborne and New Orleans's Battalion of Color," 34; Pitcavage, "Ropes of Sand," 483.

141. Aline Helg, *Slave No More: Self-Liberation Before Abolitionism in the Americas* (Chapel Hill: University of North Carolina Press, 2019), 191.

142. Thompson, "National Newspaper and Legislative Reactions to Louisiana's Deslondes Slave Revolt of 1811," 16; Aptheker, "American Negro Slave Revolts," 523; Buman, "Historiographic Examinations of the 1811 Slave Insurrection," 325, 334.

143. Paquette, "'A Horde of Brigands?,'" 76, 77.

144. Aptheker, "American Negro Slave Revolts," 523.

145. Paquette, "'A Horde of Brigands?,'" 76, 77.

146. Rasmussen, *American Uprising*, 142.

147. Paquette, "'A Horde of Brigands?,'" 77–78.

148. Thompson, "National Newspaper and Legislative Reactions to Louisiana's Deslondes Slave Revolt of 1811," 9.

149. Wainwright, "William Claiborne and New Orleans's Battalion of Color," 35–36.

150. Kenneth R. Aslakson, *Making Race in the Courtroom: The Legal Construction of Three Races in Early New Orleans* (New York: NYU Press, 2014), 95; Louisiana State Constitution of 1812, Rutgers, https://njlaw.rutgers.edu/cgi-bin/constitution.cgi?page=1&document=LA003&zoom=120&state=LA&funct=1, accessed May 3, 2020.

151. Nathaniel Millett, "Slavery and the War of 1812," *Tennessee Historical Quarterly* 71, no. 3 (Fall 2012): 186.

152. Lorenzo J. Greene, "The Negro in the War of 1812 and the Civil War," *Negro History Bulletin* 14, no. 6 (March 1951): 133; Pitcavage, "Ropes of Sand," 482.

153. Millett, "Slavery and the War of 1812," 196.

154. C. Edward Skeen, *Citizen Soldiers in the War of 1812* (Lexington: University Press of Kentucky, 1999), 39; Greene, "The Negro in the War of 1812 and the Civil War," 133.

155. Nicholas J. Johnson, David B. Kopel, George A. Mocsary, and Michael P. O'Shea, *Firearms Law and the Second Amendment: Regulation, Rights, and Policy* (New York: Wolters Kluwer Law and Business, 2012), 250.

156. Robert L. Kerby, "The Militia System and the State Militias in the War of 1812," *Indiana Magazine of History* 73, no. 2 (June 1977): 103, 105.

157. Wainwright, "William Claiborne and New Orleans's Battalion of Color," 38.

158. Millett, "Slavery and the War of 1812," 187.

159. Wainwright, "William Claiborne and New Orleans's Battalion of Color," 36.

160. Aslakson, *Making Race in the Courtroom*, 95–96; Gene Allen Smith, "'Sons of Freedom': African Americans Fighting the War of 1812," *Tennessee Historical Quarterly* 71, no. 3 (Fall 2012): 215.

161. Aslakson, *Making Race in the Courtroom*, 96.

162. Wainwright, "William Claiborne and New Orleans's Battalion of Color," 40.

163. Mary F. Berry, review of "Negro Troops of Antebellum Louisiana: A History of the Battalion of Free Men of Color," by Roland C. McConnell, in *Journal of American History* 55, no. 3 (December 1968): 654; Wainwright, "William Claiborne and New Orleans's Battalion of Color, 1803–1815," 38.

164. Quintard Taylor, *From Timbuktu to Katrina: Sources in African-American History*, Vol. 1 (Boston, MA: Thomson Wadsworth, 2008), 77; U.S. Congress, House, *Executive Documents*, 41st Cong. 2d sess., 1869–1870, vol. 13, no. 265, 350.

165. Aslakson, *Making Race in the Courtroom*, 96.

166. Greene, "The Negro in the War of 1812 and the Civil War," 133; Proenza-Coles, *American Founders*, 98.

167. Wainwright, "William Claiborne and New Orleans's Battalion of Color," 13.

168. Waldman, *The Second Amendment*, 66.

169. Fuente and Gross, *Becoming Free: Becoming Black*, 184–185. There were a number of private Black militias; see Kerr-Ritchie, "Rehearsal for War."

170. Fuente and Gross, *Becoming Free: Becoming Black*, 185.

171. Cottrol and Diamond, "The Second Amendment," 338n144.

172. Jones, *Birthright Citizens*, 107.

173. Johnson, Kopel, Mocsary, and O'Shea, *Firearms Law and the Second Amendment*, 277–278.

174. Cottrol and Diamond, "The Second Amendment," 336.

175. Johnson, Kopel, Mocsary, and O'Shea, *Firearms Law and the Second Amendment*, 277–278.

176. Jones, *Birthright Citizens*, 104–106; Steve Ekwall, "The Racist Origins of US Gun Control Laws Designed to Disarm Slaves, Freedmen, and African-Americans," https://www.sedgwickcounty.org/media/29093/the-racist-origins-of-us-gun-control.pdf, accessed April 24, 2020.

177. W. E. Burghardt Du Bois, *The Souls of Black Folk*, introductions by Nathan Hare and Alvin Poussaint (New York: Signet Classic, 1969, 1982), 43.

178. Steven Lubet, *Fugitive Justice: Runaways, Rescuers, and Slavery on Trial* (Cambridge, MA: Harvard University Press, 2010), 39.

179. Walker, *Walker's Appeal*, 27.

180. Aptheker, "American Negro Slave Revolts," 532.

181. Freeman, *The Field of Blood*.

182. Nicole Etcheson, *Bleeding Kansas: Contested Liberty in the Civil War Era* (Lawrence: University of Kansas Press, 2004).

183. Lubet, *Fugitive Justice*, 37; David M. Pletcher, *The Diplomacy of Annexation: Texas, Oregon, and the Mexican War* (Columbia: University of Missouri Press, 1973); Amy S. Greenberg, *A Wicked War: Polk, Clay, Lincoln, and the 1846 U.S. Invasion of Mexico* (New York: Alfred Knopf, 2012).

184. Nicholas Johnson, *Negroes and the Gun: The Black Tradition of Arms* (Amherst, NY: Prometheus Books, 2014), 39.

185. Dunbar, *Never Caught*, 110–152.

186. "*Prigg v. Pennsylvania*," Oyez, https://www.oyez.org/cases/1789-1850 /41us539, accessed May 7, 2020; DelBanco, *The War Before the War*, 179–180.

187. Johnson, *Negroes and the Gun*, 50.

188. David W. Blight, *Frederick Douglass: Prophet of Freedom* (New York: Simon and Schuster, 2018), 205.

189. Leslie M. Alexander, *African or American? Black Identity and Political Activism in New York City, 1784–1861* (Urbana: University of Illinois Press, 2008); Leslie M. Harris, *In the Shadow of Slavery: African Americans in New York City, 1626–1863* (Chicago: University of Chicago Press, 2003); DelBanco, *The War Before the War*, 179.

190. Jackson, *Force and Freedom*, Location, 988.

191. Jonathan Daniel Wells, *Blind No More: African American Resistance, Free-Soil Politics, and the Coming of the Civil War* (Athens: University of Georgia Press, 2019), 43–70.

192. Johnson, *Negroes and the Gun*, 50.

193. Jackson, *Force and Freedom*, Location, 153, 1033, 1239.

194. Blight, *Frederick Douglass*, 245.

195. Johnson, *Negroes and the Gun*, 37.

196. Johnson, *Negroes and the Gun*, 62.

197. William Parker, "The Freedman's Story: An Escaped Slave Tells His Story—Including His Account of His Violent Showdown with Slave-Catchers in Pennsylvania," *The Atlantic*, March 1866, https://www.the atlantic.com/magazine/archive/1866/03/the-freedmans-story-continued

/308738, accessed April 29, 2020; Jones, *Birthright Citizenship*, 103; DelBanco, *The War Before the War*, 34.

198. Jackson, *Force and Freedom*, Location, 1075, 1081, 1088; Parker, "The Freedman's Story."

199. Johnson, *Negroes and the Gun*, 64; Jackson, *Force and Freedom*, Location, 1088; Parker, "The Freedman's Story."

200. Blight, *Frederick Douglass*, 244.

201. Johnson, *Negroes and the Gun*, 64; Jackson, *Force and Freedom*, 1106.

202. James J. Robbins, *Report of the Trial of Castner Hanway for Treason, in the Resistance of the Execution of the Fugitive Slave Law of September, 1850* (Philadelphia: King and Baird, 1852), found in "Christiana Treason Trial (1851)," Digital Bookshelf: Records and Court Cases, www.housedivided.dickinson.edu/ugrr/case_1851.htm, accessed May 6, 2020.

203. "Christiana Treason Trial (1851)."

204. "Christiana Treason Trial (1851)."

205. Johnson, *Negroes and the Gun*, 64–65; "Christiana Treason Trial (1851)."

206. Johnson, *Negroes and the Gun*, 61.

207. Litwack, "The Federal Government and the Free Negro, 1790–1860," 274.

208. Jackson, *Force and Freedom*, Location 600, 605, 611; Richard B. Kielbowicz, "The Law and Mob Law in Attacks on Antislavery Newspapers, 1833–1860," *Law and History Review* 24, no. 3 (Fall 2006): 559.

209. Cottrol and Diamond, "The Second Amendment," 342; C. G. Woodson, "The Negroes of Cincinnati Prior to the Civil War," *Journal of Negro History* 1, no. 1 (January 1916): 14–15.

210. Fuente and Gross, *Becoming Black, Becoming Free*, 185.

211. Cottrol and Diamond, "The Second Amendment," 340–342; Johnson, *Negroes and the Gun*, 74; Jackson, *Force and Freedom*, Location 558.

212. Stephen Chambers, "Our Hidden History: Race Riots Gave Birth to Providence Police," *Providence Journal*, July 18, 2020 https://www .providencejournal.com/story/opinion/2020/07/18/our-hidden-hist ory-race-riots-gave-birth-to-providence-police/42593079, accessed December 13, 2020.

213. Johnson, *Negroes and the Gun*, 35.

214. "The Trial of Celia, a Slave (1855): Trial Testimony," http://law2.umkc .edu/faculty/projects/ftrials/celia/celiaaccount.html, accessed May 8, 2020.

215. Johnson, Kopel, Mocsary, and O'Shea, *Firearms Law and the Second Amendment Regulations, Rights, and Policy*, 252, 274–276.

216. Henry Louis Gates Jr. and Jennifer Burton, *Call and Response: Key Debates in African American Studies* (New York: W. W. Norton and Co., 2011), 86–130.

217. Litwack, "The Federal Government and the Free Negro, 1790–1860," 262, 272.

218. Jones, *Birthright Citizens*, 1, 3, 11.

219. Kat Eschner, "President James Buchanan Directly Influenced the Outcome of the Dred Scott Decision," *Smithsonian Magazine*, March 6, 2017, https://www.smithsonianmag.com/smart-news/president-james -buchanan-directly-influenced-outcome-dred-scott-decision-180962329, accessed May 8, 2020.

220. *Dred Scott v. Sandford*, 60 U.S. 393 (1857), https://www.law.cornell.edu /supremecourt/text/60/393, accessed May 9, 2020.

221. Jackson, *Force and Freedom*, Location, 1954.

222. *Dred Scott v. Sandford*, 60 U.S. 393 (1857); Wayne D. Moore, *Constitutional Rights and Powers of the People* (Princeton, NJ: Princeton University Press, 1996), 13–36.

223. Statistics on Civil War and Medicine, Department of History, Ohio State University, https://ehistory.osu.edu/exhibitions/cwsurgeon/cw surgeon/statistics, accessed May 9, 2020.

224. Jackson, *Force and Freedom*, Location, 252.

CHAPTER THREE: THE RIGHT TO KILL NEGROES

1.  "Data Analysis: African Americans on the Eve of the Civil War," Table 1, https://www.bowdoin.edu/~prael/lesson/tables.htm, accessed October 25, 2020.

2.  Ron Chernow, *Grant* (New York: Penguin Press, 2017), 841.

3.  Heather Cox Richardson, *How the South Won the Civil War: Oligarchy, Democracy, and the Continuing Fight for the Soul of America* (New York: Oxford University Press, 2020); Eric Foner, *The Second Founding: How the Civil War and Reconstruction Remade the Constitution* (New York: W.W. Norton, 2019), 24; Paul D. Escott, *The Worst Passions of Human Nature: White Supremacy in the Civil War North* (Charlottesville: University of Virginia Press, 2020), 124–142.

4.  Carol Anderson, *White Rage: The Unspoken Truth of Our Racial Divide* (New York: Bloomsbury, 2016, 2017), 15–18; Louisiana Democratic Platform, October 2, 1865, in Walter Lynwood Fleming, ed., *Documentary History of Reconstruction*, Vol. 1 (Cleveland, OH: A. H. Clark, 1906), 229.

5.  Carl Schurz, *Report on the Condition of the South* (New York: Arno Press, 1969, 2012), Kindle, 153; Annette Gordon-Reed, *Andrew Johnson*, American Presidents series, ed. Arthur M. Schlesinger Jr. and Sean Wilentz (New York: Times Books, 2011), 118.

6.  W. E. B. Du Bois, *Black Reconstruction in America: The Oxford W. E. B. Du Bois*, ed. Henry Louis Gates, vol. 6, *Black Reconstruction in America* (New York: Oxford University Press, 2016), Kindle, Location 4641.

7.  Equal Justice Initiative, "Reconstruction in America: Racial Violence After the Civil War, 1865–1876," https://eji.org/wp-content/uploads/2020/07/reconstruction-in-america-report.pdf, accessed October 28, 2020.

8.  Nicholas Johnson, *Negroes and the Gun: The Black Tradition of Arms* (Amherst, NY: Prometheus Books, 2014), 79.

9.  Du Bois, *Black Reconstruction in America*, Kindle, Location 4761, 4766, 4767, 4772.

10.  Nicholas J. Johnson, David B. Kopel, George A. Mocsary, and Michael P. O'Shea, *Firearms Law and the Second Amendment: Regulation, Rights, and Policy* (New York: Wolters Kluwer Law and Business, 2012), 291.

11.  Johnson, *Negroes and the Gun*, 80–82.

12.  Abraham Lincoln, "Gettysburg Address," November 19, 1863, Bliss Copy, http://www.abrahamlincolnonline.org/lincoln/speeches/gettysb urg.htm, accessed November 1, 2020.

13.  Richardson, *How the South Won the Civil War*.

14.  Johnson, *Negroes and the Gun*, 80; Du Bois, *Black Reconstruction in America*, Kindle, Location 16230.

15.  Johnson, *Negroes and the Gun*, 79–80.

16.  Equal Justice Initiative, "Reconstruction in America," 13.

17.  Andrew K. Diemer, *The Politics of Black Citizenship: Free African Americans in the Mid-Atlantic Borderland, 1817–1863* (Athens: University of Georgia Press, 2016), 186.

18.  Bruce Catton, *The Army of the Potomac: Glory Road* (New York: Doubleday, 1952), 212; David W. Blight, *Frederick Douglass: Prophet of Freedom* (New York: Simon and Schuster, 2018), 391–397; Laura F.

Edwards, *A Legal History of the Civil War and Reconstruction: A Nation of Rights* (New York: Cambridge University Press, 2015), Kindle, 84.

19. Le'Trice D. Donaldson, *Duty Beyond the Battlefield: African American Soldiers Fight for Racial Uplift, Citizenship, and Manhood, 1870–1920* (Carbondale: Southern Illinois University Press, 2020), 2.

20. Andrew F. Lang, "Republicanism, Race, and Reconstruction: The Ethos of Military Occupation in Civil War America," *Journal of the Civil War Era* 4, no. 4 (December 2014): 566, 572–573.

21. Adam Fairclough, *The Revolution That Failed: Reconstruction in Natchitoches* (Gainesville: University Press of Florida, 2018), 55.

22. Lang, "Republicanism, Race, and Reconstruction," 565–566. Emphasis in the original.

23. Aaron Astor, "'I Wanted a Gun': Black Soldiers and White Violence in Civil War and Postwar Kentucky and Missouri," in *The Great Task Remaining Before Us: Reconstruction as America's Continuing Civil War*, ed. Paul A. Cimbala and Randall M. Miller (New York: Fordham University Press, 2010), 46.

24. Lang, "Republicanism, Race, and Reconstruction," 574.

25. Bruce E. Baker, *This Mob Will Surely Take My Life: Lynchings in the Carolinas, 1871–1947* (London: Continuum, 2008), 46.

26. Fairclough, *The Revolution That Failed*, 55.

27. Richard C. Cortner, *A Mob Intent on Death: The NAACP and the Arkansas Riot Cases* (Middletown, CT: Wesleyan University Press, 1988), 18.

28. Johnson, *Negroes and the Gun*, 79.

29. Charles Lane, *The Day Freedom Died: The Colfax Massacre, the Supreme Court, and the Betrayal of Reconstruction* (New York: Henry Holt, 2008), Kindle, 104.

30. Lang, "Republicanism, Race, and Reconstruction," 575.

31. Johnson, *Negroes and the Gun*, 81–82.

32. Kidada E. Williams, *They Left Great Marks on Me: African American Testimonies of Racial Violence from Emancipation to World War I* (New York: New York University Press, 2012), 43.

33. Fairclough, *The Revolution That Failed*, 42, 46–48.

34. Foner, *The Second Founding*, 86.

35. Johnson, *Negroes and the Gun*, 78–79.

36. Laura F. Edwards, *A Legal History of the Civil War and Reconstruction: A Nation of Rights* (New York: Cambridge University Press, 2015), Kindle, 88.

37. Blight, *Frederick Douglass*, 473–475.

38. Lang, "Republicanism, Race, and Reconstruction," 575–576.

39. "America's Historical Documents: The 13th Amendment to the U.S. Constitution: Abolition of Slavery," National Archives, https://www .archives.gov/historical-docs/13th-amendment, accessed November 1, 2020.

40. Foner, *The Second Founding*, 41; Du Bois, *Black Reconstruction in America*, Location 4533, 4535.

41. Blight, *Frederick Douglass*, 473.

42. Foner, *The Second Founding*, 74; Legal Information Institute, "Incorporation Doctrine," https://www.law.cornell.edu/wex/incorpora tion_doctrine, accessed October 4, 2020.

43. Robert Whitaker, *On the Laps of Gods: The Red Summer of 1919 and the Struggle for Justice That Remade a Nation* (New York: Crown, 2008), Kindle, 25.

44. Johnson, *Negroes and the Gun*, 82.

45. Donald E. Reynolds, "The New Orleans Riot of 1866, Reconsidered," *Louisiana History: The Journal of the Louisiana Historical Association* 5, no. 1 (Winter 1964): 5–27; Bobby L. Lovett, "Memphis Riots: White Reaction to Blacks in Memphis, May 1865–July 1866," *Tennessee Historical Quarterly* 38, no. 1 (Spring 1979): 9–33; Lee W. Formwalt, "The Camilla Massacre of 1868: Racial Violence as Political Propaganda," *Georgia Historical Quarterly* 71, no. 3 (Fall 1987): 399–426; Lorraine Boissoneault, "The Deadliest Massacre in Reconstruction-Era Louisiana Happened 150 Years Ago: In September 1868, Southern White Democrats Hunted Down Around 200 African-Americans in an Effort to Suppress Voter Turnout," *SmithsonianMag.com*, September 28, 2018, https://www.smithsonianmag.com/history/story-deadliest-massacre-reconstruction-era-louisiana-180970420, accessed November 14, 2020.

46. Lane, *The Day Freedom Died*, Kindle, 18–19.

47. Williams, *They Left Great Marks on Me*, Kindle, 25–26.

48. Baker, *This Mob Will Surely Take My Life*, 9–41.

49. Eric Foner, *Reconstruction: America's Unfinished Revolution, 1863–77*, updated ed. (New York: HarperCollins, 2014), Kindle, 577.

50. Foner, *Reconstruction*, 739–740.

51. Foner, *Reconstruction*, 738–739.

52. Lang, "Republicanism, Race, and Reconstruction," 568; Baker, *This Mob Will Surely Take My Life*, 15.

53. Foner, *Reconstruction*, 587.

54. Foner, *Reconstruction*, 739.

55. Foner, *Reconstruction*, 725.

56. LeeAnna Keith, *The Colfax Massacre: The Untold Story of Black Power, White Terror, and the Death of Reconstruction* (New York: Oxford University Press, 2008), Kindle, Location 109.

57. Lane, *The Day Freedom Died*, 91.

58. Lane, *The Day Freedom Died*, 9, 93–94.

59. Chernow, *Grant*, 759; Lane, *The Day Freedom Died*, 20.

60. A. Leon Higginbotham Jr., *Shades of Freedom: Racial Politics and Presumptions of the American Legal Process*, vol. 2 (New York: Oxford University Press, 1996), 88; Chernow, *Grant*, 759.

61. *United States v. Cruikshank*, 92 U.S. 542 (1875).

62. Chernow, *Grant*, 759.

63. Foner, *Reconstruction*, 751–752.

64. Foner, *Reconstruction*, 751.

65. Foner, *Reconstruction*, 752; Chernow, *Grant*, 840.

66. Dorothy Sterling, ed., *The Trouble They Seen: The Story of Reconstruction in the Words of African Americans* (Cambridge, MA: Da Capo Press, 1994), 463–464.

67. Chernow, *Grant*, 841.

68. Williams, *They Left Great Marks on Me*, 62–63, 89; Senate Committee to Inquire into Alleged Frauds and Violence in the Elections of 1878 with the Testimony and Documentary Evidence, 45th Cong., 3d sess., 1879, S. Rep. 855, 411–429; Lee W. Formwalt, "The Camilla Massacre of 1868: Racial Violence as Political Propaganda," *Georgia Historical Quarterly* 71, no. 3 (Fall 1987): 399–426.

69. Whitaker, *On the Laps of Gods*, 27.

70. Anderson, *White Rage*, 32–38.

71. Blight, *Frederick Douglass*, 710.

72. Nan Elizabeth Woodruff, *American Congo: The African American Freedom Struggle in the Delta* (Cambridge, MA: Harvard University Press, 2003, 2020), Kindle, Location 84.

73. Senate Committee to Inquire into Alleged Frauds and Violence in the Elections of 1878 with the Testimony and Documentary Evidence, 45th Cong., 3d sess., 1879, S. Rep. 855, 423.

74. Woodruff, *American Congo*, Location 74, 1511.

75. Williams, *They Left Great Marks on Me*, 115–116.

76. Williams, *They Left Great Marks on Me*, 96.

77. Whitaker, *On the Laps of Gods*, 36.

78. Philip Dray, *At the Hands of Persons Unknown: The Lynching of Black America* (New York: Random House, 2002); Patrick Phillips, *Blood at the Root: A Racial Cleansing in America* (New York: W. W. Norton, 2016), 1–65; Equal Justice Initiative, "Lynching in America: Confronting the Legacy of Racial Terror" (2015), 4–6, https://lynchinginamerica.eji .org/report, accessed October 4, 2020.

79. Higginbotham, *Shades of Freedom*, 141.

80. Melissa N. Stein, *Measuring Manhood: Race and the Science of Masculinity, 1830–1934* (Minneapolis: University of Minnesota Press, 2015), 251–275; *Ethnic Notions*, dir. Marlon Riggs, 56 minutes, California Newsreel, 1987; Kali N. Gross, *Colored Amazons: Crime, Violence, and Black Women in the City of Brotherly Love, 1880–1910* (Durham, NC: Duke University Press, 2006); Khalil Gibran Muhammad, *The Condemnation of Blackness: Race, Crime, and the Making of Modern Urban America* (Cambridge, MA: Harvard University Press, 2010); Talitha L. LeFlouria, *Chained in Silence: Black Women and Convict Labor in the New South* (Chapel Hill: University of North Carolina Press, 2015); Dray, *At the Hands of Persons Unknown*, 5.

81. James W. Loewen, *Sundown Towns: A Hidden Dimension of American Racism* (New York: New Press, 2005), Kindle, 327.

82. David Fort Godshalk, *Veiled Visions: The 1906 Atlanta Race Riot and the Reshaping of American Race Relations* (Chapel Hill: University of North Carolina Press, 2005), Kindle, 39.

83.   Francis James Grimké, *The Atlanta Riot: 1906* (Washington, DC: unknown publisher, 1906, 2020), Kindle, Location 126; Gregory Mixon and Clifford Kuhn, "Atlanta Race Riot of 1906," *New Georgia Encyclopedia*, https://www.georgiaencyclopedia.org/articles/history-arc haeology/atlanta-race-riot-1906, accessed November 9, 2020; Mark Bauerlein, *Negrophobia: A Race Riot in Atlanta, 1906* (San Francisco: Encounter Books, 2001), 92.

84.   Godshalk, *Veiled Visions*, 36; Bauerlein, *Negrophobia*, 86.

85.   Bauerlein, *Negrophobia*, 124.

86.   Godshalk, *Veiled Visions*, 38.

87.   Bauerlein, *Negrophobia*, 93–132.

88.   Godshalk, *Veiled Visions*, 88.

89.   Godshalk, *Veiled Visions*, 85.

90.   Godshalk, *Veiled Visions*, 90, 96, 99, 100; Bauerlein, *Negrophobia*, 139.

91.   Grimké, *The Atlanta Riot*, Location 201.

92.   Godshalk, *Veiled Visions*, 99, 100.

93.   Godshalk, *Veiled Visions*, 102.

94.   Godshalk, *Veiled Visions*, 102; Jay Winston Driskell Jr., *Schooling Jim Crow: The Fight for Atlanta's Booker T. Washington High School and the Roots of Black Protest Politics* (Charlottesville: University of Virginia Press, 2014), 88.

95.   Grimké, *The Atlanta Riot*, Location 206, 209, 210, 214.

96.   Driskell, *Schooling Jim Crow*, 88; Godshalk, *Veiled Visions*, 102.

97.   Grimké, *The Atlanta Riot*, Location 209.

98.   Godshalk, *Veiled Visions*, 102.

99.   Arthur W. Rowell to his mother, letter, [September 24, 1906], Box 1, File 3, Arthur W. Rowell Papers, Stuart A. Rose Manuscript, Archives, and Rare Book Library, Emory University.

100.  Godshalk, *Veiled Visions*, 103.

101.  Godshalk, *Veiled Visions*, 103.

102.  Godshalk, *Veiled Visions*, 99, 104.

103.  Grimké, *The Atlanta Riot*, Location 116.

104.  Godshalk, *Veiled Visions*, 107.

105.  Godshalk, *Veiled Visions*, 98, 107.

106.  Louis R. Harlan, *Booker T. Washington: The Wizard of Tuskegee, 1901–1915*, vol. 2 (New York: Oxford Paperbacks, 2020), Kindle, Location 4188, 4193.

107.  Godshalk, *Veiled Visions*, 138.

108.  William Baker, *The Brownsville Texas Incident of 196: The True and Tragic Story of a Black Battalion's Wrongful Disgrace and Ultimate Redemption* (Cranberry Township, PA: Red Engine Press, 2020), Kindle, Location 412, 429, 446.

109.  Donaldson, *Duty Beyond the Battlefield*, 151.

110.  Edmund Morris, *Theodore Rex* (New York: Modern Library, 2002), Kindle, 453–454.

111.  Harlan, *Booker T. Washington*, Location 4328, 4330; Morris, *Theodore Rex*, 453.

112.  Morris, *Theodore Rex*, 454.

113.  Harlan, *Booker T. Washington*, Location 4328, 4330; Morris, *Theodore Rex*, 454; Donaldson, *Duty Beyond the Battlefield*, 72.

114.  Morris, *Theodore Rex*, 454.

115. Morris, *Theodore Rex*, 454, 455, 464.

116. Morris, *Theodore Rex*, 464–465.

117. Harlan, *Booker T. Washington*, Location 4333, 4338, 4339, 4343, 4347; Baker, *The Brownsville Texas Incident of 1906*, Location 311.

118. Harlan, *Booker T. Washington*, Location 4376, 4378, 4404, 4720.

119. Morris, *Theodore Rex*, 511; Sam Roberts, "William Baker, Who Righted a 1906 Army Racial Wrong, Dies at 86," *New York Times*, October 8, 2018.

120. Harlan, *Booker T. Washington*, Location 4404, 4425, 4428.

121. The Austro-Hungarian, Russian, German, and Ottoman Empires collapsed because of World War I.

122. Drew Gilpin Faust, *This Republic of Suffering: Death and the American Civil War* (New York: Vintage Books, 2009).

123. "The Battle of the Somme," History.com, November 4, 2019, https://www.history.com/topics/world-war-i/battle-of-the-somme, accessed November 15, 2020; Thomas D. Morgan, "The Legacy of Verdun," *Army History*, no. 46 (Fall 1998–Winter 1999): 23–26.

124. "President Woodrow Wilson's Fourteen Points," January 8, 1918, Avalon Project, https://avalon.law.yale.edu/20th_century/wilson14.asp, accessed November 15, 2020.

125. Lloyd E. Ambrosius, "Making the World Safe for Democracy," in *Woodrow Wilson and American Internationalism*, Cambridge Studies in US Foreign Relations (Cambridge: Cambridge University Press, 2017), 43–62.

126. Ross Kennedy, "'A Net of Intrigue and Selfish Rivalry': Woodrow Wilson and Power Politics During World War I," *Proceedings of the American Philosophical Society* 159, no. 2 (June 2015): 156–157.

127. James Mennell, "African-Americans and the Selective Service Act of 1917," *Journal of Negro History* 84, no. 3 (Summer 1999): 275–278.

128. Douglas S. Massey, "The Past and Future of American Civil Rights," *Daedalus* 140, no. 2 (Spring 2011): 40; Mennell, "African-Americans and the Selective Service Act of 1917," 276.

129. Whitaker, *On the Laps of Gods*, 40.

130. Mennell, "African-Americans and the Selective Service Act of 1917," 283.

131. Robert V. Haynes, "The Houston Mutiny and Riot of 1917," *Southwestern Historical Quarterly* 76, no. 4 (April 1973): 420–421; James M. SoRelle, "The 'Waco Horror': The Lynching of Jesse Washington," *Southwestern Historical Quarterly* 86, no. 4 (April 1983): 517–536.

132. Haynes, "The Houston Mutiny and Riot of 1917," 423–427.

133. Haynes, "The Houston Mutiny and Riot of 1917," 421.

134. Donaldson, *Duty Beyond the Battlefield*, 71–72; Haynes, "The Houston Mutiny and Riot of 1917," 428.

135. Donaldson, *Duty Beyond the Battlefield*, 72; Haynes, "The Houston Mutiny and Riot of 1917," 429.

136. Donaldson, *Duty Beyond the Battlefield*, 73–74; Theodore Kornweibel Jr., *"Investigate Everything": Federal Efforts to Compel Black Loyalty During World War I* (Bloomington: University of Indiana Press, 2002), 171–174.

137. Donaldson, *Duty Beyond the Battlefield*, 4.

138. Whitaker, *On the Laps of Gods*, 40; Ronald R. Krebs, *Fighting for Rights: Military Service and the Politics of Citizenship* (Ithaca, NY: Cornell University Press, 2006), 126.

139. Krebs, *Fighting for Rights*, 124.

140. Peter N. Nelson, *A More Unbending Battle: The Harlem Hellfighters' Struggle for Freedom in WWI and Equality at Home* (New York: Basic Civitas, 2009).

141. Cameron McWhirter, *Red Summer: The Summer of 1919 and the Awakening of Black America* (New York: Henry Holt, 2011), Kindle, 56.

142. Donaldson, *Duty Beyond the Battlefield*, 154.

143. McWhirter, *Red Summer*, 51.

144. Whitaker, *On the Laps of Gods*, 45–46.

145. McWhirter, *Red Summer*, 13.

146. McWhirter, *Red Summer*, 98–104.

147. Whitaker, *On the Laps of Gods*, 53.

148. Claire Hartfield, *A Few Red Drops: The Chicago Race Riot of 1919* (Boston: Clarion Books, Houghton Mifflin Harcourt, 2018), Kindle, 23.

149. McWhirter, *Red Summer*, 173–180.

150. Whitaker, *On the Laps of Gods*, 3.

151. Pete Daniel, *The Shadow of Slavery: Peonage in the South, 1901–1969* (Urbana: University of Illinois Press, 1972), 1–42.

152. Ida B. Wells-Barnett, *The Arkansas Race Riot* (Chicago: Aquila, 1920), Kindle, Location 186.

153. Whitaker, *On the Laps of Gods*, 8–9.

154. Whitaker, *On the Laps of Gods*, 14.

155. Cortner, *A Mob Intent on Death*, 7.

156. Whitaker, *On the Laps of Gods*, 87.

157. Cortner, *A Mob Intent on Death*, 8.

158. Cortner, *A Mob Intent on Death*, 8.

159. Wells-Barnett, *The Arkansas Race Riot*, Location 214.

160. Griff Stockley, Brian K. Mitchell, and Guy Lancaster, *Blood in Their Eyes: The Elaine Massacre of 1919* (Fayetteville: University of Arkansas, 2020), Kindle, 98.

161. Woodruff, *American Congo*, Location 1219, 1225–1226.

162. Wells-Barnett, *The Arkansas Race Riot*, Location 211–217; Woodruff, *American Congo*, Location 1230; Whitaker, *On the Laps of Gods*, 91, 94; *Moore vs. the State of Arkansas* (1919), no. 955, transcript of record, filed May 24, 1920, 93, https://www.google.com/books/edition/Records_and_Briefs_of_the_United_States/Wuvx1PMXOIQC?q=%22out+unarmed,+holding+up+their+hands+and+some+of+them+running+and+trying%22+to+get+away%C2%A0.%C2%A0.%C2%A0.+They+were+shot+down+and+killed.&gbpv=1&bsq=%22out%20unarmed,%20holding%20up%20their%20hands%20and%20some%20of%20them%20running%20and%20trying%22#f=false, accessed February 15, 2021

163. Woodruff, *American Congo*, Location 1219; Whitaker, *On the Laps of Gods*, 102, 104; Stockley, Mitchell, and Lancaster, *Blood in Their Eyes*, Kindle, 11–12; Cortner, *A Mob Intent on Death*, 11.

164. Whitaker, *On the Laps of Gods*, 111–112.

165. Whitaker, *On the Laps of Gods*, 118.

166. Stockley, Mitchell, and Lancaster, *Blood in Their Eyes*, 12; Woodruff, *American Congo*, Location 1467; Whitaker, *On the Laps of Gods*, 126.

167. Stockley, Mitchell, and Lancaster, *Blood in Their Eyes*, 97.

168. Stockley, Mitchell, and Lancaster, *Blood in Their Eyes*, 97; Wells-Barnett, *The Arkansas Race Riot*, Location 87–88, 282, 292–293, 335.

169. Cortner, *A Mob Intent on Death*, 16–18.

170. Whitaker, *On the Laps of Gods*, 121; Woodruff, *American Congo*, Location 1537–1538; Wells-Barnett, *The Arkansas Race Riot*, Location

1212. The NAACP, through years of litigation, secured the release of the men convicted to death row and to prison terms.

CHAPTER FOUR: HOW CAN I BE UNARMED WHEN MY BLACKNESS IS THE WEAPON THAT YOU FEAR?

1.   Joshua Bloom and Waldo E. Martin, *Black Against Empire: The History and Politics of the Black Panther Party* (Berkeley: University of California Press, 2016), Kindle, Location 1027.

2.   [Oakland Police Department], "The Black Panther Movement," Mulford Act Files, firearmspolicy.org/resources, accessed October 7, 2020.

3.   "Solons Assail Armed Band Entering Capitol," *Sacramento Bee*, May 3, 1967.

4.   Thomas J. Sugrue, *Sweet Land of Liberty: The Forgotten Struggle for Civil Rights in the North* (New York: Random House, 2008), 133.

5.   Scott Kurashige, *The Shifting Grounds of Race: Black and Japanese Americans in the Making of Multiethnic Los Angeles* (Princeton, NJ: Princeton University Press, 2008), 270.

6.   Bloom and Martin, *Black Against Empire*, Location 668.

7.   Bloom and Martin, *Black Against Empire*, Location 668.

8.   Bloom and Martin, *Black Against Empire*, Location 673, 676.

9.   Robert O. Self, *American Babylon: Race and the Struggle for Postwar Oakland* (Princeton, NJ: Princeton University Press, 2003), 78.

10.  Donna Jean Murch, *Living for the City: Migration, Education, and the Rise of the Black Panther Party in Oakland, California* (Chapel Hill: University of North Carolina Press, 2010), Kindle, 38–39.

11.  Bloom and Martin, *Black Against Empire*, Location 1116.

12.  Bloom and Martin, *Black Against Empire*, Location 1027, 1031, 1039.

13. "Loving Your Enemies, Sermon Delivered at the Detroit Council of Churches' Noon Lenten Services," March 7, 1961, Martin Luther King Jr. Research and Education Institute, Stanford University, https://kinginsti tute.stanford.edu/king-papers/documents/loving-your-enemies-sermon -delivered-detroit-council-churches-noon-lenten, accessed January 2, 2021.

14. Bloom and Martin, *Black Against Empire*, Location 1032–1060; Adam Winkler, *Gun Fight: The Battle Over the Right to Bear Arms in America* (New York: W. W. Norton, 2011, 2013), 236–237.

15. Bobby Seale, *Seize the Time: The Story of the Black Panther Party and Huey P. Newton* (Baltimore, MD: Black Classic Press, 1991), 91.

16. Bloom and Martin, *Black Against Empire*, Location 1118–1140.

17. Bloom and Martin, *Black Against Empire*, Location 1259.

18. Black Panther Party for Self Defense: What We Want What We Believe, Mulford Act Files, firearmspolicy.org/resources, accessed October 7, 2020. Emphasis in the original.

19. Black Panther Party for Self Defense: What We Want What We Believe, Mulford Act Files, firearmspolicy.org/resources, accessed October 7, 2020. Emphasis in the original.

20. Lance Hill, *The Deacons for Defense: Armed Resistance and the Civil Rights Movement* (Chapel Hill: University of North Carolina Press, 2004); Timothy B. Tyson, *Radio Free Dixie: Robert F. Williams and the Roots of Black Power* (Chapel Hill: University of North Carolina Press, 1999); Akinyele Omowale Umoja, *We Will Shoot Back: Armed Resistance in the Mississippi Freedom Movement* (New York: NYU Press, 2013); Charles E. Cobb Jr., *This Nonviolent Stuff'll Get You Killed: How Guns Made the Civil Rights Movement Possible* (Durham, NC: Duke University Press, 2016); Simon Wendt, "'Urge People Not to Carry Guns': Armed Self-Defense in the Louisiana Civil Rights Movement and the Radicalization of the Congress of Racial Equality,"

*Louisiana History: The Journal of the Louisiana Historical Association* 45, no. 3 (Summer 2004): 267–273.

21. Bayard Rustin speech at Grand Valley State College in Michigan, March 25, 1985, *Bayard Rustin Papers* (Frederick, MD: University Publications of America, 1988), Reel 2; J. Mills Thornton III, *Dividing Lines: Municipal Politics and the Struggle for Civil Rights in Montgomery, Birmingham, and Selma* (Tuscaloosa: University of Alabama Press, 2002); Robert Weems Jr., *Desegregating the Dollar: African American Consumerism in the Twentieth Century* (New York: New York University Press, 1998).

22. Wendt, "'Urge People Not to Carry Guns,'" 275–276.

23. Hazel Erskine, "The Polls: Demonstrations and Race Riots," *Public Opinion Quarterly* 31, no. 4 (Winter 1967–1968): 665.

24. Erskine, "The Polls," 674.

25. Lawrence Davies, "Reagan Brands Those in Riots 'Mad Dogs Against the People,'" *New York Times*, July 26, 1967, https://www.nytimes.com /1967/07/26/archives/reagan-brands-those-in-riots-mad-dogs-against -the-people.html, accessed January 4, 2021.

26. Roper Center, "Black, White, and Blue: Americans' Attitudes on Race and Police," September 22, 2015, https://ropercenter.cornell.edu/blog /black-white-and-blue-americans-attitudes-race-and-police, accessed January 3, 2021; Carol Anderson, *White Rage: The Unspoken Truth of Our Racial Divide* (New York: Bloomsbury, 2016), 103–105; Elizabeth Kai Hinton, *From the War on Poverty to the War on Crime: The Making of Mass Incarceration in America* (Cambridge, MA: Harvard University Press, 2016); Charles Holden, Zach Messitte, and Jerald Podair, "Channeling Spiro Agnew in the Baltimore Riots," *Baltimore Sun*, May 9, 2015, https://www.baltimoresun.com/opinion/bs-ed-freddie-gray-agnew -20150509-story.html, accessed January 5, 2021; Lauren Pearlman, *Democracy's Capital: Black Political Power in Washington, D.C., 1960s– 1970s* (Chapel Hill: University of North Carolina Press, 2019), 139–178.

27. Jeffrey M. Jones, "Confidence in Police Drops to 10-Year Low," Gallup, November 10, 2005, https://news.gallup.com/poll/19783/confidence -local-police-drops-10year-low.aspx, accessed January 3, 2021.

28. [Oakland Police Department], "The Black Panther Party for Self Defense is an extremely militant . . . ," n.d., Mulford Act Files, firearms policy.org/resources, accessed October 7, 2020.

29. [Oakland Police Department], Request for Changes in Legislation Concerning the Control of Firearms, n.d., Mulford Act Files, firearms-policy.org/resources, accessed October 7, 2020; Bloom and Martin, *Black Against Empire*, Location 1118–1140.

30. Jerry Belcher, "It's All Legal: Oakland's Black Panthers Wear Guns, Talk Revolution," *San Francisco Examiner*, April 30, 1967, found in Mulford Act Files, firearmspolicy.org/resources, accessed October 7, 2020.

31. [Oakland Police Department], "The Black Panther Party for Self Defense is an extremely militant . . ."

32. [Oakland Police Department], "The Black Panther Movement," n.d., Mulford Act Files, firearmspolicy.org/resources, accessed October 7, 2020.

33. Don Mulford to Ronald Reagan, April 21, 1967, Mulford Act Files, fire-armspolicy.org/resources, accessed October 7, 2020.

34. Winkler, *Gun Fight*, 239.

35. Emilie Raymond, *From My Cold, Dead Hands: Charlton Heston and American Politics* (Lexington: University Press of Kentucky, 2006), 243, 244.

36. Tod Sloan, handwritten notes, n.d., https://sites.law.duke.edu/second thoughts/wp-content/uploads/sites/13/2020/04/Ted-Sloan-Notes-1967 -Mulford-Papers.pdf, accessed December 20, 2020.

37. Bloom and Martin, *Black Against Empire*, Location 1271, 1280, 1283.

38.　"Capitol Is Invaded," *Sacramento Bee*, May 2, 1967; "'Panther' Invasion Riles Legislature," *Los Angeles Herald Examiner*, May 3, 1967, Mulford Act Files, firearmspolicy.org/resources, accessed October 7, 2020; Ed Salzman, "Gun Control Bill Runs Into Trouble," *Oakland Tribune*, May 12, 1967, Mulford Act Files, firearmspolicy.org/resources, accessed October 7, 2020; "Capitol Flurry in Gun Protest," *San Francisco Chronicle*, May 3, 1967, Mulford Act Files, firearmspolicy.org/resources, accessed October 7, 2020.

39.　Bloom and Martin, *Black Against Empire*, Location 1291–1297. For the role of women, see Ashley D. Farmer, *Remaking Black Power: How Black Women Transformed an Era* (Chapel Hill: University of North Carolina Press, 2017).

40.　"Black Panthers Disrupt Assembly," *San Francisco Chronicle*, May 3, 1967.

41.　Cynthia Deitle Leonardatos, "California's Attempts to Disarm the Black Panthers," *San Diego Law Review* 36 (1999), 971–972.

42.　Leonardatos, "California's Attempts to Disarm the Black Panthers," 971.

43.　"Solons Assail Armed Band Entering Capitol," *Sacramento Bee*, May 3, 1967.

44.　Don Mulford to Arthur E. de la Barra, June 22, 1967, https://sites.law .duke.edu/secondthoughts/wp-content/uploads/sites/13/2020/04 /Mulford-Letter-1.pdf, accessed December 20, 2020.

45.　Leonardatos, "California's Attempts to Disarm the Black Panthers," 973.

46.　Don Mulford to Ronald Reagan, April 21, 1967, https://sites.law.duke .edu/secondthoughts/wp-content/uploads/sites/13/2020/04/Mulford -Letter-3.pdf, accessed December 20, 2020; John A. Nejedly to Ronald Reagan, April 20, 1967, Mulford Act Files, firearmspolicy.org/resources, accessed October 7, 2020.

47.　Jack Lindsey to Don Mulford, May 19, 1967, Mulford Act Files, firearms policy.org/resources, accessed October 7, 2020.

48. Don Mulford to John K. Jamison, May 24, 1967, Mulford Act Files, fire-armspolicy.org/resources, accessed October 7, 2020; Jack Lindsey to Don Mulford, May 19, 1967, Mulford Act Files, firearmspolicy.org/resources, accessed October 7, 2020.

49. Nick Wing, "Here's How the Nation Responded When a Black Militia Group Occupied a Government Building," *Huffington Post*, December 21, 2016, https://www.huffpost.com/entry/black-panthers-california-1967_n_568accfce4b014efe0db2f40, accessed January 5, 2021.

50. Winkler, *Gun Fight*, 245.

51. Anderson, *White Rage*, 102.

52. "'Panther' Invasion Riles Legislature," *Los Angeles Herald Examiner*.

53. "Black Panther Episode Was a Senseless Thing," *Sacramento Bee*, May 4, 1967, Mulford Act Files, firearmspolicy.org/resources, accessed October 7, 2020.

54. "Stronger Gun Laws Needed," *Los Angeles Times*, May 4, 1967, Mulford Act Files, firearmspolicy.org/resources, accessed October 7, 2020.

55. Stephen D'Arrigo Jr., letter to the editor, *San Jose News*, May 10, 1967, Mulford Act Files, firearmspolicy.org/resources, accessed October 7, 2020.

56. Salzman, "Gun Control Bill Runs Into Trouble."

57. Winkler, *Gun Fight*, 245–246.

58. Peter N. Carroll, *It Seemed like Nothing Happened: America in the 1970s* (New Brunswick: Rutgers University Press, 1982, 1990), 20.

59. Richard A. Oppel Jr., "How M.L.K.'s Death Helped Lead to Gun Control in the U.S., *New York Times*, April 3, 2018, https://www.nytimes.com/2018/04/03/us/martin-luther-king-1968-gun-control-act.html, accessed January 20, 2020.

60. Olivia B. Waxman, "How the Gun Control Act of 1968 Changed America's Approach to Firearms—and What People Get Wrong About That History," *Time*, October 30, 2018, https://time.com/5429002/gun-control-act-history-1968, accessed December 11, 2020.

61. Max Arthur Herman, *Summer of Rage: An Oral History of the 1967 Newark and Detroit Riots* (New York: Peter Lang, 2013), Kindle, 9–13; Bloom and Martin, *Black Against Empire*, Location 1838, 1842, 1859.

62. Winkler, *Gun Fight*, 250.

63. Niraj Warikoo, "43 Fatal Victims of the Detroit Riot of 1967," *Detroit Free Press*, July 27, 2017, https://www.freep.com/story/news/detroitriot/2017/07/23/victims-detroit-riot-1967/499550001, accessed January 31, 2021; Herman, *Summer of Rage*, 185–187.

64. Winkler, *Gun Fight*, 250.

65. Frances Stead Sellers, "Assassinations of 1968 Led the NRA to Become the Lobbying Force It Is Today," *Oakland Press*, May 29, 2018, https://www.theoaklandpress.com/news/nation-world-news/assassinations-of-1968-led-the-nra-to-become-the-lobbying-force-it-is-today, accessed December 11, 2020.

66. "Rifle Club: Anti-Riot Plan—Shotguns in Urban Homes," *San Francisco Chronicle*, May 8, 1967, Mulford Act Files, firearmspolicy.org/resources, accessed October 7, 2020.

67. Oppel, "How M.L.K.'s Death Helped Led to Gun Control in the U.S."

68. Oppel, "How M.L.K.'s Death Helped Led to Gun Control in the U.S."

69. Michael Waldman, *The Second Amendment: A Biography* (New York: Simon and Schuster, 2014), 89.

70. Waldman, *The Second Amendment*, 89.

71. Waldman, *The Second Amendment*, 83; Adam Winkler, "The Secret History of Guns," *The Atlantic*, September 2011, https://www.theatlantic

.com/magazine/archive/2011/09/the-secret-history-of-guns/308608, accessed December 11, 2020.

72. Jonathan Simon, *Governing Through Crime: How the War on Crime Transformed American Democracy and Created a Culture of Fear* (New York: Oxford University Press, 2007), 22–23.

73. Susan D. Greenbaum, *Blaming the Poor: The Long Shadow of the Moynihan Report on Cruel Images About Poverty* (New Brunswick, NJ: Rutgers University Press, 2015), 91.

74. Linda K. Mancillas, *Presidents and Mass Incarceration: Choices at the Top, Repercussions at the Bottom* (Santa Barbara, CA: Praeger, 2018), Kindle, 30.

75. Heather Cox Richardson, *How the South Won the Civil War: Oligarchy, Democracy, and the Continuing Fight for the Soul of America* (New York: Oxford University Press, 2020), 172; Angie Maxwell and Todd G. Shields, *The Long Southern Strategy: How Chasing White Voters in the South Changed American Politics* (New York: Oxford University Press, 2019).

76. Anderson, *White Rage*, 104–105.

77. Mancillas, *Presidents and Mass Incarceration*, 31; Gil Newbold, "Stop Coddling Criminals," letter to the editor, *Washington Post*, December 10, 1988, https://www.washingtonpost.com/archive/opinions/1988/12/10 /stop-coddling-criminals/5fbfa167-55eb-4de6-b61b-e866bfdeb1bf, accessed January 11, 2021; Ken Kreigsman, "Coddling Criminals Doesn't Stop Crime," letter to the editor, *Orlando Sentinel*, March 7, 1993, https://www.orlandosentinel.com/news/os-xpm-1993-03-07-93030 50648-story.html, accessed January 11, 2021; Radley Balko, "John McCain: We Must Stop Coddling Criminals," *Reason*, October 28, 2008, https://reason.com/2008/10/28/john-mccain-we-must-stop-coddl, accessed January 11, 2021.

78. Nicholas Lemann, "The Unfinished War," *The Atlantic*, December 1988, https://www.theatlantic.com/past/docs/politics/poverty/lemunf1.htm, accessed January 11, 2021.

79. Betsy Pearl, "Ending the War on Drugs: By the Numbers," Center for American Progress, June 27, 2018, https://www.americanprogress.org /issues/criminal-justice/reports/2018/06/27/452819/ending-war-drugs -numbers, accessed January 12, 2021.

80. Eric Primm, Robert M. Regoli, and John D. Hewitt, "Race, Fear, and Firearms: The Roles of Demographics and Guilt Assignment in the Creation of a Political Partition," *Journal of African American Studies* 13, no. 1 (March 2009): 67–68.

81. Jennifer L. Eberhardt, *Biased: Uncovering the Hidden Prejudice That Shapes What We See, Think, and Do* (New York: Viking, 2019), 6.

82. Lloyd Vries, "Cops Defend Shooting 92-Year-Old Woman," CBS News, https://cbsnews.com/news/cops-defend-shooting-92-year-old -woman, accessed November 29, 2015; Brenda Goodman, "Police Kill Woman, 92, in Shootout in Her Home," *New York Times*, November 23, 2006, https://www.nytimes.com/2006/11/23/us/23atlanta.html, accessed December 16, 2020; ACLU, "Kathryn Johnston and Police System Failure: What Can Congress Do About It?," https://www.aclu.org/other/kathryn -johnston-and-police-system-failure, accessed December 16, 2020.

83. Vries, "Cops Defend Shooting 92-Year-Old Woman."

84. Goodman, "Police Kill Woman, 92, in Shootout in Her Home."

85. Daniel J. Merrett, "Crimes and Offenses, Defenses to Criminal Prosecutions: Provide That Person Who Is Attacked Has No Duty to Retreat; Provide Immunity from Prosecution," *Georgia State University Law Review* 23, no. 1 (Fall 2006): 27–35.

86. Vries, "Cops Defend Shooting 92-Year-Old Woman."

87. Vries, "Cops Defend Shooting 92-Year-Old Woman."

88. ACLU, "Kathryn Johnston and Police System Failure."

89. ACLU, "Kathryn Johnston and Police System Failure"; Goodman, "Police Kill Woman, 92, in Shootout in Her Home."

90. Goodman, "Police Kill Woman, 92, in Shootout in Her Home."

91. Tessa Duvall, "Fact Check 2.0: Debunking 9 Widely Shared Rumors in the Breonna Taylor Police Shooting," *Louisville Courier Journal*, October 14, 2020, https://www.courier-journal.com/story/news/crime /2020/06/16/breonna-taylor-fact-check-7-rumors-wrong/5326938002, accessed December 16, 2020; Nicholas Bogel-Burroughs, "Louisville Officer Who Shot Breonna Taylor Will Be Fired," *New York Times*, December 29, 2020, https://www.nytimes.com/2020/12/29/us/louisville -officer-fired-jaynes-breonna-taylor.html, accessed December 30, 2020; Radley Balko, "Correcting the Misinformation About Breonna Taylor," *Washington Post*, September 24, 2020, https://www.washingtonpost .com/opinions/2020/09/24/correcting-misinformation-about-breonna -taylor, accessed December 16, 2020; NAACP Legal Defense Fund, "Justice Denied: A Call for a New Grand Jury Investigation into the Killing of Breonna Taylor," November 2020, https://www.naacpldf.org /wp-content/uploads/LDF_10272020_BreonnaTaylor-11.pdf, accessed December 16, 2020; Malachy Browne, Anjali Singhvi, Natalie Reneau, and Drew Jordan, "How the Police Killed Breonna Taylor," *New York Times*, December 28, 2020, https://www.nytimes.com/video/us/10000 0007348445/breonna-taylor-death-cops.html?s=03, accessed December 28, 2020.

92. Zak Cheney-Rice, "It Sure Looks like Daniel Cameron Lied About Breonna Taylor's Killing," *NY Magazine*, September 30, 2020, https:// nymag.com/intelligencer/2020/09/daniel-cameron-lied-about-grand -jury-louisville-police-breonna-taylor.html, accessed December 16, 2020; Balko, "Correcting the Misinformation About Breonna Taylor."

93. NAACP Legal Defense Fund, "Justice Denied."

94. Cheney-Rice, "It Sure Looks like Daniel Cameron Lied About Breonna Taylor's Killing."

95. Emily Shapiro, "AG Cameron Defends Decision to Not Advise Breonna Taylor Grand Jury of More Charges," ABC News, October 31, 2020,

https://abcnews.go.com/US/ag-cameron-defends-decision-advise -breonna-taylor-grand/story?id=73940937, accessed December 16, 2020.

96. Duvall, "Fact Check 2.0"; Bogel-Burroughs, "Louisville Officer Who Shot Breonna Taylor Will Be Fired"; NAACP Legal Defense Fund, "Justice Denied."

97. Tim Stickings, Keith Griffith, and Karen Ruiz, "Cops Release Photos That Were Tagged 'Partners in Crime' from Breonna Taylor's Boyfriend's Phone That Show Them Both Holding Gun Believed to Be the One He Used to Fire at Police as Messages Also Suggest He Was Selling Drugs," *Daily Mail*, October 8, 2020, https://www.dailymail.co .uk/news/article-8816249/Louisville-police-release-details-Taylor -investigation.html?, accessed October 8, 2020.

98. Responses on Twitter to *Daily Mail* article on LMPD release of photos of Breonna Taylor with a gun, October 8, 2020, https://twitter.com /search?q=Daily%20Mail%20Breonna%20Taylor%20Gun&src=typed_ query, accessed October 8, 2020.

99. Caroline E. Light, *Stand Your Ground: A History of America's Love Affair with Lethal Self-Defense* (Boston: Beacon Press, 2017), 149–162.

100. Charles Broward, "NAACP Weighs in on What They Say Is a 'Stand Your Ground' Case Against Jacksonville Woman," *Florida Times-Union*, April 21, 2012, https://www.jacksonville.com/article/20120421 /NEWS/801254470, accessed December 29, 2020.

101. Ryan Devereaux, "Florida's Stand-Your-Ground Law Put to Test in Marissa Alexander Conviction," *The Guardian*, May 17, 2012, https://www.theguardian.com/world/2012/may/17/stand-your-ground -marissa-alexander, accessed December 29, 2020.

102. Maine Domestic Abuse Homicide Review Panel, *Building Bridges Towards Safety and Accountability*, 10th annual report, April 2014,

https://www.maine.gov/ag/dynld/documents/10th%20Biennnial%20
Report%20-FINAL%204-23-14.pdf, accessed January 14, 2021.

103. Devereaux, "Florida's Stand-Your-Ground Law Put to Test in Marissa
Alexander Conviction."

104. Mike Spies, "The N.R.A. Lobbyist Behind Florida's Pro-Gun Policies,"
*New Yorker*, March 5, 2018, https://www.newyorker.com/magazine/2018
/03/05/the-nra-lobbyist-behind-pro-gun-policies, accessed August 8,
2018.

105. Adam Weinstein, "The Trayvon Martin Killing, Explained," *Mother
Jones*, March 18, 2012, http://www.motherjones.com/politics/2012
/03/what-happened-trayvon-martin-explained#newvideo, accessed
March 17, 2016.

106. Karen Grigsby Bates, "Stand Your Ground Laws Complicate Matters
for Black Gun Owners," *Code Switch*, NPR, February 27, 2017,
https://www.keranews.org/2017-02-27/stand-your-ground-laws-compli
cate-matters-for-black-gun-owners, accessed August 13, 2018.

107. Lindsay Peoples, "Marissa Alexander Fired a Warning Shot at Her
Abusive Husband and Was Sentenced to 20 Years. Now She's Free,"
*The Cut*, March 29, 2017, https://www.thecut.com/2017/03/marissa
-alexander-case-stand-your-ground-florida.html, accessed August 24,
2018.

108. Devereaux, "Florida's Stand-Your-Ground Law Put to Test in Marissa
Alexander Conviction."

109. Christine Hauser, "Florida Woman Whose 'Stand Your Ground'
Defense Was Rejected Is Released," *New York Times*, February 7, 2017,
https://www.nytimes.com/2017/02/07/us/marissa-alexander-released
-stand-your-ground.html, accessed December 29, 2020.

110. Mariame Kaba, "Black Women Punished for Self-Defense Must Be
Freed from Their Cages," *The Guardian*, January 3, 2019, https://www

.theguardian.com/commentisfree/2019/jan/03/cyntoia-brown-marissa -alexander-black-women-self-defense-prison, accessed January 3, 2019.

111. Hauser, "Florida Woman Whose 'Stand Your Ground' Defense Was Rejected Is Released."

112. Devereaux, "Florida's Stand-Your-Ground Law Put to Test in Marissa Alexander Conviction."

113. Zerlina Maxwell, "How Stand Your Ground Laws Failed Marissa Alexander," *Essence*, January 29, 2015, https://www.essence.com /news/how-stand-your-ground-laws-failed-marissa-alexander, accessed December 29, 2020.

114. Weinstein, "The Trayvon Martin Killing, Explained."

115. Adam Weinstein, "Trayvon Shooter's 911 Calls: Potholes, Piles of Trash—and Black Men," *Mother Jones*, March 22, 2012, https://www .motherjones.com/politics/2012/03/trayvon-shooters-911-calls-potholes -piles-trash-black-men, accessed December 23, 2020.

116. Weinstein, "The Trayvon Martin Killing, Explained."

117. Madison Gray, "Report: Police Initially Wanted to Make Arrest in Trayvon Martin Case," *Time*, March 29, 2012, http://newsfeed.time .com/2012/03/29/report-police-initially-wanted-to-make-arrest-in -trayvon-martin-case, accessed March 17, 2016.

118. Weinstein, "The Trayvon Martin Killing, Explained."

119. "Ex-Sanford Police Chief Tells Local 6 Why He Didn't Arrest George Zimmerman," ClickOrlando.com, July 12, 2013, http://www .clickorlando.com/news/zimmerman/ex-sanford-police-chief-tells -local-6-why-he-didnt-arrest-george-zimmerman, accessed March 17, 2016.

120. Vivian Kuo, "Fatal Shooting of Florida Teen Turned Over to State Attorney," CNN, March 15, 2012, http://www.cnn.com/2010/03/14 /justiceflorida-teen-shooting, accessed March 17, 2016.

121. Kuo, "Fatal Shooting of Florida Teen Turned Over to State Attorney."

122. Zerlina Maxwell, "The Thug-ification of Trayvon," *The Grio*, March 28, 2012, http://thegrio.com/2012/03/28/the-thug-ification-of-trayvon-mar tin-smear-campaign-distracts-from-the-case, accessed March 7, 2016; Eric Boehlert, "Trayvon Martin and Why the Right-Wing Media Spent 16 Months Smearing a Dead Teenager," *Huffington Post*, September 16, 2013, https://www.huffpost.com/entry/trayvon-martin-and-why-th_b _3611111, accessed February 16, 2021.

123. Leonard Pitts, "Who Was the Real Thug—Trayvon Martin or George Zimmerman?," *Dallas Morning News*, November 25, 2013, http://www .dallasnews.com/opinion/latest-columns/20131124-who-was-the-real -thug—trayvon-martin-or-george-zimmerman.ece, accessed March 7, 2016.

124. Jack Kerwick, "Trayvon Martin: A Child, or a Thug Wannabe?," *New American*, July 15, 2013, http://www.thenewamerican.com/reviews /opinion/item/15986-trayvon-martin-a-child-or-a-thug-wannabe, accessed March 7, 2016.

125. Carol Anderson, "Respectability Will Not Save Us: On the History of Respectability Politics and Their Failure to Keep Black Americans Safe," *Literary Hub*, August 9, 2017, https://lithub.com/respectability -will-not-save-us, accessed January 15, 2021.

126. Hauser, "Florida Woman Whose 'Stand Your Ground' Defense Was Rejected Is Released."

127. Mike Schneider, "Instructions to the Jury Were at the Forefront of the Zimmerman Verdict," *Business Insider*, July 14, 2013, https://www .businessinsider.com/instructions-to-the-jury-were-at-the-forefront-of -the-zimmerman-verdict-2013-7, accessed January 15, 2021.

128. Sofie Werthan, "Even the NRA Disagrees with Florida Sheriff Who Cited 'Stand Your Ground' in Parking-Space Killing," *Slate*, August 3, 2018, https://slate.com/news-and-politics/2018/08/the-nra-says-florida

-sheriffs-interpretation-of-stand-your-ground-law-is-wrong-in-markeis
-mcglockton-case.html, accessed August 31, 2018.

129. Weinstein, "The Trayvon Martin Killing, Explained."

130. Spies, "The N.R.A. Lobbyist Behind Florida's Pro-Gun Policies."

131. Erin Meisenzahl-Peace, "'Stand Your Ground' Laws Are Racist, New
Study Reveals," *Vice*, December 1, 2015, https://broadly.vice.com/en_us
/article/nz8pek/stand-your-ground-laws-are-racist-new-study-reveals,
accessed July 22, 2018.

132. Laura Bult, "A Timeline of 1,944 Black Americans Killed by Police,"
*Vox*, June 30, 2020, https://www.vox.com/2020/06/30/21306843/black
-police-killings, accessed January 14, 2021.

133. Eberhardt, *Biased*, 35, 36, 62.

134. Carol Anderson, "Florida Shooter Saw Black, Thought 'Threat,'" CNN
.com, February 12, 2014, https://www.cnn.com/2014/02/12/opinion
/anderson-dunn-trial/index.html, accessed January 16, 2021.

135. Andres Jaurequi, "Cops Who Killed John Crawford III at Ohio Walmart
Shot Him 'On Sight': Attorney," *Huffington Post*, August 27, 2014,
http://www.huffingtonpost.com/2014/08/27/john-crawford-killed
-walm_n_5721676.html, accessed November 29, 2015.

136. Audrey Hackett, "Through the Lens of Race: The 911 Call," *Yellow
Springs News*, August 4, 2016, https://ysnews.com/news/2016/08/through
-the-lens-of-race-the-911-call, accessed January 16, 2021.

137. Elahe Izadi, "Ohio Wal-Mart Surveillance Video Shows Police Shooting
and Killing John Crawford III," *Washington Post*, September 24, 2014,
https://www.washingtonpost.com/news/post-nation/wp/2014/09/25
/ohio-wal-mart-surveillance-video-shows-police-shooting-and-killing
-john-crawford-iii, accessed September 14, 2019.

138. Jon Swaine, "'It Was a Crank Call': Family Seeks Action Against 911
Caller in Wal-Mart Shooting," *The Guardian*, September 26, 2014,

https://www.theguardian.com/world/2014/sep/26/walmart-ohio -shooting-charges-911-calller-john-crawford, accessed January 16, 2021.

139. Swaine, "'It Was a Crank Call'"; Dan MacGuill, "The Death of John Crawford III," *Snopes*, August 14, 2018, https://www.snopes.com/fact -check/john-crawford-police-shooting-meme, accessed January 16, 2021.

140. MacGuill, "The Death of John Crawford III."

141. Izadi, "Ohio Wal-Mart Surveillance Video Shows Police Shooting and Killing John Crawford III."

142. MacGuill, "The Death of John Crawford III."

143. Jaurequi, "Cops Who Killed John Crawford III at Ohio Walmart Shot Him 'On Sight.'"

144. Swaine, "'It Was a Crank Call.'"

145. Hackett, "Through the Lens of Race."

146. Shaila Dewan and Richard A. Oppel Jr., "In Tamir Rice Case, Many Errors by Cleveland Police, Then a Fatal One," *New York Times*, January 22, 2015, http://nyti.ms/1AVZBhs, accessed March 21, 2016.

147. Adam Ferrise, "Cleveland Officer Who Shot Tamir Rice Had 'Dismal' Handgun Performance for Independence Police," Cleveland.com, December 3, 2014, http://impact.cleveland.com/metro/print.html?entry =/2014/12/cleveland_police_officer_who_s.html, accessed March 22, 2016.

148. Dewan and Oppel, "In Tamir Rice Case, Many Errors by Cleveland Police, Then a Fatal One."

149. Dewan and Oppel, "In Tamir Rice Case, Many Errors by Cleveland Police, Then a Fatal One."

150. Anderson, "Respectability Will Not Save Us."

151. German Lopez, "Cleveland Police Shooting of Tamir Rice: City to Pay $6 Million After 12-Year-Old's Death," *Vox*, April 25, 2016, https://www .vox.com/2014/11/24/7275297/tamir-rice-police-shooting, accessed January 17, 2021.

152. German Lopez, "The Police's Story About the Shooting of 12-Year-Old Tamir Rice Doesn't Match the Video," *Vox*, December 3, 2014, http://www.vox.com/2014/12/3/7326243/tamir-rice-police-contradictions, accessed March 22, 2016.

153. John P. Coyne and Kantele Franko, "Tamir Rice, Boy Shot Dead by Cleveland Police, Did Not Point Replica Gun at Officer," *Huffington Post*, November 24, 2014, http://www.huffingtonpost.com/2014/11 /24/tamir-rice-boy-shot-cleveland-police_n_6211064.html, accessed February 5, 2016.

154. Bryan L. Adamson, "Don't Understand the Connection Between Tamir Rice's Killing and His Parents' History? Join the Club," *Huffington Post*, February 3, 2015, http://www.huffingtonpost.com/bryan-l-adamson /tamir-rice-media_b_6265114.html, accessed February 5, 2016; Kim Palmer, "Reports Find Police Shooting of Tamir Rice 'Reasonable,'" *Huffington Post*, October 12, 2015, https://www.huffpost.com/entry /reports-find-police-shooting-of-tamir-rice-reasonable_n_561a7b5be4 b0082030a2eb1e, accessed March 22, 2016; Leon Neyfakh, "Was the Shooting of Tamir Rice 'Reasonable'? The Bad Supreme Court Standard That Lets Cops Who Kill Go Free," *Slate*, October 14, 2015, https://slate .com/news-and-politics/2015/10/tamir-rice-shooting-were-officer-tim -loehmanns-actions-reasonable.html, accessed February 5, 2016; Timothy Williams and Mitch Smith, "Cleveland Officer Will Not Face Charges in Tamir Rice Shooting Death," *New York Times*, December 28, 2015, http://nyti.ms/1ZxCYyp, accessed February 5, 2016.

155. Christina Coleman, "Prosecutor Smears Mother of Tamir Rice, Says Family Is 'Economically Motivated,'" *NewsOne*, November 9, 2015, https://newsone.com/3245405/prosecutor-smears-mother-of-tamir -rice-says-family-is-economically-motivated, accessed March 7, 2016;

Adamson, "Don't Understand the Connection Between Tamir Rice's Killing and His Parents' History?"

156. Williams and Smith, "Cleveland Officer Will Not Face Charges in Tamir Rice Shooting Death."

157. Anderson, "Respectability Will Not Save Us."

158. Joseph P. Williams, "Tamir Rice Shooting: Not Just a Tragedy," *US News and World Report*, December 29, 2015, http://usnews.com/news/articles/2015-12-29/tamir-rice-shooting-not-just-a-tragedy, accessed February 5, 2016.

159. Charles P. Pierce, "The Tamir Rice Shooting Reveals the Darkness at the Heart of Open Carry Laws: Ohio's Law Clearly Does Not Apply to Everyone," *Esquire*, December 29, 2015, http://www.esquire.com/news-politics/politics/news/a40818/tamir-rice-shooting-open-carry, accessed March 7, 2016.

160. Roshae Harrison, "A Teen Activist Gives Her Personal Take on 'The Hate U Give,'" *Vice*, October 30, 2018, https://www.vice.com/en/article/evwyq4/the-hate-u-give-movie-review-teen-activist, accessed December 22, 2020.

## EPILOGUE: RACISM LIES AROUND LIKE A LOADED WEAPON

1. Stefan Sykes, "19-Year-Old Charged with Illegally Supplying Gun to Kyle Rittenhouse: The Friend of Rittenhouse, 17, Purchased the Gun Later Used to Allegedly Fatally Shoot Two Men in Kenosha, Wisconsin, Prosecutors Say," NBC News, November 10, 2020, https://www.nbcnews.com/news/us-news/19-year-old-charged-illegally-supplying-gun-kyle-rittenhouse-n1247307, accessed January 18, 2021; Robert Klemko and Greg Jaffe, "A Mentally Ill Man, a Heavily Armed Teenager and the Night Kenosha Burned," *Washington Post*, October 3, 2020, https://www.washingtonpost.com/nation/2020/10/03/kenosha-shooting-victims/?arc404=true, accessed October 3, 2020.

2.    Eric Litke, "Fact Check: Police Gave Kyle Rittenhouse Water and Thanked Him Before Shooting," *USA Today*, August 29, 2020, https://www.usatoday.com/story/news/factcheck/2020/08/29/fact-check-video-police-thanked-kyle-rittenhouse-gave-him-water/5661804002, accessed October 24, 2020.

3.    Jemima McEvoy, "Video of Police Ignoring Suspected Kenosha Shooter Sparks Calls of Injustice," *Forbes*, August 26, 2020, https://www.forbes.com/sites/jemimamcevoy/2020/08/26/video-of-police-ignoring-suspected-kenosha-shooter-sparks-calls-of-injustice/?sh=453d06db4f9b, accessed January 20, 2021.

4.    Jeremy Lambe, "Attorneys Pounce on Kyle Rittenhouse's Reported Well-Regulated Militia Defense," *Law and Crime*, September 1, 2020, https://lawandcrime.com/high-profile/attorneys-pounce-on-kyle-rittenhouses-reported-well-regulated-militia-legal-defense, accessed December 16, 2020; Faith Karimi, "Kenosha Shooting Suspect Called a Friend to Say He 'Killed Somebody,' Police Say, and Then Shot Two Others," CNN, August 28, 2020, https://www.cnn.com/2020/08/28/us/kyle-rittenhouse-kenosha-shooting/index.html, accessed October 24, 2020.

5.    Brooke Newman, "ASU Conservatives Raising Funds for Kenosha Protest Shooter Kyle Rittenhouse," AZcentral.com, August 29, 2020, https://www.azcentral.com/story/news/education/2020/08/28/asu-college-republicans-united-kyle-rittenhouse-fundraiser/5662895002, accessed October 24, 2020; " 'God Is on Your Side': Christian Crowdfunding Site Raises over $500K for Kyle Rittenhouse, with Donors Describing Him as a 'American Hero Acting in Self-Defense' When He Shot and Killed Two Protesters in Kenosha," *Daily Mail*, September 29, 2020, https://www.dailymail.co.uk/news/article-8785185/God-Christian-crowdfunding-site-raises-500K-Kyle-Rittenhouse.html, accessed October 24, 2020.

6.    Julia Ainsley, "Internal Document Shows Trump Officials Were Told to Make Comments Sympathetic to Kyle Rittenhouse," NBC News,

October 1, 2020, https://www.nbcnews.com/politics/national-security
/internal-document-shows-trump-officials-were-told-make-comments
-sympathetic-n1241581?, accessed October 24, 2020.

7.    Michael Thau, "Kyle Rittenhouse Did Nothing Wrong. Conservatives
Throwing Him Under the Bus Need to Cut It Out Now," *Red State*,
September 4, 2020, https://redstate.com/michael_thau/2020/09/04/the
-only-thing-mass-covid-testing-achieves-is-a-permanent-fake-pandemic
-sustained-by-false-positives-n253527, accessed January 20, 2020.

8.    Klemko and Jaffe, "A Mentally Ill Man, a Heavily Armed Teenager and
the Night Kenosha Burned."

9.    Press briefing by Press Secretary Kayleigh McEnany, August 31, 2020,
James S. Brady Press Briefing Room, 1:03 p.m. EDT, https://www
.whitehouse.gov/briefings-statements/press-briefing-press-secretary
-kayleigh-mcenany-8-31-2020, accessed October 24, 2020.

10.   Remarks by President Trump before Air Force One departure, Joint Base
Andrews, MD, September 1, 2020, 11:23 a.m. EDT, https://www.whitehouse
.gov/briefings-statements/remarks-president-trump-air-force-one
-departure-joint-base-andrews-md-090120, accessed October 28, 2020.

11.   Mahita Ganjan and Sanya Mansoor, "'Good Guys with Guns' Can
Rarely Stop Mass Shootings, and Texas and Ohio Show Why," *Time*,
August 7, 2019, https://time.com/5644578/good-guys-with-guns-el
-paso-dayton, accessed January 20, 2021.

12.   Editorial Board, "Police Killed Two Good Guys with Guns. Arming
More People Isn't the Answer," *Washington Post*, November 30, 2018,
https://www.washingtonpost.com/opinions/police-killed-two-good
-guys-with-guns-arming-more-people-isnt-the-answer/2018/11/30/08a2
34cc-f1f0-11e8-80d0-f7e1948d55f4_story.html, accessed December 3,
2018; Carl Takei and Paige Fernandez, "Does the Second Amendment
Protect Only White Gun Owners?," ACLU, December 5, 2018,
https://www.aclu.org/blog/racial-justice/race-and-criminal-justice

/does-second-amendment-protect-only-white-gun-owners, accessed December 5, 2018.

13. Jamil Smith, "The 'Good Guy with the Gun' Is Never Black," *Rolling Stone*, November 27, 2018, https://www.rollingstone.com/politics /politics-features/good-guy-with-gun-760557, accessed November 27, 2018; Takei and Fernandez, "Does the Second Amendment Protect Only White Gun Owners?"; Daniel Victor, "Black Man Killed by Police in Alabama Was Shot from Behind, Autopsy Shows," *New York Times*, December 4, 2018, https://www.nytimes.com/2018/12/04/us/alabama -mall-shooting-autopsy.html, accessed December 4, 2018.

14. Smith, "The 'Good Guy with the Gun' Is Never Black."

15. Smith, "The 'Good Guy with the Gun' Is Never Black."

16. John Eligon, "A White Officer Shoots a Black Colleague, Deepening a Racial Divide," *New York Times*, January 15, 2020, https://www.nytimes .com/2019/11/24/us/st-louis-race-police.html, accessed February 29, 2020.

17. Eligon, "A White Officer Shoots a Black Colleague, Deepening a Racial Divide."

18. Matt Wilstein, "Trevor Noah Gets Serious About Alabama Mall Shooting Victim: Black Men Will Never Be 'Good Guy with a Gun,'" *Daily Beast*, November 27, 2018, https://www.thedailybeast.com/trevor -noah-gets-serious-about-alabama-mall-shooting-victim-black-men -will-never-be-good-guy-with-a-gun, accessed November 27, 2018.

19. Wilstein, "Trevor Noah Gets Serious About Alabama Mall Shooting Victim."

20. Mark V. Tushnet, *Out of Range: Why the Constitution Can't End the Battle over Guns* (New York: Oxford University Press, 2007); David E. Young, ed., *The Origin of the Second Amendment: A Documentary History of the Bill of Rights, 1787–1792*, 2d ed. (Ontanagon, MI: Golden Oaks Books, 2001); Nicholas J. Johnson, "Firearms Policy and the Black

Community: An Assessment of the Modern Orthodoxy," *Connecticut Law Review* 45, no. 1491 (2013): 1493, 1495.

21. *United States v. Miller,* 307 U.S. 174 (1939); John Paul Stevens, "The Supreme Court's Worst Decision of My Tenure: *District of Columbia v. Heller* Recognized an Individual Right to Possess a Firearm Under the Constitution. Here's Why the Case Was Wrongly Decided," *The Atlantic,* May 14, 2019, https://www.theatlantic.com/ideas/archive /2019/05/john-paul-stevens-court-failed-gun-control/587272, accessed January 18, 2021; *District of Columbia v. Heller,* 554 U.S. 570 (2008); *McDonald v. Chicago* 561 U.S. 742 (2010).

22. *Toyosaburo Korematsu v. United States,* 323 U.S. 214 (1944).

23. B. M. Chiperfield, "The Legal Status of the National Guard Under the Army Reorganization Bill," *Journal of the American Institute of Criminal Law and Criminology* 7, no. 5 (January 1917): 673.

24. Michael Waldman, "How the NRA Rewrote the Second Amendment," Brennan Center for Justice, May 20, 2014, https://www.brennancenter .org/our-work/research-reports/how-nra-rewrote-second-amendment, accessed August 6, 2020.

# INDEX

# A NOTE ON THE AUTHOR

CAROL ANDERSON is the Charles Howard Candler Professor and Chair of African American Studies at Emory University. She is the author of *One Person, No Vote*, longlisted for the National Book Award and a finalist for the PEN/John Kenneth Galbraith Award; *White Rage*, a *New York Times* bestseller and winner of the National Book Critics Circle Award; *Bourgeois Radicals*; and *Eyes off the Prize*. She was named a Guggenheim Fellow for Constitutional Studies. She lives in Atlanta, Georgia.